Turning the Right Corner

DIRECTIONS IN DEVELOPMENT
Environment and Sustainable Development

Turning the Right Corner

Ensuring Development through a Low-Carbon Transport Sector

Andreas Kopp, Rachel I. Block, and Atsushi Iimi

THE WORLD BANK
Washington, D.C.

© 2013 International Bank for Reconstruction and Development / The World Bank
1818 H Street NW, Washington DC 20433
Telephone: 202-473-1000; Internet: www.worldbank.org

Some rights reserved

1 2 3 4   16 15 14 13

This work is a product of the staff of The World Bank with external contributions. Note that The World Bank does not necessarily own each component of the content included in the work. The World Bank therefore does not warrant that the use of the content contained in the work will not infringe on the rights of third parties. The risk of claims resulting from such infringement rests solely with you.

The findings, interpretations, and conclusions expressed in this work do not necessarily reflect the views of The World Bank, its Board of Executive Directors, or the governments they represent. The World Bank does not guarantee the accuracy of the data included in this work. The boundaries, colors, denominations, and other information shown on any map in this work do not imply any judgment on the part of The World Bank concerning the legal status of any territory or the endorsement or acceptance of such boundaries.

Nothing herein shall constitute or be considered to be a limitation upon or waiver of the privileges and immunities of The World Bank, all of which are specifically reserved.

Rights and Permissions

This work is available under the Creative Commons Attribution 3.0 Unported license (CC BY 3.0) http://creativecommons.org/licenses/by/3.0. Under the Creative Commons Attribution license, you are free to copy, distribute, transmit, and adapt this work, including for commercial purposes, under the following conditions:

Attribution—Please cite the work as follows: Kopp, Andreas, Rachel I. Block, and Atsushi Iimi. 2013. *Turning the Right Corner: Ensuring Development through a Low-Carbon Transport Sector.* Directions in Development. Washington, DC: World Bank. doi:10.1596/978-0-8213-9835-7. License: Creative Commons Attribution CC BY 3.0

Translations—If you create a translation of this work, please add the following disclaimer along with the attribution: *This translation was not created by The World Bank and should not be considered an official World Bank translation. The World Bank shall not be liable for any content or error in this translation.*

All queries on rights and licenses should be addressed to the Office of the Publisher, The World Bank, 1818 H Street NW, Washington, DC 20433, USA; fax: 202-522-2625; e-mail: pubrights@worldbank.org.

ISBN (paper): 978-0-8213-9835-7
ISBN (electronic): 978-0-8213-9890-6
DOI: 10.1596/978-0-8213-9835-7

Cover photo: The cover photo is the copyrighted property of 123RF Limited, its Contributors, or Licensed Partners and is being used with permission under license. This photo may not be copied or downloaded without permission from 123RF Limited.

Library of Congress Cataloging-in-Publication Data

Kopp, Andreas.
Turning the right corner : ensuring development through a low-carbon transport sector / Andreas Kopp, Rachel I Block, Atsushi Iimi.
    pages cm
Includes bibliographical references.
ISBN 978-0-8213-9835-7 — ISBN 978-0-8213-9890-6
 1. Transportation—Environmental aspects. 2. Sustainable development. 3. Emissions trading. I. Title.
 HE147.65.K66 2013
 629.04028'6—dc23   2013008680

Contents

Foreword		*xi*
Acknowledgments		*xiii*
Abbreviations		*xv*

Overview	**Transport Efficiency Promotes Development and Protects the Environment**	**1**
	Climate Policies, Transport, and Development	2
	The Direction of Transport Greenhouse Gas Emissions	2
	The Effect of Technology Innovation on Emissions	3
	The Effect of the Modal Composition of Transport	9
	Transport Adaptation Needs	11
	Climate Change and Transport Financing Gaps	13
	The Inadequacy of Current Carbon Finance	14
	Transport Reforms and Climate Policy Costs	15
	Integrating Supply and Demand	16
	Note	17
	References	17
Chapter 1	**Transport, Mobility, Emissions, and Development**	**21**
	The Relationship between Mobility and Development	21
	Climate Risks from Transport	23
	Dealing with Inertia in Infrastructure	25
	Low-Carbon Transport and Development	31
	Annex 1A Characteristics of the Transport Sector	33
	References	36
Chapter 2	**Avoiding Future Disruption of Services**	**39**
	Threats to Transport Infrastructure and Operations	39
	Preserving Resilient and Least-Cost Transport as the Climate Changes	52
	Standards and the Resilience of Transport Infrastructure	52
	Fundamentals of Transport Adaptation	64
	Information	64
	Decision-Making Tools	66

	Notes	67
	References	69
Chapter 3	**Integrating Sector-Wide Reforms for Mitigation**	**75**
	Technology: Necessary, Promising, but Still Far Off	76
	Demand-Side Transport Policies for Mitigation	105
	Designing Transport Projects from a Broader Point of View	125
	Notes	126
	References	127
Chapter 4	**Climate-Resilient Investment in Transport**	**135**
	Financing Mitigation and Adaptation	135
	Insufficient Financing Available	141
	Economics of Climate-Resilient Transport Financing and Mitigation	146
	Generating New Resources	150
	Conclusion	152
	Annex 4A City Examples: How Carbon Pricing Can Produce Benefits	154
	Notes	156
	References	157

Boxes

1.1	Characteristics of the Transport Sector	22
2.1	Impact of Sea-Level Rise and Cyclones on Transport Infrastructure in Bangladesh	40
2.2	The 1997–98 El Niño and Transport and Reconstruction in Kenya, Peru, and Ecuador	41
2.3	Minimizing the Costs of Extreme Events: The Role of Transport	47
2.4	Starting the Adaptation Process: Asking the Right Questions	50
2.5	Advancing the Adaptation Process: Assessing Risk and Defining a Strategy	51
2.6	Failures and Successes in Disaster Recoveries	55
2.7	Standards Updating: Examples	56
2.8	Monitoring Corruption	61
2.9	Manila: Public Transport Resilience to Extreme Events	62
2.10	A Five-Step Risk-Assessment Approach to Infrastructure Design	65
3.1	Rail Companies: Energy Consumers but also Electricity Producers	84
3.2	How Multimodality Affects Emissions: ASIF Decomposition	90
3.3	Demand for High-Speed Rail	93
3.4	Building Greener Transport Infrastructure	99
3.5	Information and Consumer Vehicle Choice	114
3.6	Policy Options Compared	123

4.1	IEA Assumptions in Estimating Mitigation Investment Needs	137
4.2	Methods of Estimating Adaptation Investment Needs	139
4.3	A Numerical Example of Road Management: Applying HDM-4	142
4.4	Blending Carbon Finance Resources in Transport: An Example	145

Figures

O.1	Road Transport Energy Consumption and per Capita Income	2
O.2	Motorization and Income	3
O.3	Transport Consumption of Oil Long-Term	4
O.4	Transport Oil Demand, OECD and Non-OECD Countries, 2007–30	5
O.5	The Optimistic View: Transport-Related CO_2 Emissions through 2030	6
O.6	The Optimistic View: Technical Standards for New Vehicles	6
O.7	The Pessimistic View: Transport the Predominant Emitter by 2095, Even with Carbon Pricing Leading to a Greenhouse Gas Concentration of 450 ppm	7
O.8	The Pessimistic View: Transport and Carbon Capture and Storage	8
O.9	Passenger Car Density and Income, 2003	9
1.1	Total Transport CO_2 Emissions, by Transport Mode	23
1.2	Actual and Projected Transport CO_2 Emissions, 1980–2030	25
1.3	Malaysia: Costs of Landslides, 1973–2007	26
1.4	Price Differences and per Capita Gasoline Consumption, Selected Countries	31
1A.1	Road Freight and Average Income, 2006	33
1A.2	Road Passenger Transport and Average Income, 2006	34
1A.3	Rail Freight Transport and Average Income, 2006	34
1A.4	Rail Passenger Transport and Average Income, 2006	35
1A.5	Motorization and Income, 2005	35
1A.6	Passenger Car Density and Income, 2003	36
2.1	Framework for Defining Vulnerability	49
2.2	Deterioration of Paved Roads over Time	53
2.3	Paved Roads by Region, 2005	54
2.4	Africa: Roads in Poor Condition (Cross-Country Average Based on Latest Data)	57
2.5	Road Roughness and Maintenance Frequency over Time	57
2.6	The Philippines: Vessels Entering and Maritime Accidents	58
2.7	Effect of Overloading on Road Roughness	60
2.8	Reasons for Flight Cancellations, United States	60
3.1	Paths of Automobile Use	76
3.2	World Transport CO_2 Emissions by Vehicle Type, 2000	77
3.3	Average Fuel Consumption, United States and European Union, 1978–2008	77
3.4	Diesel Share of Total Gasoline and Diesel Fuel Use	78

3.5	Estimated Emissions Reduction by 2050 and Costs by Vehicle and Fuel Type	79
3.6	GHG Intensity of Electricity Generation, by Region (IEA Baseline Scenario)	80
3.7	Passenger Aircraft: CO_2 Normalized Energy Efficiency	82
3.8	Railway Traffic by Region	83
B.3.1	Energy Production Trends in Japanese Railways	85
3.9	Willingness to Pay for Ethanol, United States	86
3.10	Sugar Production Costs as an Input to Ethanol Production	87
3.11	Long Distance Travel Time, Sweden	92
3.12	Maximum Speed of High-Speed Trains	93
3.13	High-Speed Rail Construction Costs	94
3.14	Marginal Emissions Abatement Costs in Mexico	96
3.15	Average Jet Fuel Prices	97
3.16	Emissions from Logistics Activities	98
3.17	Average Freight Cost and Empty Trip Rate	99
3.18	Individual Transport Emissions and Population Density	100
3.19	Modal Share, Selected Cities in Asia	102
3.20	Passenger Car Travel, Fuel Economy, and Average Fuel Prices, 1998	107
3.21	Passenger Car Use and Average Fuel Prices, 1998	108
3.22	Fuel Taxation by Country (Percentage of Retail Gasoline Price)	108
3.23	Fuel Taxation (Percentage of Retail Gasoline Price), 1970–2009	109
B3.5.1	The United Kingdom Respondents Familiar with New Vehicle Technologies	114
3.24	U.S. Fuel Economy Standards and Actual Performance	116
3.25	Total Vehicle Emissions by Base Year	118
3.26	Singapore: Quota Premiums for Passenger Cars	120
3.27	Fuel Consumption and CO_2 Emissions per Vehicle-km	121
B3.6.1	Mexico: Expected Net Mitigation Benefits, Various Transport Intervention	125
4.1	Cumulative Incremental Transport Investment by Mode	137
4.2	Cumulative Incremental Transport Investment by Regions and Sectors	138
4.3	Road Network and Population by Region, 2005	140
B4.3.1	Road Maintenance Costs, Actual Maintenance, and Climate Change: An Example	142
4.4	Potential Annual Emission Reduction (Gt CO_2eq)	143
4.5	Climate Funds and Transition to Low-Carbon Technologies	146
4.6	Actual Transport Spending and Estimated Requirements, Sub-Saharan Africa	147
4.7	Average Particulate Matter Emissions, 10 Micrometers or Less, 2006	150
4.8	Implicit Subsidies to Gasoline and Diesel, 2007–08	151

Maps

1.1	Per Capita Transport Energy Use, 2006	24
3.1	Corridor IV (Thessaloniki–Sofia–Hungary) and Corridor X (Thessaloniki–Skopje–Belgrade–Hungary)	104
3.2	Rail Sections, Durres-Skopje-Sofia, along Corridor VIII	105

Tables

2.1	Effects of Pavement and Weather on Road Accidents	58
2.2	Reported Overloading, Southern African Development Community, 2004	59
2.3	Japan: Macro Logistics Costs	62
3.1	Fuel Economy Standards for Passenger Cars, United States and European Union, and Japan	78
3.2	Top Global Hybrid Vehicle Markets, 2009	79
3.3	Boeing 747 Average Fuel Efficiency	82
3.4	Railway Diesel Fuel Consumption, Selected Countries	84
B3.2.1	ASIF Decomposition, Selected Developed Countries, 1973–95 (1973 = 100)	90
3.5	Average CO_2 Emission Factors by Vehicle Type, United Kingdom	91
3.6	Transport Modes Used before the MRT Blue Line Opened in Bangkok	91
3.7	Estimated Emissions Reduction by the MRT Blue Line in Bangkok	91
3.8	Average CO_2 Emission Factors, Road and Rail Freight, United Kingdom	95
3.9	Average Vehicle-km Traveled, Selected Urban Areas	100
3.10	Trip Purpose by Bicycle	101
3.11	Road Users Killed, by Transport Mode, as a Percentage of Total Fatalities	103
3.12	Costs and Benefits, Selected Nonmotorized Modes	103
3.13	Energy Consumption, Door-to-Door Transportation	103
3.14	Corridors between Thessaloniki, Greece, and Nish, Serbia, Compared	104
3.15	Relative Costs of Driving and Mass Transit in Selected Cities	106
3.16	Effectiveness of Major Price Policies in Reducing Transport Emissions	106
B3.5.1	Hybrid Markets in the United States	115
3.17	Major Quantitative Regulations for Emissions Mitigation	116
3.18	Prohibitions on Imported Used Cars and Tires	117
3.19	Vehicle Classification of Singapore's Quota System	119
B3.6.1	Fuel Taxes and Fuel Economy Standards: Cost and Emissions Benefits	124
4.1	Reduction of Energy-Related Emissions by 2050, by Sector	136
4.2	Average Annual Incremental Mitigation Investment by 2030	136

4.3	Average Annual Incremental Adaptation Cost through 2050	138
4.4	U.S. Civil Aviation Safety Assessment, 2008	140
4.5	Annual Adaptation and Infrastructure Deficits	141
4.6	Global Environment Facility Funding, 1991–2010	144
4.7	CTF-Endorsed Country Investment Plans	144
4.8	Estimated Costs External to Transport, United States	147
4.9	Estimated Costs External to Transport, OECD Averages	148
4.10	Transport Fatality and Injury, Japan, FY2008/09	149
4.11	Road Traffic Injury and Fatality Rates	149
4.12	Emission Reduction: Effect, Benefits, and Fiscal Potential of Various Interventions	152
4A.1	External Costs of Passenger Transport, Washington, 2007	155

Foreword

Growth and development are primarily a matter of mobility. Mobility of people for access to employment, education, and health; mobility of goods to supply the world markets that ensure the dynamism of economic activity. In our globalized economy, it is the infrastructure and transport services that underpin trade, linking production centers to consumption areas, integrating territories beyond administrative boundaries, and thus offering everyone the opportunity to contribute to value creation, as well as to enjoy its benefits.

So mobility has value. So much value, actually, that when looking into options on how to set the transport sector on a low carbon path, those cutting down on mobility can hardly be entertained, such is the risk that they would significantly undermine development. In other words, stop moving, emit less, is not an option.

Then the challenge becomes: how to progress toward low-carbon mobility? And how do we finance such a transformation in transport patterns, so as to make it sustainable? And what will the role of technology be in helping along this route?

Those are some of the key questions this report seeks to answer. Or when the answer is not that straightforward, at least to provide some fertile avenues for further analysis and better understanding of the mechanisms through which transport may help make sustainable and inclusive green growth possible.

Transport is too often taken for granted. Without a deliberate policy agenda to steer the sector toward a sustainable future where mobility is provided to people and freight while simultaneously protecting the planet from increased congestion and ineluctable asphyxia, this evolution is unlikely to happen by itself. Or mobility will be curbed, under pressure from emerging crisis conditions, with development and growth being among the first casualties. And as is so often the case in these situations, the poor are likely to suffer the most, with social inclusion giving way to survival of the fittest.

So now is the time to think through those issues and propose clear policy choices, which will hopefully help chart a way toward the future we—and our children—aspire to live in.

Jose Luis Irigoyen
Director
Transport, Water, and Information and
Communication Technologies
The World Bank

Acknowledgments

This report was prepared by the Transport and Climate Change team led by Andreas Kopp, with Atsushi Iimi and Rachel Block contributing chapter inputs. Marianne Fay provided crucial support to the project. Isabela Manelici helped with useful comments and invaluable editorial assistance. Monica Moldovan and Xavier Muller have masterly done the final formatting. The report has benefited much from the discussions of the World Bank regions' advisory committee, with Charles Crochet, Georges Bianco Darido, Ke Fang, Elisabeth Goller, Jean-Roger Gorham, Carolina Monsalve, Ziad Nakat, and Tomas S. Serebrisky. The generous support is gratefully acknowledged.

Abbreviations

ABI	Association of British Insurers
BRT	bus rapid transit
CAFE	Corporate Average Fuel Economy
CARS	car allowance rebate system
CCS	carbon capture and storage
CDM	clean development mechanism
CH_4	methane
CIF	Climate Investment Funds
CNG	compressed natural gas
CO_2	carbon dioxide
CSIRO	Commonwealth Scientific and Industrial Research Organization
CTF	Clean Technology Fund
EACC	economics of adaptation to climate change
EAR	economic amplification ratio
EC	European Commission
EU	European Union
ESALF	equivalent standard axle load factor
GCAM	Global Change Assessment Model
GDP	gross domestic product
GEF	Global Environment Facility
GHG	greenhouse gas
HDM	Highway Development and Management Model
HOT	high-occupancy toll
HOV	high-occupancy vehicle
IAMS	integrated assessment models
IEA	International Energy Agency
IPCC	Intergovernmental Panel on Climate Change
IRI	international roughness index
Ktoe	kilotons oil equivalent

LPG	liquefied petroleum gas
LRT	light rail transit
MRT	metro rail transit
NAMA	Nationally Appropriate Mitigation Action
NCAR	National Center for Atmospheric Research
N_2O	nitrous oxide
NO_2	nitrogen dioxide
OECD	Organisation for Economic Co-operation and Development
PNNL	Pacific Northwest National Laboratory
RDM	robust decision making
SAR	special administrative region
SNP	structural number of the pavement
SO_2	sulfur dioxide
SSATP	Sub-Saharan Africa Transport Policy Program
SUVs	sport-utility vehicles
SWIFT	structured what if technique
TJ	terajoule
UNFCCC	United Nations Framework Convention on Climate Change
UTTP	Mexico Municipal Transport Project

OVERVIEW

Transport Efficiency Promotes Development and Protects the Environment

Affordable transport services are crucial for development. They connect rural areas to sales opportunities and inputs, and nations to export markets and foreign technologies. Affordability refers not just to consumer prices but also to all costs to society: the time losses due to congestion, the sometimes dramatic consequences of accidents, the health costs of local pollution, and the damage that severe climate events inflict on the population. Transport decisions, particularly those for infrastructure investments, will determine these costs for decades to come, offering opportunities to countries whose transport systems are not yet mature.

Recognition of climate implications in transport, unlike other sectors, has had a slow start. One reason is that the transition to a low-carbon context appears to be more costly than in other sectors. But broadening the policy agenda to shift behavior changes the cost picture completely, especially measures to reduce congestion, local air pollution, safety risks, and energy imports.

Policies to guide demand to low-emission modes and technologies must be part of investment programs and projects. Such policies can reduce transport demand in the longer run by changing the economic geography of cities and countries. But that will take close coordination of transport, environmental, and health policies. This report's main messages are these:

- Climate policies should not compromise transport's contribution to development.
- If past trends continue, transport greenhouse gas emissions will increase dramatically.
- Innovations in engine technologies will not produce deep cuts in emissions.
- To avoid a vicious lock-in, cutting emissions urgently requires a new modal composition for infrastructure and transport services.
- Reducing transport's vulnerability to climate change starts with better maintenance and management of infrastructure.

- Climate change widens financing gaps in transport.
- Current carbon finance is inadequate to address transport's needs.
- Benefits to transport from broad sector reforms would reduce the cost of climate policies.
- Integrating supply and demand actions requires institutional change and coordination.

Climate Policies, Transport, and Development

Lower transport costs drive urbanization and growth. High local demand leads to higher productivity because unit costs for larger firms are lower and access to specialized inputs is easier. Lower transport costs increase competition in smaller cities and regions, further concentrating production and increasing productivity. Movement of workers to larger cities puts pressure on wages, leading to a new virtuous cycle of larger local markets, greater production scale, and higher real incomes (Krugman 1991). Putting development first, therefore, climate policies for transport should not come at the expense of mobility (World Bank 2008a).

The Direction of Transport Greenhouse Gas Emissions

Because development and the demand for mobility go hand in hand, energy use in transport increases with per capita income. The main driver of increased fuel use is the expansion of roads, but high levels of national development are possible with very large differences in transport energy consumption. The high-income Asian economies, which developed rapidly after World War II, define the lower bound of per capita energy consumption (figure O.1). Numerous European countries have low per capita energy consumption for road transport relative

Figure O.1 Road Transport Energy Consumption and per Capita Income

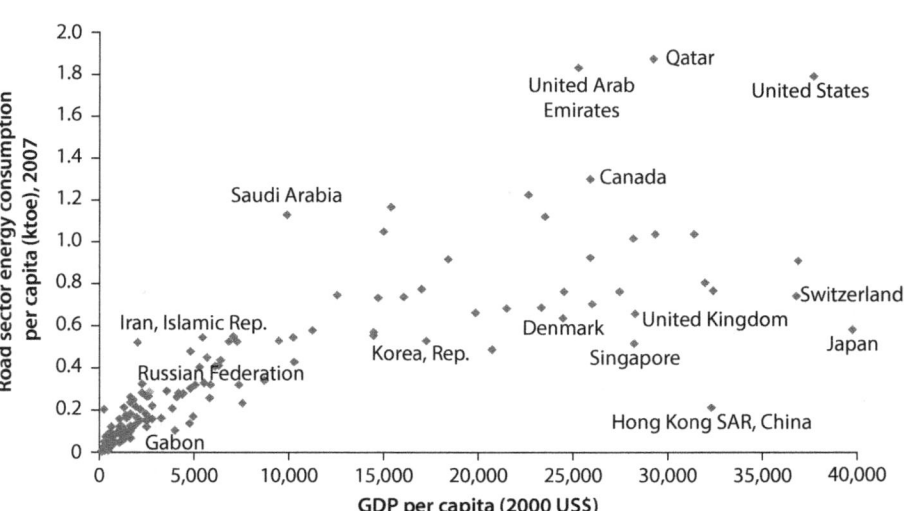

Source: World Bank 2010d.
Note: GDP = gross domestic product, ktoe = kilotons oil equivalent.

Figure O.2 Motorization and Income

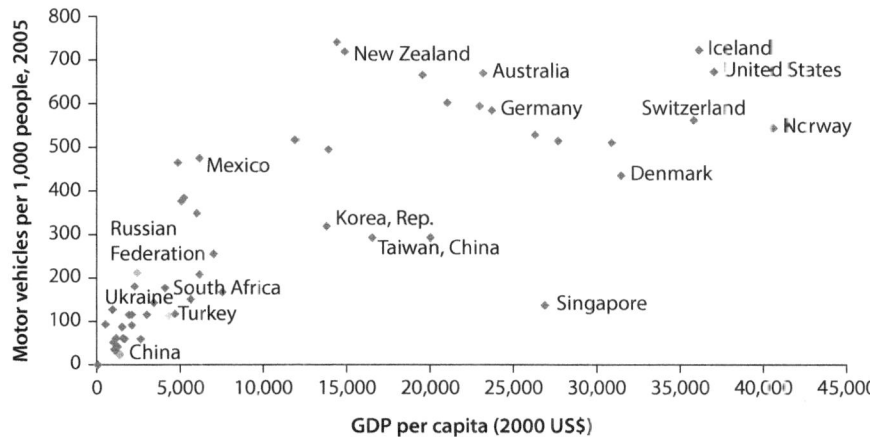

Source: World Bank 2010d.
Note: GDP = gross domestic product.

to income, and Canada, the United States, and some oil-producing countries have very high consumption. Some of the differences can be explained by geography, but others are due to energy demand policies and technology differences.

Motorization has driven the expansion of roads and the increase in energy use. It accelerates in most countries at per capita incomes of $5,000–$10,000 (figure O.2). There is no direct link between motorization and development; small countries with high per capita incomes, in particular, have large differences in motorization.

Projecting patterns of motorization and energy use into the future, the transport sector would eventually become the main consumer of oil (figure O.3). Absolute oil consumption would increase dramatically until 2030, and alternative sources of energy would have minor impact. Longer-term scenarios suggest that the trend would continue until the century ends. Deep cuts in transport greenhouse gas emissions through fuel substitution are expected to be possible with the emergence of new biofuel feedstocks that do not compete with food production and require less water—or as fuel cell cars become economically viable.

If today's developing countries repeat what has happened in developed countries, almost all the increase in transport oil demand would come from non–Organisation for Economic Co-operation and Development (OECD) countries. China, India, and the Middle East would see the largest increase (figure O.4). Progress in engine technologies would reduce fossil fuel consumption in some parts of the OECD, but such savings in non-OECD countries would be far exceeded by the rise in motorization.

The Effect of Technology Innovation on Emissions

Unlike other sectors, where mitigation is mainly about replacing the fuel-using technologies of a small number of users whose reactions are highly predictable,

Figure O.3 Transport Consumption of Oil Long-Term

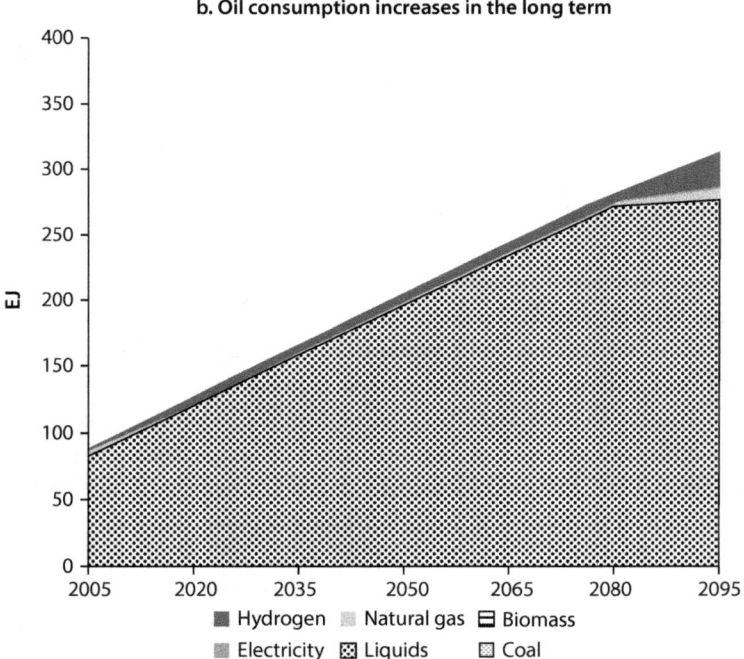

a. Oil consumption increases in the medium term

Source: OECD/IEA 2009b, figure 1.4, p. 79.

b. Oil consumption increases in the long term

Source: Clarke 2007.
Note: EJ = exajoule.

mitigating greenhouse gases in transport is a matter of changing the behavior of an enormous number of people. Billions of consumers make separate decisions about whether to use a car, which type of car to use, which type of fuel to use, and which length of trip to take. Reducing emissions in transport thus involves shifting a large number of consumers toward cleaner technologies.

Figure O.4 Transport Oil Demand, OECD and Non-OECD Countries, 2007–30

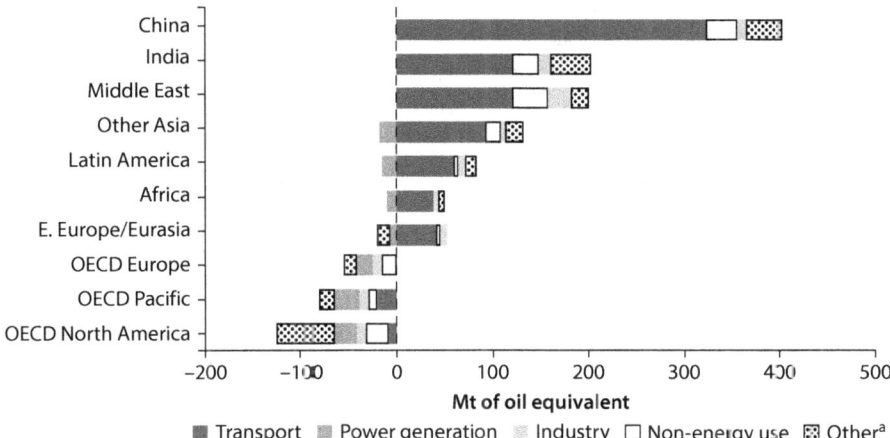

Source: OECD/IEA 2009b, figure 1.6, p. 82.
Note: Mt = metric ton, OECD = Organisation for Economic Co-operation and Development.
a. Includes residential, services, agriculture, and other energy sectors.

Because climate change is a global policy problem, climate policies require global agreement. To achieve the 2°C cap on average global temperature increase over preindustrial times, by 2100 carbon prices will have to increase to $700 a ton (Clarke and others 2007a). The more a country invests in roads, the more the carbon price will affect the price of a passenger-km or a ton-km. And the less a country has done to reduce transport greenhouse gas emissions, the more painful the transition to a low-carbon regime will be.

Differences in European and North American auto technologies illustrate this point. North America consumes four to six times more gasoline per head in transport than Europe. Why? Because Europe unilaterally implemented higher fuel prices. If all OECD countries had the low fuel prices of the United States, fuel use would have been 30 percent higher throughout the OECD. Conversely, if all countries had the high gas prices of Italy, the United Kingdom, or the Netherlands, OECD gasoline consumption would have been 44 percent lower, for an annual savings of 8.5 billion tons of carbon dioxide (CO_2). If all countries had U.S. fuel prices, the OECD would have used more than twice as much gasoline (133 percent more) than if all countries had Dutch prices (Sterner 2007).

How much will the transport sector be able to cut greenhouse gas emissions? Global scenarios vary, mainly because of differing expectations for progress in engine technologies. To some extent the answers depend on how much technical progress will be possible in other sectors, particularly power. They do not assume that there will be less use of transport or a significant change in means of transport. Technology optimists and pessimists do differ, however, in their assumptions about how to bring about a transition in the sector.

The optimists expect substantial technical progress in all countries, leading by 2030 to emission cuts of 30 percent compared to business as usual. But not even the optimists believe that emissions can be reduced from current levels in coming decades (figure O.5). The optimists assume that transport emission cuts will be achieved by internationally agreed emission standards for vehicles. Emissions per km of new cars would be reduced through better gasoline and diesel internal combustion engines, better lighting and air conditioning, better tires, and the rapid growth of plug-in hybrids and electric vehicles (figure O.6). Heavy-duty vehicles will benefit from spillovers of technical progress in light-duty vehicles. The aviation fleet will reduce emissions in accord with international efficiency agreements and reduce its average fuel consumption from 4.6 liters per 100 revenue passenger-km to 2.6 liters in 2030.

Pessimists expect a far slower spread of plug-in vehicles and electric cars and see high barriers to adoption of advanced vehicle technologies in developing countries (Calvin and others 2009; Clarke and others 2007b). They assume that

Figure O.5 The Optimistic View: Transport-Related CO_2 Emissions through 2030

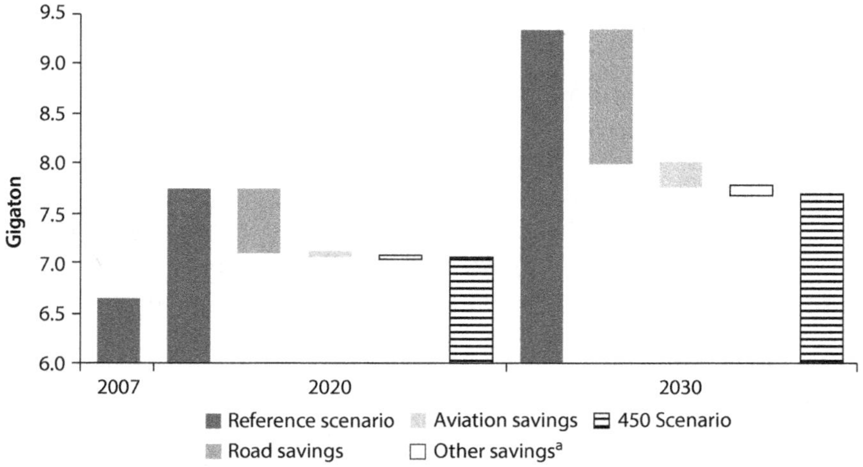

Source: OECD/IEA 2009b, figure 6.9, p. 237.
a. Includes rail, pipeline, domestic navigation, international marine bunkers, and other non-specified transport.

Figure O.6 The Optimistic View: Technical Standards for New Vehicles

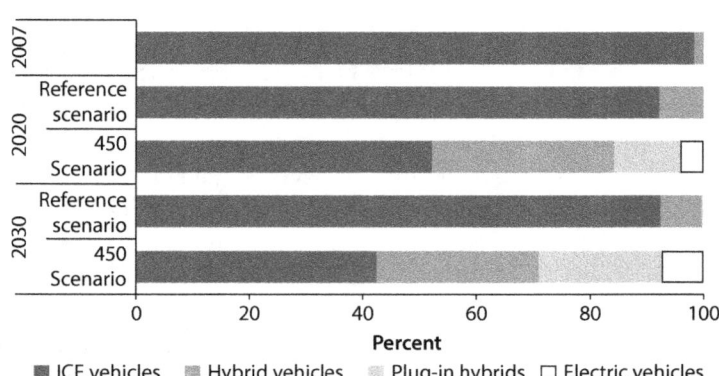

Source: OECD/IEA 2009b, figure 6.10, p. 239.

plug-in hybrids will be adopted only in developed countries due, for example, to the recycling risks of battery technologies and the high costs of infrastructure for alternative fuels. In developing countries, emission reductions must rely on advanced internal combustion engine technologies that can achieve 35 miles per gallon for gasoline engines and 37 for diesel (Kim and others 2006). In the MiniCam model of the Pacific Northwest National Laboratory (PNNL), consumers and firms choose between different vehicles and modes of transport. Choices are driven not by technical vehicle standards but by a universal carbon price that holds for other sectors as well. The transport sector will, under the pessimistic assumptions about progress in vehicle technology, grow into the main emitter, even with a carbon price regime that stabilizes greenhouse gas concentrations at 450 ppm (figure O.7). It takes the lead by 2050, when its emissions will have increased by 47 percent over 2005.

Pessimists expect that the prominence of transport as a greenhouse gas emitter could be amplified by rapid technical progress in the energy sector. A recent PNNL scenario based on the Global Change Assessment Model (GCAM), the successor to the MiniCam model, sees much greater potential for biofuel use in transport. The GCAM also covers agricultural production and land use, with biofuel production reacting to the carbon price (Luckow, Wise, and Dooley 2010). It is the first scenario to take into account how technical developments in

Figure O.7 The Pessimistic View: Transport the Predominant Emitter by 2095, Even with Carbon Pricing Leading to a Greenhouse Gas Concentration of 450 ppm

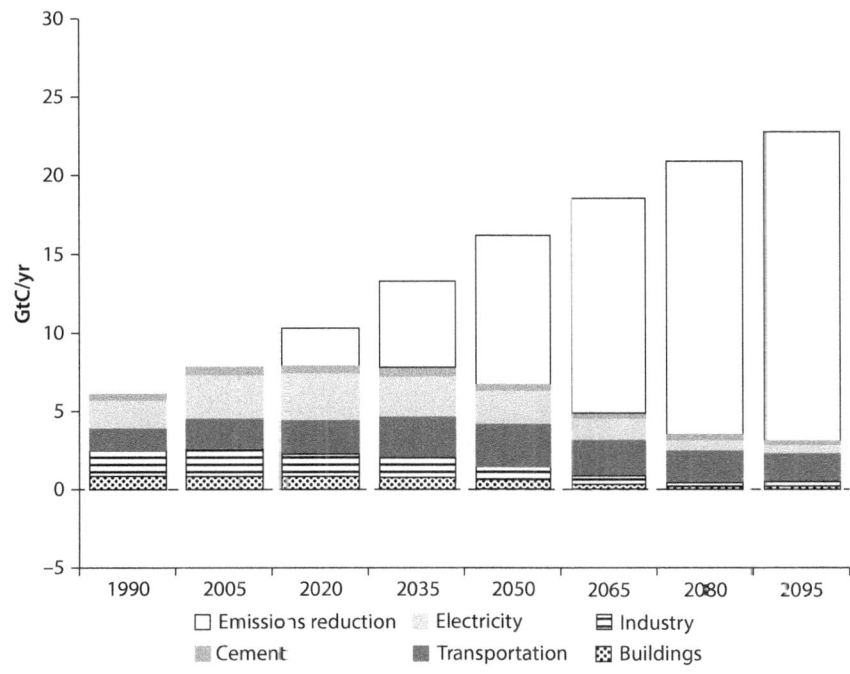

Source: Clarke and Calvin 2008.
Note: GtC/yr = gigatons of carbon per year. ppm = parts per million.

different sectors interact through their impact on the carbon price. Even if there were large-scale use of biomass, however, transport might remain the main polluter, depending less on technical developments in transport than on the availability of carbon capture and storage (CCS). Without CCS, a high carbon price will lead to massive substitution of biofuels for gasoline and diesel. With CCS, much lower carbon prices are needed to get to the 450 ppm stabilization level, removing the pressure to find substitutes for fossil fuels (figure O.8)

Figure O.8 The Pessimistic View: Transport and Carbon Capture and Storage

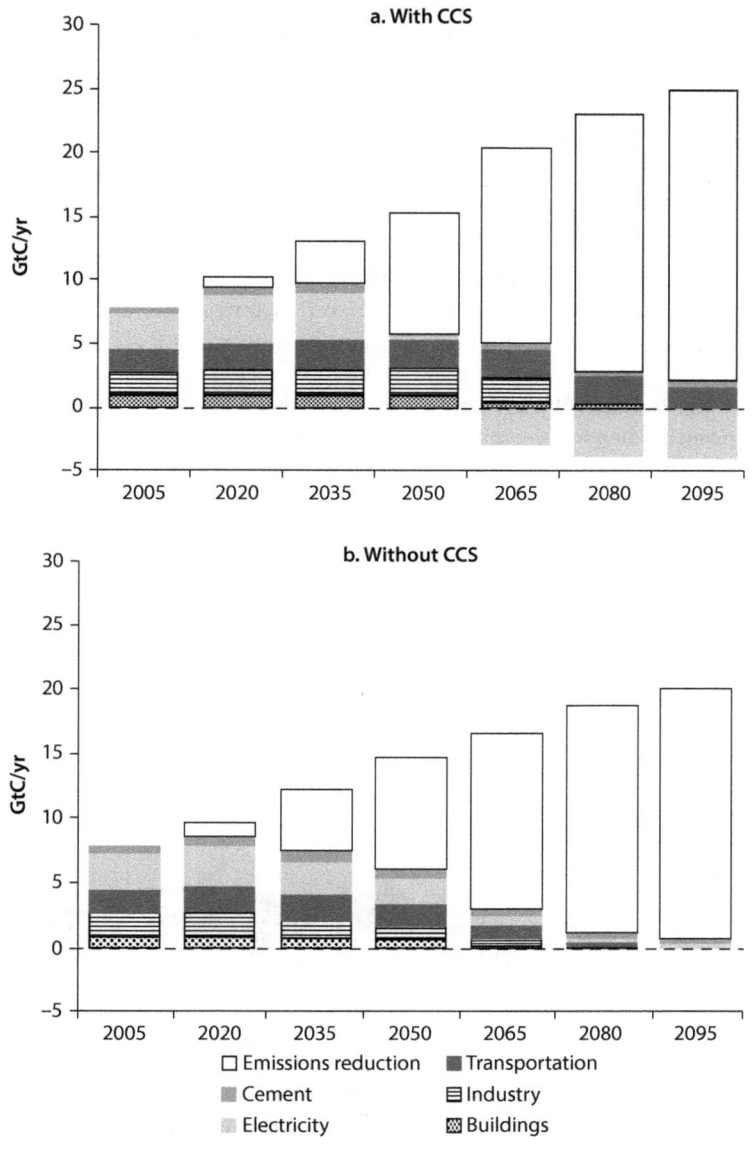

Source: Luckow, Wise, and Dooley 2010.
Note: CCS = carbon capture and storage; GtC/yr = gigatons of carbon per year.

Figure O.9 Passenger Car Density and Income, 2003

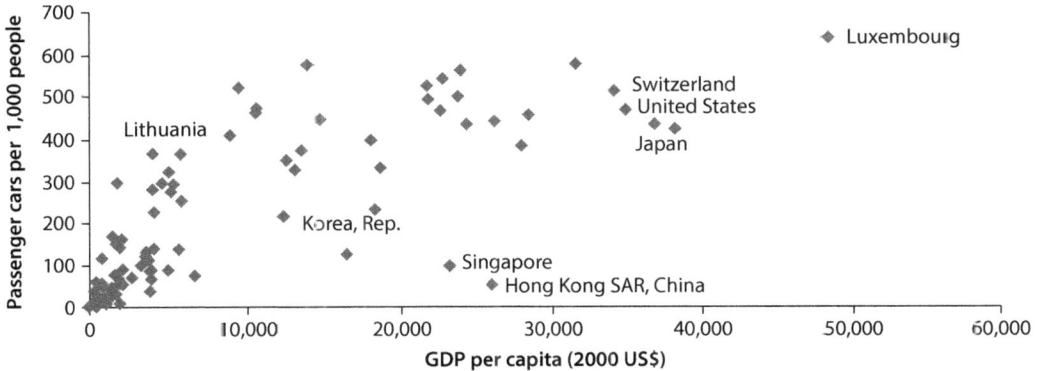

Source: World Bank 2010d.

Without the rapid emergence and global adoption of low-carbon engine technologies, deep cuts in transport greenhouse gas emissions will depend on shifts in mode. Transport emissions can be reduced below the levels envisaged in the scenarios by shifting from

- road transport to rail and waterborne modes
- air transport to rail
- Individual car use to urban mass transit.

Transport is less emissions-intensive in economies were the role of roads is smaller (figure O.9).[1] The Republic of Korea; Singapore; Hong Kong SAR, China; and Japan are all at the lower bound. Countries with low-carbon transport demonstrate that a balanced modal structure is not correlated with low growth. In fact, the "development miracles" of the late 20th century have fairly low shares of road transport and low emissions per passenger-km and ton-km.

Finding alternatives to road transport will be a challenge for rapidly growing cities in developing countries. Megacities Singapore; Seoul; Hong Kong SAR, China; and Tokyo have all combined accessibility and mobility with low emissions by directing transport toward a balanced modal structure. Thirty years ago in Hong Kong SAR, China, car ownership doubled in a decade, and time lost to congestion exploded. The integration of road building, a massive expansion of mass transit, and demand management halved vehicle ownership by 1985—by then 10 percent of the passenger cars were taxis—drastically reducing travel times without making the city less attractive for business (Cullinane 2002). It ranks second on the infrastructure index of the Global Competitiveness Report and second on its goods market efficiency index.

The Effect of the Modal Composition of Transport

The durability of transport equipment, the longevity of its infrastructure, and high fixed costs mean that current investments lock in the modal structure of transport for decades. The high costs that would result from failing to establish a low-carbon transport infrastructure system early on would persist for many years, and the inertia of consumer preferences for many transport attributes other than energy efficiency exacerbates the infrastructure lock-in. That calls for prompt action because of the long time lags between policy implementation and sector changes. Slow changes in the modal composition of infrastructure drastically increase the costs of mitigation because the capital stock has no alternative use (Lecocq, Hourcade, and Ha-Duong 1998). To change travel behavior and the modal choices of users of transport systems thus requires long adjustment periods.

Consumers who buy a vehicle incur high fixed costs. A change in fuel costs or taxes affects only a small part of total expenditures on the car. With changing fuel prices, fuel-inefficient cars lose value on the resale market. The lower price on the resale market translates into a capital loss if the car is sold. If that loss cannot be recaptured by switching to a more fuel-efficient vehicle, substitutes for energy-inefficient transport equipment will be introduced only with the technical depreciation of polluting vehicles.

Most roads are used for more than 70 years (Haraldsson and Jonsson 2008), and the expected lifetime of Dutch bridges is 84 years (Van Noortwijk and Klatter 2004). Once investments have been made, the expenditures are sunk. Economic analysis of a switch from an existing infrastructure network to a new one—say, with a different modal structure—would compare the costs of operating the current system with the high costs of new networks. If past national policies have produced heavy car-dependence, modal shifts are very costly in the short term. But countries at early stages of development can reduce future transport costs substantially by investing in infrastructure that supports low-carbon modes.

The immediate path-dependence of infrastructure induces a secondary path-dependence in settlement patterns. Reliance on road transport and a high share of individual car use favor dispersed settlement, with jobs widely separated from residential locations and long commuting distances. This further constrains the opportunities to reduce the greenhouse gas emissions of urban transport. Changing the modal composition of urban transport then faces the barrier that mass transit cannot serve dispersed settlements.

Shalizi and Lecocq (2009) describe the different dimensions of transport infrastructure lock-in. The U.S. interstate highway program of the 1960s, for instance, determined later investments in state road projects, strengthening road sector network effects and pre-empting expansion of other types of infrastructure like rail. Shalizi and Lecocq see the sprawl of U.S. cities as induced by the build-up of the interstate highway system.

The consumption inertia in transport is reflected in a low price elasticity of transport demand—for developed countries between 0.23 and 0.27. That is, a 10 percent increase in fuel prices would reduce fuel consumption by 2.3–2.7 percent. The temporary lock-in of consumer decisions for vehicle choice is evident in long-term price elasticities that are three to four times higher than short-term elasticities. The difference reflects the time required for consumers to change their transport equipment, and possibly their residence. The emphasis of

U.S. infrastructure policy on roads has reduced transport's responsiveness to price signals, such as the costs of carbon (Hughes, Knittel, and Sperling 2005).

A more flexible modal composition of transport infrastructure increases the opportunities to respond to future changes in energy and emission prices. The price elasticities for European countries well endowed with public transport are 20 percent above the global average (Goodwin, Dargay, and Hanly 2004; Graham and Glaister 2004). And the more the flexibility, the smaller the future adjustment costs and the risk that climate action will increase transport costs.

Transport Adaptation Needs

Transport is not simply a major emitter of greenhouse gases and contributor to climate change. It is also threatened by it. Climate policies for transport have to address two risks: the physical risk of transport disruptions due to extreme weather events, and the policy risk of an emission-intensive transport sector, with limited opportunities to respond to future climate policy imperatives.

Climate change, particularly the higher frequency of extreme weather events, will disrupt transport services more often. Storms and floods will damage costly infrastructure and interrupt access to villages and cities, sometimes for days. Interruptions to commuting and intermediate goods deliveries will lead to production losses. Inventories to protect production against climate-induced supplies irregularities will bind up large amounts of capital. With transport services less reliable, trade relations will become less attractive, and the benefits of a greater division of labor will not materialize. Trucking and other transport-intensive sectors might relocate to regions where they will be less exposed to extreme weather events. If, then, the transport sector is not made more resilient to changing weather conditions, the lower reliability of transport services could have huge development costs.

Adaptation will reduce the risk of extended interruptions to transport. Adaptation concerns management of infrastructure in the short run, and designs and location criteria for infrastructure facilities in the longer run. Threatening the reliability of transport are higher average temperatures, fewer very cold days, earlier spring thaws, and later autumn freezes. Droughts will become more likely in continental areas, while the intensity of rainfall will increase, particularly in coastal areas. Accelerated hydrological cycles will further intensify rainfall and wind storms.

These climatic and hydrological changes will affect infrastructure operations and maintenance. Extreme temperatures can expand and erode surface pavements and buckle rail tracks. Intense rainfall slows road and rail traffic, and flooding completely disrupts it. In aviation, climate change requires larger drainage systems to cope with more intense rainfall, and longer runways and load restrictions to respond to the higher heat during liftoff.

Climate change will exacerbate the deficits in infrastructure administration common in many countries. In many countries maintenance services are underresourced. The value of losses of infrastructure assets often exceeds by far the maintenance spending required to avoid them (Foster and Briceno-Garmendia 2010). Climate change will increase demand for maintenance services to ensure that transport services stay reliable. The follow-on effects of increased landslides, flash floods, and erosion of land transport services will also require expansion of emergency services to avoid long interruptions. Because emergency services are often financed from maintenance budgets, more weather-related emergencies would worsen maintenance fiscal deficits (World Bank 2010c).

Because the consequences of climate change for transport will vary greatly among geoclimatic regions, adaptation must be specific to local conditions. The smaller the geographic area, the more uncertain are any predictions related to climate change, and fine-tuning current climate models will not entirely eliminate the uncertainty. Recurrent assessments of weather-related risks should generate as needed new regulatory frameworks, new institutions, and new policies. The process should periodically produce an action plan, updated in the light of new information on local climate conditions and the consequences for transport (Fay, Ebinger, and Block 2010).

The higher demand for maintenance may alter the tradeoff between capital investment and maintenance. The higher costs of more resilient new investment could bring high future savings in retrofitting or more frequent and costly maintenance. Resolving this tradeoff depends on institutional changes to increase maintenance capacity.

The longevity of transport infrastructure calls for a long planning horizon and a process to update decision rules for investing in infrastructure. A first low-cost step is to change the decision rules for locating new facilities. Assessing rising risks from changing weather conditions and avoiding high-risk sites is economical insurance against climate-related disruptions. But inertia in planning locations can have very high costs. Inundations of more than one meter completely destroy roads. With its current location decisions, for example, Bangladesh risks losing more than 10,000 km of roads (Dasgupta and others 2010).

The biggest challenge for long-term infrastructure planning is to avoid looking only at the past. Because local climates can change abruptly, past changes may not inform what might happen. Standard updating procedures—based on recording weather events and revising the probabilities of their occurrence—can distract from crucial adaptation measures. What is needed are decision tools that can incorporate information from forward-looking nonlinear models. Robust decision making, a process designed for use when probability distributions are unknown, gives proper attention to the possibility of high-impact events even if there is a very low probability that they will occur (Lempert and Collins 2007).

In the longer run, new building codes need to counter short-termism and the temptation to save on capital expenditures. Short-termism manifests itself in overdiscounting the future costs of retrofitting or replacement. New standards can be put in place if new facilities are built and there is progress in predicting climate change (Meyer 2008).

Climate Change and Transport Financing Gaps

Adaptation and mitigation policies will lead to more incremental financial demands. Global scenarios suggest that a large part of mitigation is in vehicle substitution, a cost borne by private households. Yet most incremental costs for adaptation are infrastructure costs. Because the scenarios underrate the modal shift in cutting greenhouse gas emissions, they also underestimate the added costs of redirecting the sector to less road and more rail, waterway, and nonmotorized transport. For interurban transport, the rail infrastructure costs per passenger-km for the San Francisco–Los Angeles corridor are more than twice aviation infrastructure costs, and 15 percent higher than the costs of highways (Levinson, Kanafani, and Gillen 1999). Within cities, the costs for light rail infrastructure alone are at least three times those for bus systems (Zimmerman n.d.).

Incremental financial needs for transport infrastructure will add to the deficits in the sector's fiscal resources. Many studies have found underinvestment in transport infrastructure, independent of the incremental costs of responding to climate change (Bougheas, Demetriades, and Mamuneas 2000; Canning and Bennathan 2000; Esfahani and Ramirez 2003). And in many countries, chronic underinvestment in transport maintenance has reduced infrastructure asset values by more than the required maintenance would have cost (Foster and Briceno-Garmendia 2010).

The incremental costs of adaptation compound these deficits. Funding requirements for adaptation are estimated by assessing how much new investment will be needed in infrastructure, multiplying that value by the share of infrastructure considered vulnerable, and multiplying that result by a mark-up factor for likely increases in infrastructure facilities costs (UNFCCC 2007). A median value for the transport share in national infrastructure investment is 20 percent. Using that assumption, the global incremental financial demands for transport would be $1.6–$26 billion a year (the wide range is due to differences in definitions of what constitutes infrastructure vulnerability). Another way of identifying the incremental funding requirements is to use cost functions that couple macroeconomic data with engineering information on expected infrastructure cost increases for infrastructure. A recent World Bank study using this approach arrives at an estimated $10 billion for additional investment and maintenance costs. The incremental annual adaptation investment is estimated to be $7.2 billion a year until 2030, which is a small share of the baseline investment (World Bank 2010a).

These estimates could underestimate the true incremental costs for two reasons:

- They neglect the infrastructure gaps of developing countries; closing those gaps will increase the additional capital costs. They also neglect the fact that capital costs will be higher because investments must reduce future maintenance requirements.
- They implicitly assume that current maintenance expenditures are optimal for maintaining the value of transport infrastructure. But actual expenditures are

far lower than what is needed. Fay and Yepes (2003) estimate that true maintenance needs are 3.3 percent of gross domestic product (GDP) in low-income countries, 2.5 percent in lower middle-income countries, and 1.4 percent in upper middle-income countries (Estache and Fay 2010). With actual maintenance expenditures often below 1 percent of GDP, the true deficit in maintenance expenditures might thus be large.

The estimated incremental costs for mitigation are far higher. The only estimate for additional spending to mitigate transport greenhouse gas emissions is that of the International Energy Agency (IEA): $100 billion a year between 2010 and 2020, moving up to $300 billion in 2030. Most of the additional spending is for investment in low-emission vehicles. That explains the exponential increase after 2020, which is the point at which plug-in hybrids and electric vehicles would become economically viable (leading to an increment of $52–$159 billion). For low-income and middle-income countries, the scenario underestimates the additional infrastructure investment needed ensure seamless multi-modality of infrastructure because it assigns only a small role to modal shifts.

The Inadequacy of Current Carbon Finance

Carbon finance covers only a very small share of the additional costs for transport adaptation and mitigation activities. Transport does not get much from the Clean Development Mechanism, the most important carbon finance mechanism for curbing greenhouse gas emissions. Of more than 2,200 registered projects, only three are transport projects. The greenhouse gas savings of all three projects add up to less than 300,000 tons of CO_2-equivalent (CO_2 eq), with a mere 0.1 percent of investments. Within the accounting and evaluation standards of the Clean Development Mechanism and its focus on reducing emissions by technology substitution rather than behavioral change, the transport projects look to be less effective in reducing emissions than projects of other sectors.

The transport sector fares not much better with the Global Environment Facility, which provides grants to innovative projects that benefit the global environment; in the past 20 years only 28 transport projects have been approved, for a total of $182.4 million (6.4 percent of all resources allotted). Transport figures more heavily in the country programs of the Clean Technology Fund (CTF), which has a broader multisectoral approach. The CTF provides limited grants, concessional loans, and partial risk guarantees to help countries scale up clean technology initiatives to transform their development path. In half the CTF country plans, transport is a priority, though its share varies considerably between countries. Transport receives on average 16.7 percent of CTF funding and 23 percent of the total investment, including leveraged government funding, multilateral development bank financing, and private investment. Total transport investment (CTF and leveraged) is $8.4 billion.

The carbon finance resources now spent on transport are a tiny share of needs. If transport policies follow a narrow climate change agenda, the high costs of climate action in transport make it unlikely that this will ever change. So far the narrow agenda focuses on reducing CO_2 by changing the technology. If the benefits of less local air pollution, reduced congestion, and greater transport safety are also considered, the prospects for more climate finance will improve. Projects confined to the supply side, without demand incentives, risk a mismatch of supply and demand. They are likely to wastefully underuse transport capacity. It would be more effective to incorporate demand measures to induce behavioral change—reducing uncertainty about the balance of supply and demand and increasing the domain of actions eligible for carbon finance. Thus a broad transport reform agenda that prices in climate, health, and congestion costs would better balance supply and demand and reduce emissions.

Transport Reforms and Climate Policy Costs

Measures to reduce greenhouse gas emissions will reduce congestion costs, local air pollution, and safety risks. Reducing these social impacts of transport will also reduce greenhouse gas emissions. Educating users about transport environmental, safety, and congestion costs will reduce its social costs. Without policies to do so, transport users have no opportunity to learn about health costs due to air pollution and no incentives to change their behavior to reduce them. The policy deficit in making such costs felt is enormous. The highest social costs are due to

- Congestion
- Local air pollution
- Road accidents
- Greenhouse gas emissions

Efforts to reduce these costs do more to reduce greenhouse gas emissions than a narrow climate change agenda (Parry 2007). Moreover, reducing them would produce revenues to finance the transition to low-carbon transport.

An obvious reform step, one that would reduce the social costs of transport and create fiscal opportunities, is to remove subsidies that give the wrong signals. Most important are subsidies for gasoline and diesel. The U.S. pump prices for gasoline and diesel are a good approximation to tax-free and subsidy-free consumer prices (GTZ 2009). In comparison, many developing countries subsidize gasoline and diesel, with substantial consequences for government spending. The Islamic Republic of Iran could save $20 billion a year, and Saudi Arabia $12 billion, by removing transport fuel subsidies. Poorer countries could also have major savings. If it cut its transport fuel subsidies, Myanmar could save more than $300 million. The Islamic Republic of Iran and Colombia are now making substantial strides toward reducing transport subsidies.

The most direct way to convey the costs of transport related to climate change is to price carbon. A gallon of gasoline contains 0.0024 tons of carbon (Parry, Walls, and Harrington 2007). Hypothetical carbon prices of $20, $30, or $300 per ton of carbon would translate into an additional 5, 12, or 72 cents per gallon of gasoline. The carbon price would thus change consumer prices moderately. If there were no changes in travel behavior, the hypothetical carbon charges would bring the United States annual revenues of $10 billion, $24 billion, or $145 billion.

The fiscal consequences of charging for local air pollution differ—in some cases, as in the United States and European Union, they are very high. For the Los Angeles area, containing the health costs of local pollution ranged from 1 to 8 cents per mile in 2000 (Small and Kazimi 1995). Given the number of vehicle miles driven in the area, such charges would produce revenues of $400 million to $3.3 billion. The health costs for Beijing were estimated at $3.5 billion in 2007, equivalent to 3.5 percent of local GDP (Creutzig and He 2009). Similar estimates can be made for congestion and accident costs. Signaling the true costs of transport to users could open considerable opportunities to address the chronic underfinancing of transport and the incremental costs to transport of climate policies.

Those measures would also generate substantial income and welfare benefits. By maximizing the development gains from limiting greenhouse gas emissions, local air pollution, and the costs of congestion and accidents, they produce not only revenues but also net benefits for consumers. Rough estimates suggest that the revenue potential could even be higher than the additional funding required for the transition to a low-carbon regime. If so, making transport more efficient would even make it possible to reduce taxes that are harmful to growth and welfare. A broad reform agenda to make the sector efficient provides far more powerful incentives to reduce greenhouse gas emissions than a narrow climate policy program that implicitly assumes that all other inefficiencies have been removed. An efficient transport sector thus protects the environment and advances development—win, win.

Integrating Supply and Demand

Climate policies in transport have suffered from a disconnect between infrastructure and environmental policymaking and implementation. They have focused on increasing the capacity of infrastructure for low-emission modes and setting regulatory standards. Yet the less the horizontal coordination between supply and demand policies, the greater the uncertainty about how emissions can be effectively reduced. The expansion of mass transit in the United States, for example, led to higher average emissions per passenger-km in public transport than in individual car use due to smaller loads for buses and rail systems (Small and van Dender 2007). Isolated subsectoral agendas can thus have unintended negative effects. By contrast, London's congestion charges were accompanied by a massive increase in bus capacity, which avoided the mismatch. The broad sector reform proposed here requires horizontal coordination not only between different aspects of transport policymaking but also between departments as diverse as finance, land use regulation, security, and health.

The different spatial dimensions of the social costs of transport require vertical coordination of different jurisdictional levels. Because greenhouse gas emissions create global damage, ideally they should be addressed globally. The scenarios of the PNNL show how globally agreed carbon prices could lead all emitting sectors to lower their emissions to arrive at targeted atmospheric concentrations. The local health costs of air pollution can differ greatly by city and region. Policy measures to address these costs should thus differ locally. Congestion and transport safety are similarly local.

Competition between countries, regions, and cities requires vertical coordination to avoid a race to the bottom. Even if there were a collective agreement on climate action, it could be difficult for individual governments to commit to climate policies. The difficulty is that they want to benefit from collective climate actions without reducing emissions. To counter this, higher jurisdictions must frame and coordinate local policies to reduce greenhouse gas emissions. The Indian Sustainable Urban Transport Project is an example of a national strategy to avoid a race by cities to the bottom (World Bank 2009a).

Individual projects to reduce the carbon intensity of transport need to be combined with programmatic policies. The difficulty of including transport in carbon finance mechanisms like the Clean Development Mechanism illustrates this point: Uncertainty over whether bus or rail projects will attract car users or minibus users could prompt the conclusion that transport investments are less effective than other sectors in reducing emissions. The discussion of Nationally Appropriate Mitigation Actions (NAMA) recognizes that programmatic and multisectoral policies can enhance the role of transport in global climate policy.

Note

1. This translates into a mirror image in per capita emissions in transport (see figure O.1).

References

Anderson, J. E., and E. von Wincoop. 2004. "Trade Costs." *Journal of Economic Literature* 42: 691–751.

Baumert, K. A., T. Herzog, and J. Pershing. 2005. *Navigating the Numbers: Greenhouse Gas Data and International Climate Policy*. Washington, DC: World Resources Institute.

Bougheas, S., P. Demetriades, and T. Mamuneas. 2000. "Infrastructure, Specialization and Economic Growth." *Canadian Journal of Economics* 33: 506–22.

Calvin, K., J. Edmonds, B. Bond-Laberty, L. Clarke, S. Kim, P. Kyle, S. J. Smith, A. Thomson, and M. Wise. 2009. "Limiting Climate Change to 450 ppm CO_2 Equivalent in the 21st Century." *Energy Economics* 3: S107–120.

Canning, D., and D. Bennathan. 2000. "The Social Rate of Return on Infrastructure Investment." Policy Research Working Paper 2390, World Bank, Washington, DC.

Clarke, L. 2007. "Transportation Technology and Climate Change. Fuel Economy Technology Trends and Policy Options." Paper presentation at the ICCT.

Clarke, L., and K. Calvin. 2008. "Sectoral Approaches in International and National Policy." Paper presented at the 2nd International Expert Meeting on Bottom-up Based Analysis on Mitigation Potential.

Clarke, L., J. Edmonds, H. Jacoby, H. Pitcher, J. Reilly, and R. Richels. 2007a. *Scenarios of Greenhouse Gas Emissions and Atmospheric Concentrations.* Sub/report 2.1 A of Synthesis and Assessment Product 2.1, U.S. Climate Change Science Program and the Subcommittee on Global Change Research, Washington, DC.

Clarke, L, J. Lurz, M. Wise, J. Edmonds, S. Kim, S. J. Smith, and H. Pitcher. 2007b. "Model Documentation for the MiniCam Climate Change Science Program. Stabilization Scenarios: CCSP Product 2.1a." PNNL 16735, Pacific Northwest National Laboratory, Richland, Washington, DC.

Creutzig, F., and D. He. 2009. "Climate Change Mitigation and Co-Benefits of Feasible Transport Demand Policies in Beijing." *Transportation Research, Part D* 14: 120–31.

Cullinane, S. 2002. "The Relationship between Car Ownership and Public Transport Provision: A Case Study of Hong Kong." *Transport Policy* 9: 29–39.

Dasgupta, S., M. Huq, K. Huq, M. Ahmed, N. Mukherjee, M. Khan, K. Pandey. 2010. "Vulnerability of Bangladesh to Cyclones in a Changing Climate." Policy Research Working Paper 5280, World Bank, Washington, DC.

Dasgupta, S., B. Laplante, C. Meisner, D. Wheeler, and D. Yan. 2007. "The Impact of Sea Level Rise on Developing Countries: A Comparative Analysis." Policy Research Working Paper 4136, World Bank, Washington, DC.

Esfahani, H., and M. Ramirez. 2003. "Institiutions, Infrastructure and Economic Growth." *Journal of Development Economics* 70: 433–77.

Estache, A., and M. Fay, eds. 2010. "Current Debates on Infrastructure Policy." In *World Bank, Globalization and Growth. Implications for a Post-Crisis World*, 151–94. Washington, DC: World Bank.

Fay, M., J. Ebinger, and R. Block. 2010. *Adapting to Climate Change in Eastern Europe and Central Asia.* Washington, DC: World Bank.

Fay, M., and T. Yepes. 2003. "Investing in Infrastructure. What Is Needed, 2000 to 2010?" Policy Research Working Paper 3102, World Bank, Washington, DC.

Foster, V., and C. Briceno-Garmendia. 2010. Africa's Infrastructure. A Time for Transformation. Washington, DC: World Bank.

GTZ (Gesellschaft für Technische Zusammenarbeit). 2009. *International Fuel Prices.* 6th edition. Eschborn, Germany: GTZ.

Goodwin, P., J. Dargay, and M. Hanly. 2004. "Elasticities of Road Traffic and Fuel Consumption with Respect to Price and Income: A Review." *Transport Reviews* 24: 275–92.

Graham, D., and S. Glaister. 2004. "Road Traffic Demand: A Review." *Transport Reviews* 24 261–74.

Haraldsson, M., and L. Jonsson. 2008. "Estimating the Economic Lifetime of Roads Using Replacement Data." Working Paper 2008:5, VTI Solna, Sweden.

Hughes, J., C. Knittel, and D. Sperling. 2006. "Evidence of a Shift in the Short-Run Price Elasticity of Gasoline Demand." UCD-ITS-RR 06-16, Institute of Transportation Studies, University of California, Davis, CA.

Kim, J. H., J. Edmonds, J. Lurz, S. Smith, and M. Wise. 2006. "The Objects Framework for Integrated Assessment: Hybrid Modeling of Transportation." *Energy Journal* 27: 63–91.

Krugman, P. R. 1991. *Geography and Trade*. Cambridge, MA: MIT Press.

Lecocq, F., J. Hourcade, and M. Ha-Duong. 1998. "Decision-Making under Uncertainty and Inertia Constraints: Sectoral Implications of the When Flexibility." *Energy Economics* 20: 539–55.

Lempert, R. J., and M. Collins. 2007. "Managing the Risk of Uncertain Threshold Responses: Comparison of Robust, Optimum, and Precautionary Approaches." *Risk Analysis* 27: 1009–26.

Levinson, D., A. Kanafani, and D. Gillen. 1999. "Air, High Speed Rail, or Highway: A Cost Comparison in the California Corridor." *Transportation Quarterly* 53: 123–32.

Loehman, E., S. Berg, A. Arroyo, R. Hedinger, J. Schwartz, M. Shaww, R. W. Fahien, V. H. De, R. P. Fishe and D. E. Rio. 1997. "Distributional Analysis of Regional Benefits and Cost of Air Quality Control." *Journal of Environmental Economics and Management* 34: 107–26.

Luckow, P., M. Wise, and J. Dooley. 2010. "Biomass Energy for Transport and Electricity: Large Scale Utilization under Low CO_2 Concentration Scenarios." PNNL-19124, Pacific Northwest National Laboratory, Richland, Washington, DC.

Meyer, M. D. 2008. "Design Standards for U.S. Transportation Infrastructure: The Implications of Climate Change." Background paper, U.S. National Research Council, Washington, DC.

National Research Council of the National Academies. 2008. "Potential Impacts of Climate Change on U.S. Transportation." Special Report 290, Transportation Research Board, Washington, DC.

Neumann, J. E., and J. C. Price. 2009. *Adapting to Climate Change: The Public Policy Response—Public Infrastructure* Washington, DC: Resources for the Future.

OECD (Organisation for Economic Co-operation and Development)/IEA (International Energy Agency). 2009a. *Transport, Energy and CO_2. Moving Towards Sustainability*. Paris: IEA.

———. 2009b. *World Energy Outlook 2009*. Paris: IEA.

———. 2010. *Energy Technology Perspectives 2010. Scenarios and Strategies to 2050*. Paris: IEA.

Parry, I. W. 2007. "Are the Costs of Reducing Greenhouse Gases from Passenger Vehicles Negative?" *Journal of Urban Economics* 62: 273–93.

Parry, I. W., M. Walls, and W. Harrington. 2007. "Automobile Externalities and Policies." *Journal of Economic Literature* 45: 373–99.

Shalizi, Z., and F. Lecocq. 2009. "Climate Change and the Economics of Targeted Mitigation in Sectors with Long-lived Capital Stock." Policy Research Working Paper 5063, World Bank, Washington, DC.

Small, K. A., and C. Kazimi. 1995. "On the Costs of Air Pollution from Motor Vehicles." *Journal of Transport Economics and Policy*, 29: 7–32.

Small, K., and K. van Dender. 2007. "Long-Run Trends in Transport Demand, Fuel Price Elasticities and Implications of the Oil Outlook for Transport Policy." Discussion Paper 2006-16, OECD/ITF, Paris.

Sterner, T. 2007. "Fuel Taxes: An Important Instrument for Climate Policy." *Energy Policy* 35: 3194–02.

UNFCCC (United Nation Framework Convention on Climate Change). 2007. *Investment and Financial Flows to Address Climate Change.* Bonn, Germany: UNFCCC.

van Noortwijk, J., and H. Klatter. 2004. "The Use of Lifetime Distributions in Bridge Maintenance and Replacement Modeling." *Computers and Structures* 82: 1091–99.

World Bank. 2008a. *Development and Climate Change: A Strategic Framework for the World Bank.* Washington, DC: World Bank.

———. 2008b. *Safe, Clean and Affordable... Transport for Development.* The World Bank Group's Transport Business Strategy for 2008–2012. Washington, DC: World Bank.

———. 2009a. "Project Appraisal Document. Sustainable Urban Transport Project (SUTP)." Report No 51145-IN, World Bank, Washington, DC.

———. 2009b. *Reshaping Economic Geography. World Development Report 2009.* Washington, DC: World Bank.

———. 2010a. *The Costs to Developing Countries of Adapting to Climate Change. New Methods and Estimates.* Washington, DC: World Bank.

———. 2010b. *Development and Climate Change. World Development Report 2010.* Washington, DC: World Bank.

———. 2010c. *Royaume du Maroc. Adaptation du secteur du transport au changement climatique.* Washington, DC: World Bank.

———. 2010d. *World Development Indicators 2010.* Washington, DC: World Bank.

Zimmerman, S. n.d. "Comparison of Bus Rapid Transit (BRT) and Light Rail Transit (LRT) Characteristics." Mimeo World Bank, Washington, DC, 1–4.

CHAPTER 1

Transport, Mobility, Emissions, and Development

The transport sector is one of the biggest contributors to greenhouse gas (GHG) emissions, and unless there is a shift to low-carbon transport, technology that emits less GHG, and reduced transport use, it will remain so (Parry 2007). Whether it can reach emission targets depends on technical opportunities, user behavior, and infrastructure investment. Continuing business as usual in the face of global climate change could result in higher costs, less mobility, less transport support for development, and greater disruption not only of transport services but also of production reliant on these services.

So far, policies have failed to recognize the centrality of transport's role in global climate change: Joint Implementation initiatives do not include a single transport project; the Clean Development Mechanism has only three transport projects out of 2,587; and the Global Environmental Facility (GEF) has only 30 transport projects out of 2,533. One reason for the lack of new transport projects is their high cost. However, accounting for synergies between related efforts in the sector to reduce traffic congestion, air pollution, and dependence on fuel greatly increases the cost-effectiveness of reducing transport emissions.

The Relationship between Mobility and Development

Historically, affordable transport has driven development, with dramatic changes in transport kicking off rapid economic development (World Bank 2009b). Access and mobility make it possible to share facilities, goods and services, and knowledge, thus increasing productivity (box 1.1).

- Development depends on infrastructure—marketplaces, schools, hospitals, and public administration offices, for instance—to provide basic services, but infrastructure requires substantial fixed investment. A reliable and affordable transport system increases the number of users and thus reduces fixed costs.

Box 1.1 Characteristics of the Transport Sector

The transport sector has increasing returns to scale: higher demand reduces its costs. Coordinating freight trips and balancing irregular demand for deliveries increase returns for the logistics industry (figure A1.1). In the maritime sector, larger container ships reduce ton-km costs.

There is a strong positive correlation between passenger-km traveled and average incomes (figure A1.2). The United States consumes the most passenger-km by far. Switzerland, where the average income is only slightly lower than in the United States, consumes just over a third of the U.S. passenger-kms. Some small countries, such as Lithuania, consume a high level of passenger-km, whereas some middle-income countries where income has recently surged, such as the Republic of Korea, have kept passenger-km remarkably low.

In addition to per capita income, the size of a country, the history of links to former Soviet Union countries, and the history of rail infrastructure policies all affect the rail share of freight transport (figure A1.3; outliers with very high rail freight transport—Kazakhstan and the United States—have been excluded from the figure).

Across countries, differences in rail passenger-km mirror differences in road passenger-km (figure A1.4). Switzerland is the prototypical country with a high per capita income and high rail passenger-km but low road passenger-km. Compared with other rich countries, the United States has low rail passenger-km. Korea has kept rail passenger-km high throughout its rapid economic development. Former Council for Mutual Economic Assistance countries that have emphasized rail transport still have high rail passenger-km.

Car ownership typically increases dramatically when countries reach an average income of $5,000 in 2000 values (figure A1.5). Motorization in Mexico shot up at this per capita income point; but Singapore, Korea, and Taiwan, China—which have had high income growth in recent decades—have kept motorization low. Some countries, such as Switzerland, that have relatively low road passenger-km in relation to incomes nevertheless have high car ownership.

A similar picture holds for passenger car density (figure A1.6). Some small countries, such as Luxembourg and the Baltic states, have a high number of cars, both in absolute terms and relative to their population and income. The rapidly developing East Asian countries stand out for their low passenger car density. India and China have low per capita incomes but a rapidly growing middle class whose demand for cars is rising. Brazil and the Russian Federation have large populations likely to reach the income level at which car ownership increases dramatically, although their passenger car densities per 1,000 people were still low in 2003, with India at 8, China at 10, Brazil at 131, and Russia at 161.

- If transport costs are reduced, workers are more likely to commute or migrate to jobs in larger cities. The larger the local market, the more efficiently consumer goods and inputs to production are produced. The geographic concentration of production made possible by lower transport costs expands opportunities to exploit scale economies.

- Despite progress in communication technologies, the transfer of knowledge and experience still depends on face-to-face communication (for example,

Leamer 2007). Transport increases productivity by creating more opportunities for sharing technical and organizational knowledge, which is crucial to the invention or improvement of products. Ensuring mobility, and thus the opportunity for direct sharing of knowledge, is a challenge in increasingly congested megacities, particularly in developing countries.

Climate Risks from Transport

The transport sector emits the GHGs carbon dioxide (CO_2), nitrous oxide (N_2O), and methane (CH_4). Since N_2O and CH_4 emissions are small, most GHG emission inventories estimate CO_2 emissions only (IPCC/UNEP/OECD/IEA 1997; IPCC 2000). In 2005 transport accounted for about 14 percent of global GHG emissions. This is equivalent to 18 percent of global CO_2 emissions and 24 percent of CO_2 emissions from energy-related sources (Baumert, Herzog, and Pershing 2005).

Within the sector, road transport accounts for the largest share of emissions at 76 percent, followed by air transport at 12 percent and water transport at 10 percent (figure 1.1). From 1971 to 2006 global transport energy use rose steadily at 2–2.5 percent a year, about the same as economic growth (World Bank 2009b).

Figure 1.1 Total Transport CO_2 Emissions, by Transport Mode

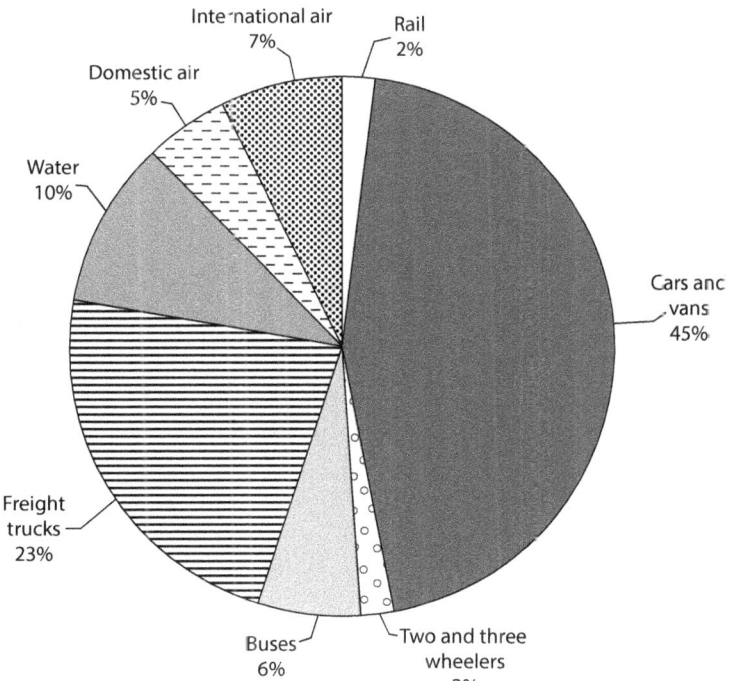

Source: World Business Council for Sustainable Development 2005 (http://www.wbcsd.org/home.aspx).
Note: CO_2 = carbon dioxide.

Behind these figures are drastic differences between countries in absolute and per capita energy consumption. Per capita energy use differs by a factor of 40–50, and the type of fuel used also differs. These differences hold even among the main consumers of fossil fuels—Australia, Europe, Saudi Arabia, Canada, and the United States. For example, Europe uses more diesel fuel per capita than North America. Many African countries use less than 70 kilotons oil equivalent (ktoe), while the United States, Canada, Saudi Arabia, and Australia have per capita consumption of 1,200–5,000 ktoe (map 1.1).

Globally, transport energy use has more than doubled since 1971, although its distribution across road, rail, aviation, and maritime transport has been fairly constant. But regional patterns of transport have changed. The road sector grew at the same pace as transport over the last two decades in developed countries, but it grew much faster, at 3.3 percent annually leading to a doubling in 20 rather than 40 years, in non-OECD (Organisation for Economic Co-operation and Development) countries. An increase in international aviation in the 1990s dominated changes in developed countries, a trend interrupted only briefly by the downturn of aviation after 9/11.

Much of the difference in per capita fuel consumption stems from differences in incomes, but there are also substantial differences between countries with similar incomes, reflecting differences in transport services consumed per capita and types of fuel. International differences in motorization and passenger-car density are paralleled in the relationship between per capita incomes and per capita energy consumption. Hong Kong SAR, China; Singapore; and Japan are examples of economies with low energy intensities that have seen rapid development in

Map 1.1 Per Capita Transport Energy Use, 2006

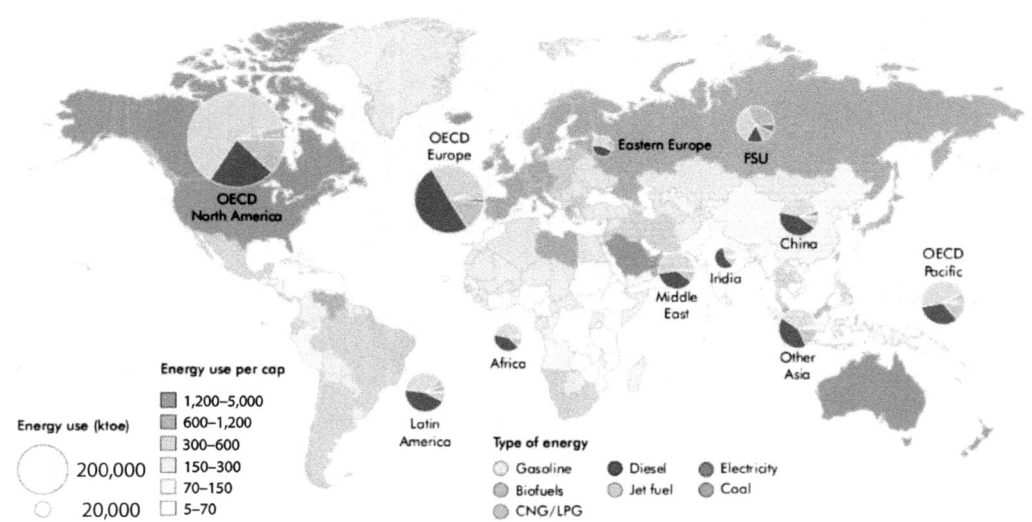

Source: OECD/IEA 2009a, figure 1.2, p. 46.
Note: CNG = compressed natural gas, FSU = former Soviet Union, LPG = liquified petroleum gas, OECD = Organisation for Economic Co-operation and Development. Does not include international shipping.

Figure 1.2 Actual and Projected Transport CO_2 Emissions, 1980–2030

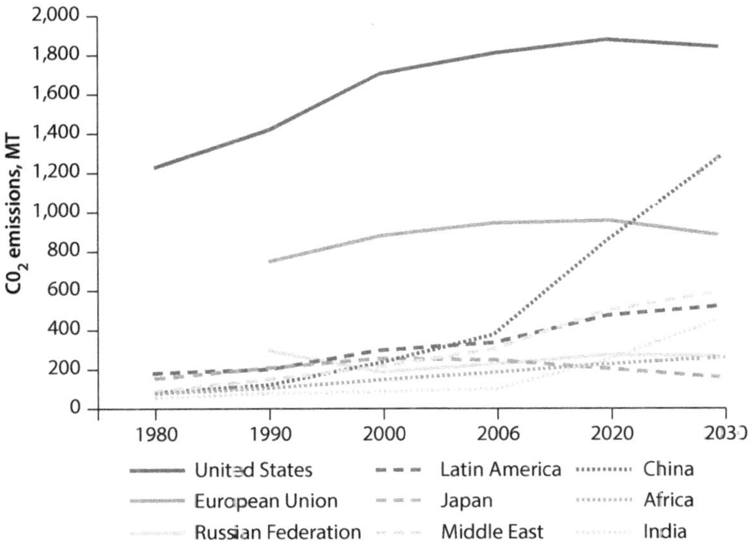

Source: OECD/IEA 2009b.

recent decades. As for fuel, the transport sector will generally remain heavily dependent on oil and will be the largest consumer of energy by 2030, increasing its consumption by about 50 percent. Emissions in North America, Europe, and Japan are projected to decline as more fuel-efficient cars are introduced and as car ownership reaches saturation. Emissions are expected to increase most in China, India, the Middle East, and Latin America (figure 1.2). A comparison of per capita emissions again shows large differences between high-income countries. These energy use differences translate directly into emission differences.

Dealing with Inertia in Infrastructure

Because transport infrastructure must be built to last, early action is needed to adapt what is already in place to likely changes in climatic conditions (and technologies) and to mitigate the kinds of problems aging infrastructure can cause.

Immediate Steps to Adapt

Transport infrastructure has a long lifetime. The effective lifetime of roads is 25–111 years, and most last more than 70 years (Haraldsson and Jonsson 2008). Bridges are expected to last at least 100 years. Since the climate is likely to change over that long a time, transport infrastructure must be made resilient to such changes.

Climate change threats include increasing mean temperatures, more frequent heat waves, more pronounced freeze-thaw cycles, heavier precipitation, stronger winds, and greater storm surges and wave heights. High temperatures can cause road surfaces and rail tracks to deform, floods and snowfalls can paralyze surface

Figure 1.3 Malaysia: Costs of Landslides, 1973–2007

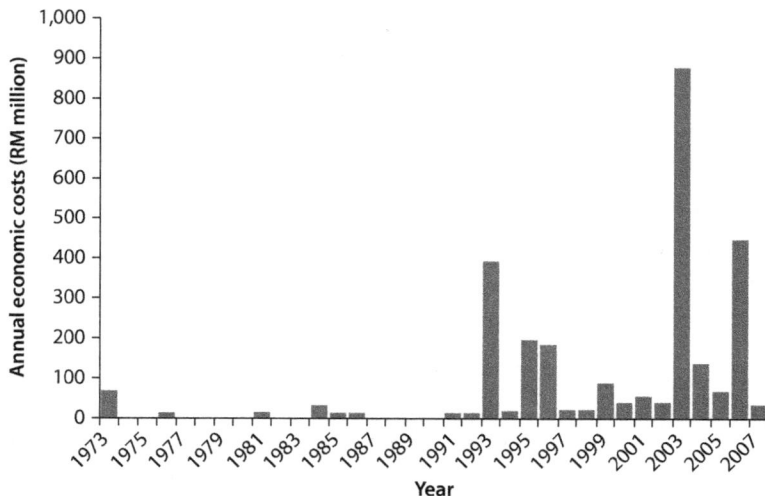

Source: Government of Malaysia 2009.

transport, and droughts can interrupt waterway transport and destabilize building foundations. Storm surges threaten harbor facilities. Rising sea levels may necessitate relocating infrastructure completely.

A major threat to road transport is landslides. In Malaysia, for example, the cost of landslides has increased dramatically (figure 1.3). Costs spiked there in 2003 when a landslide closed the highway at Bukit Lanjan in Selangor, Malaysia, precipitating a half-year of traffic congestion, road closures, and diversions in the Klang Valley that made this landslide Malaysia's most costly to date.

Changes in logistics could cushion extreme weather events. Maintaining larger inventories and more location choices could avoid irregularity in transport times, which drive up distribution costs. The cost of importing goods to the United States, for instance, is estimated to be 55 percent of their production value (Anderson and van Wincoop 2004). Higher logistics cost would be the equivalent of higher value-added taxes, which would adversely affect interregional and international trade.

Transport maintenance is already widely underfinanced and neglected, and will become more so with climate change. Better emergency services could save considerably on maintenance budgets. For example, clearing roads and railways faster after landslides or heavy snowfall could save days of production losses. Infrastructure maintenance and emergency services need serious reform.

Some transport agencies have started to systematically collect information on how climate affects transport. Transit New Zealand, for example, took climate change effects into account as it planned, constructed, and maintained its state highway network as mandated by the 2004 Resource Management (Energy and Climate Change) Amendment Act (National Research Council of the National Academies 2008). A monitoring system tracked how climate weather affected bridges, culverts, causeways, coastal roads, pavement surfaces, surface drainage, and hillside slopes. Of major concern was the threat to highways from a rise in sea level, coastal storm surges, and more frequent and more intense rainfall. The data allowed Transit New Zealand to assess infrastructure vulnerability to see whether retrofitting was needed. The conclusion was that it was less economical to retrofit bridges and culverts than to repair them as needed (Kinsella and McGuire 2005).

Historical data may not reliably predict climate change. Many climate models warn that weather changes may not be smooth but occur in discrete jumps. To protect transport from nonlinear changes, adaptation policies should be anticipatory.

The total costs of adaptation are calculated roughly as percentages of gross fixed capital formation. The United Nations (UN) Framework Convention on Climate Change (UNFCCC) has estimated that gross capital formation will be $22.3 trillion in 2030 (UNFCCC 2007), taking into account the following:

- Munich Re estimates that 0.7 percent of the gross addition to capital formation is vulnerable; the Association of British Insurers estimates 2.7 percent.

- Of the resulting totals, 5–20 percent are capital costs for adaptation, that is, $53–$650 billion. The estimates assume that infrastructure deficits in developing countries will persist and that adaptation money would thus go to developed countries with larger infrastructure endowments (Parry and others 2009). However, if infrastructure capacity in developing countries were to expand (Sachs and The UN Millennium Project 2005), the cost of adaptation in Africa would increase from $370 million to $12.3 billion, roughly in line with the World Bank estimates of Africa's infrastructure deficits (Foster and Briceno-Garmendia 2010).

- Geographic and climatic conditions as well as the local economy's transport intensity will determine the transport share in these investments. The UN Millennium Project expects road financial needs to be about 20 percent of total infrastructure needs. Global transport adaptation needs, according to the UNFCCC estimate, range from $30 to $130 billion. A recent World Bank study estimates the annual cost of transport adaptation to be $11 to $13 billion (Hughes, Chinowsky, and Strzepek 2010).

Data collection and improvement in maintenance and emergency responses to climate events are self-financing, the great uncertainty of future damages notwithstanding. Improved maintenance brings great benefits to developing countries independent of climate change (OECD/ECMT Transport Research Centre 2007). Further adaptation will then use local weather knowledge to inform design standards, use of materials, and location decisions.

Early Action and Sector Inertia
While transport is central to mitigating carbon emissions, there are several impediments to making changes. The first is that because of its high sunk costs,

infrastructure cannot be changed overnight. The second is the technological inertia in both transport mode and infrastructure design. The third is the land use nexus: that is, regulations related to construction, land use, urban planning, and so on that affect everything from settlement patterns to consumer behavior. Moreover, inconsistent energy pricing policies reinforce inertia that resists change.

The intent of transport adaptation is to reduce the negative impact of climate change on access and mobility. The Copenhagen Accord (UNFCCC 2009) expanded the concept of adaptation to include mitigation, with serious consequences for transport. If mitigation leads to higher carbon and vehicle prices, demand could shift from one transport mode to another. Some infrastructure investment would thus become adaptation investment. Because it is uncertain how a local climate will change, current measures are often reactive rather than anticipatory and largely directed to reducing maintenance costs. Some countries, in fact, use up most of their maintenance budget reacting to weather events. Responding to landslides in Morocco, for example, uses 50 percent of the road maintenance budget (World Bank 2010a).

The Forces behind Transport Sector Inertia

Infrastructure inertia: Transport infrastructure facilities tend to be large-scale, lumpy investments with high fixed costs. Capital stock turnover is low because high sunk costs make premature removal of capital costly. That is why inertia is usually modeled within integrated assessment models (IAMS) as a cost multiplier function of capital turnover increase (Lecocq, Hourcade, and Ha-Duong 1998). Consequently, changing the modal structure between roads, rail, aviation, and waterways depends on solid economic policies, especially appropriate pricing policies, such as subsidies and taxes. Because infrastructure expenditures are sunk, the opportunity cost of transport capital stock depends on maintenance. The cost of shifting transport services to low-carbon modes thus unfairly compares the marginal costs of reducing emissions within the carbon-intensive transport mode to the full (infrastructure plus operations) cost of shifting to an innovative, low-emission mode. For instance, power station networks for recharging batteries of electrically powered cars require high fixed investment. Thus, the cheapest option would appear to be marginal changes to existing infrastructure rather than investing in a new low-carbon infrastructure. However, climate change uncertainty and inertia argue for early mitigation. Socioeconomic inertia increases the cost of accelerating emissions reduction as initial targets tighten up (Ha-Duong, Grubb, and Hourcade 1997). At some point expected costs exceed the costs of premature capital removal, thus making early, forceful mitigation measures profitable. Any sound comparative economic analysis must therefore take into account inertia if it is not to omit relevant low-carbon investments.

Technological inertia: Incentives to densify the existing grid arise mostly from technology lock-in and network effects (Economides 1996) that increase the value of existing services when demand for such services grows. For example, the U.S. Interstate Highway Program launched in the 1960s has largely determined later investments in state road projects at the expense of other transport, such as rail (Shalizi and Lecocq 2009). Energy pricing policies that either subsidize fossil fuels or do not reflect the true social cost of carbon discourage innovation in energy-saving technologies and encourage consumer inertia in favor of carbon-intensive transport.

Built-environment inertia: Besides moving people and goods, transport infrastructure fosters economic development and shapes the pattern of a territory. For example, the sprawling pattern of U.S. cities may be an induced effect of the Interstate Highway Program (Shalizi and Lecocq 2009). Thus transport infrastructure must be considered as just one aspect of broader public policies for land use, regional development, and sustainable development. Changing the regulatory framework is a prerequisite to infrastructure change, although the difficulty of tracking the complex interactions between development and infrastructure planning tends to work against radical change. Early action is needed to overcome inertia and move the sector gradually to a low-carbon state. Inertia toward change stems from three factors: transport services depend on infrastructure, consumers value certain transport services that are weighted against energy savings and lower emissions, and historic infrastructure and energy-related transport policies on the demand side determine current differences in emissions.

Past Infrastructure Policies and Transport Emissions

Building infrastructure promotes self-reinforcing development. How? (1) Investments in transport infrastructure are normally large-scale, lumpy, and have high fixed costs. (2) Infrastructure has a long lifetime, extending over generations if properly maintained, which means long-term forecasting of demand for services and of the capacity needed to meet that demand. (3) Expenditures for infrastructure are sunk; once infrastructure is in place, it cannot be put to another use. Transport infrastructure also creates secondary investments in housing and other urban infrastructure that make changes in it even more costly.

Policies to change infrastructure capacity or the structure of roads, rail aviation, and waterways are thus costly. Because infrastructure spending is sunk, the opportunity cost of transport infrastructure stock depends on maintenance. Any economic analysis of the shifting of transport services to low-carbon modes will thus compare the marginal costs of reducing emissions within the high-carbon sector to the full (infrastructure plus operations) costs of shifting to a low-emission mode.

Transport infrastructure investment also largely determines settlement and land use. Prioritizing car use, for example, leads to dispersed settlement because low transport costs invite people to move to areas distant from their jobs and retail centers where housing is less costly. U.S. household data suggest that suburban households drive 31–35 percent more than urban residents (Kahn 2006). Dispersed settlements are more difficult to serve by mass transit. In the United States, for example, the share of mass transit passenger miles relative to other modes has been falling steadily for 30 years (Polzin and Chu 2005).

How responsive users are to fuel cost changes and carbon taxes is an indicator of transport inertia. There is a vast literature measuring the short-run elasticity of gasoline demand. A review of 300 studies for the United States and other developed countries found a median short-run price elasticity of −0.23 (Espey 1998). In other words, a 10 percent increase in fuel price would reduce gasoline consumption by 2.3 percent. An even higher estimated −0.27 elasticity for European countries reflects a higher share of nonmotorized transport and more public transport (Goodwin, Dargay, and Hanly 2004; Graham and Glaister 2004). Long-term elasticities are in the range of −0.6 to −1.0, about three times higher than those for the short term. The higher long-run elasticities are influenced by consumers moving in the shorter run to cars that consume less fuel or to residential locations that require less vehicle-km travel, and in the longer run making residential location decisions that result in shorter commuting and retail trips. Notably, transport has become less responsive to emission cost changes (Hughes, Knittel, and Sperling 2008; Small and van Dender 2007). During two periods that had similarly high prices, 1975–1980 and 2001–2006, short-run price elasticities went down considerably, ranging from −0.21 to −0.34 for 1975–1980 and −0.034 to −0.077 for 2001–2006 (Hughes, Knittel, and Sperling 2008). This decrease may reflect more dependence on cars as suburban development increases distances between homes and job and retail locations.

With few incentives for consumers to reduce energy use and emissions, transport policy must intervene if reduction targets are to be achieved. However, sudden and dramatic price increases in equipment and infrastructure, a cap-and-trade system, or the levying of carbon taxes would in the short term create high welfare costs (Gusdorf and Hallegatte 2007). Severe transport cost hikes would decrease demand for other goods and have a negative secondary effect on economies from infrastructure use, trade, and agglomeration.

Changing only supply-side investment could lead to a mismatch of capacity and demand without bringing down emissions much. Ideally, incentives to guide demand to less polluting modes should be put in place concurrently with the transition to low carbon use. This would limit negative secondary effects and increase political acceptability (Weyant 1993).

In contrast to what low short-run elasticities suggest, persistent incentives for changing demand can significantly influence fuel and emission intensity (figure 1.4). Per capita gasoline consumption mirrors price developments for the last two decades. A study calculated the hypothetical effect of all OECD countries adjusting permanently to the fuel tax levels of Italy, the United Kingdom, and the Netherlands (Sterner 2007). This would reduce all OECD transport carbon emissions by about 40 percent, or 270 million tons of fuel a year; in a decade 8.5 billion tons of CO_2 would thus be avoided. If all OECD countries were taxed at the level of the United States rather than of the Netherlands, however, the increase in emissions would be 133 percent.

Low-Carbon Transport and Development

Some low- and middle-income countries that have rapidly reached very high per capita incomes have kept per capita emissions very low. In the late 1970s, Hong Kong SAR, China, resembled metropolitan areas of today: It had real growth of about 10 percent a year, an influx of immigrants, and a roaring demand for private cars. Car ownership had more than doubled in a decade. The result was both a huge loss of time for passengers and freight and significant health costs from air pollution.

The Hong Kong SAR, China, transport department reacted with draconian measures (Hau 1990). In 1979 it drastically reformed transport policy, increased road capacity, improved mass transit, and introduced demand management. It trebled the license fee for cars, doubled the first registration fee (up to 90 percent of the value of an imported car), and doubled fuel taxes. Vehicle ownership plunged; by 1985 it was down to 50 percent of the 1979 value, of which taxis represented 10 percent. The public transport system incorporates an underground metro, a heavy rail line linking Hong Kong SAR, China, with mainland China, a light rail system in the northwest New Territories, and a tram on the north side of Hong Kong Island. Five private

Figure 1.4 Price Differences and per Capita Gasoline Consumption, Selected Countries

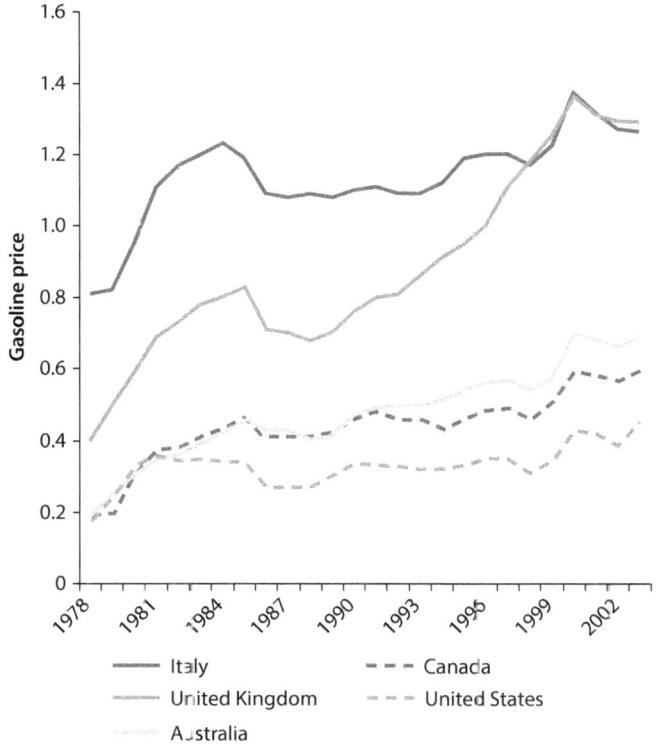

figure continues next page

Figure 1.4 Price Differences and per Capita Gasoline Consumption, Selected Countries *(continued)*

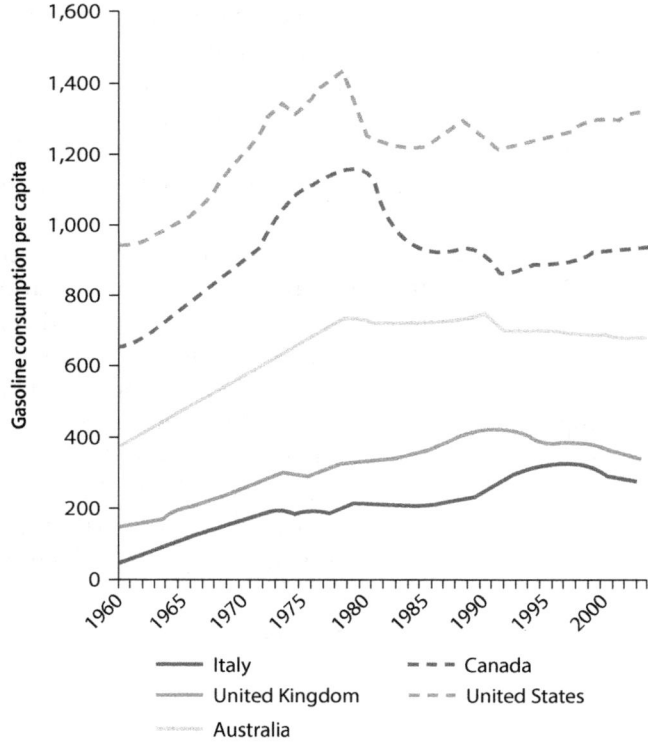

Source: Sterner 2007.

bus companies operate more than 6,000 buses. Minibuses with fixed fares and exclusive rights to operate on certain routes provide feeder services to the main bus lines. Entry to this submarket is strictly regulated and a maximum number of minibuses is set for city districts. Transfers from one mode of travel to another are synchronized to minimize time loss (Cullinane 2002).

The opening of the Island Eastern Corridor in 1987 and the Island Route of the Mass Transit Railway further reduced congestion. Tolls are levied to improve air quality and keep the city attractive. (Although road pricing had been introduced in 1985, after vehicle ownership had already significantly decreased, it has been dropped.) In the infrastructure index of the Global Competitiveness Report, Hong Kong SAR, China, ranks second, with a score of 6.54 out of 7. In goods market efficiency, it scores 5.54, second only to Singapore (World Economic Forum 2010). Hong Kong SAR, China, is a prime example of a metropolis that has retained a high level of mobility by taking a multimodal approach rather than focusing only on roads. Avoiding the congestion that plagues other megacities allows both for agglomeration economies and for sustained access and mobility for residents.

Annex 1A Characteristics of the Transport Sector

The transport sector has increasing returns to scale: higher demand reduces its costs. Coordinating freight trips and balancing irregular demand for deliveries increase returns for the logistics industry (figure 1A.1). In the maritime sector, larger container ships reduce ton-kilometer costs.

There is a strong positive correlation between passenger-km traveled and average incomes (figure 1A.2). The United States consumes the most passenger-km by far. Switzerland, however, with an average income only slightly lower than that of the United States, consumes only just over a third of U.S. passenger-km. Some small countries, such as Lithuania, consume a high level of passenger-km, whereas some middle-income countries where income has recently surged, such as Korea, have kept passenger-km remarkably low.

In addition to per capita income, the size of a country, the integration of former Soviet Union countries, and the history of rail infrastructure policies all affect the rail share of freight transport (figure 1A.3; outliers with very high rail freight transport—Kazakhstan and the United States—have been excluded from the figure).

Across countries, differences in rail passenger-km mirror differences in road passenger-km (figure 1A.4). Switzerland is the prototypical country with high per capita income and high rail passenger-km but low road passenger-km. Compared with other rich countries, the United States has low rail passenger-km. Korea has maintained high rail passenger-km throughout its rapid economic development. Former Council for Mutual Economic Assistance countries that have emphasized rail transport still have high rail passenger-km.

Figure 1A.1 Road Freight and Average Income, 2006

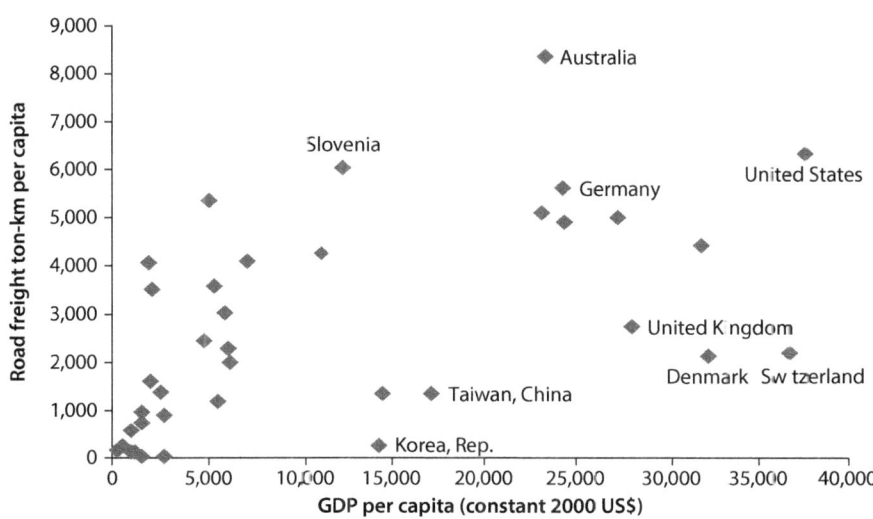

Source: World Bank 2010b.
Note: GDP = gross domestic product.

Figure 1A.2 Road Passenger Transport and Average Income, 2006

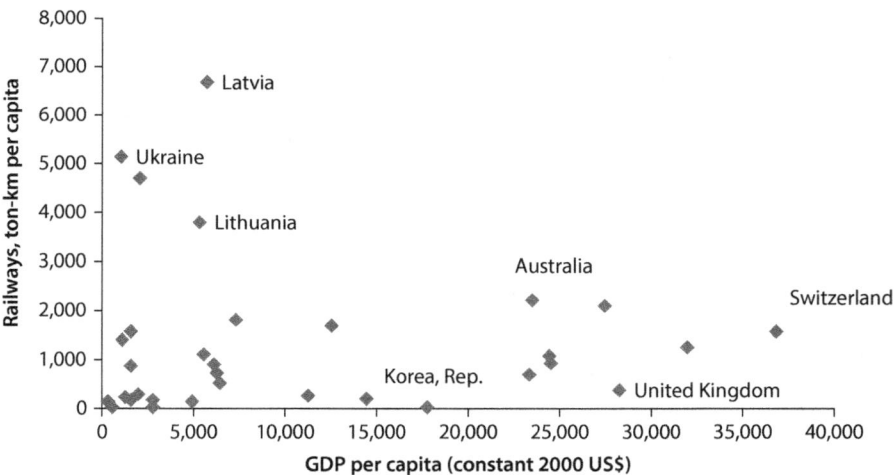

Source: World Bank 2010b.
Note: GDP = gross domestic product.

Figure 1A.3 Rail Freight Transport and Average Income, 2006

Source: World Bank 2010b.
Note: GDP = gross domestic product.

Car ownership typically increases dramatically when countries reach an average income of $5,000 in 2000 values (figure 1A.5). Motorization in Mexico shot up at this per capita income point; but Singapore, Korea, and Taiwan, China, which have all had high income growth in recent decades, have kept motorization low. Some countries, such as Switzerland, that have relatively low road passenger transport in relation to incomes nevertheless have high car ownership.

Figure 1A.4 Rail Passenger Transport and Average Income, 2006

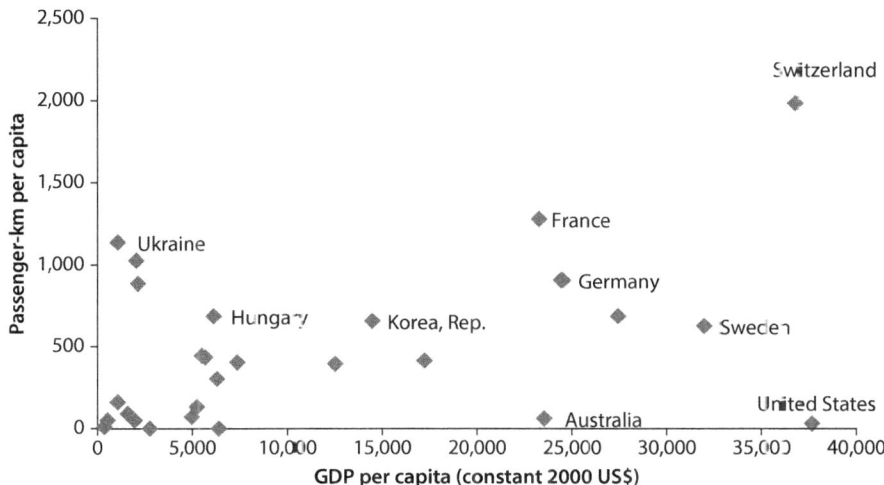

Source: World Bank 2010b.
Note: GDP = gross domestic product.

Figure 1A.5 Motorization and Income, 2005

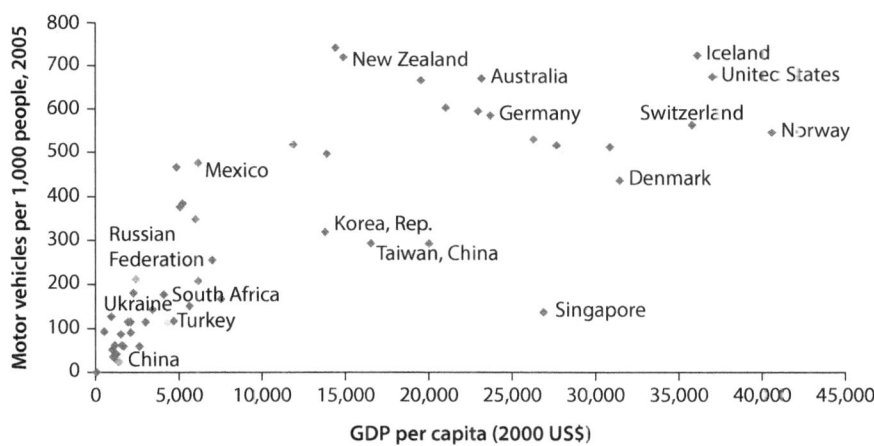

Source: World Bank 2010b.
Note: GDP = gross domestic product.

A similar picture holds for passenger car density (figure 1A.6). Some small countries, such as Luxembourg and the Baltic states, have a high number of cars, both in absolute terms and relative to their population and income. The rapidly developing East Asian countries stand out for their low passenger car density. India and China have low per capita incomes but a rapidly growing middle class whose demand for cars is rising. Brazil and Russia have large populations likely to reach the income level at which car ownership increases dramatically. However, passenger car densities per 1,000 people were still low in 2003, at 8 for India, 10 for China, 131 for Brazil, and 161 for Russia.

Figure 1A.6 Passenger Car Density and Income, 2003

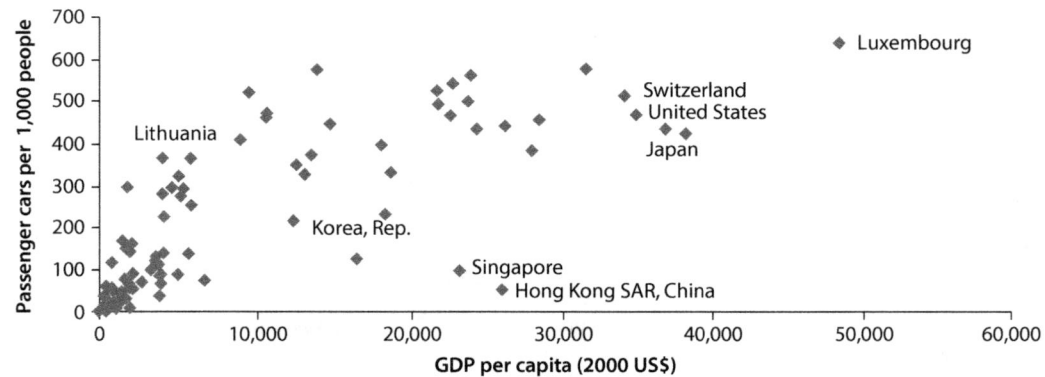

Source: World Bank 2010b.
Note: GDP = gross domestic product.

References

Anderson, J. E., and von Wincoop, E. 2004. "Trade Costs." *Journal of Economic Literature* 42: 691–751.

Baumert, K. A., Herzog, T., and Pershing, J. 2005. *Navigating the Numbers: Greenhouse Gas Data and International Climate Policy*. Washington, DC: World Resources Institute.

Cullinane, S. 2002. "The Relationship between Car Ownership and Public Transport Provision: A Case Study of Hong Kong." *Transport Policy* 9: 29–39.

Economides, N. 1996. "The Economics of Networks." *International Journal of Industrial Organization* 14 (6): 673–99.

Espey, M. 1998. "Gasoline Demand Revisited: An International Meta-Analysis of Elasticities." *Energy Economics* 20: 273–90.

Foster, V., and Briceno-Garmendia, C. 2010. *Africa's Infrastructure. A Time for Transformation*. Washington, DC: World Bank.

Goodwin, P., Dargay, J., and Hanly, M. 2004. "Elasticities of Road Traffic and Fuel Consumption with Respect to Price and Income: A Review." *Transport Reviews* 36: 275–95.

Government of Malaysia. 2009. *National Slope Master Plan 2009–2023*. Kuala Lumpur.

Graham, D., and Glaister, S. 2004. "Road Traffic Demand: A Review." *Transport Reviews* 24: 261–74.

Gusdorf, F., and Hallegatte, S. 2007. "Behaviors and Housing Inertia Are Key Factors in Determining the Consequences of a Shock in Transportation Costs." *Energy Policy* 35: 3483–95.

Haraldsson, M., and Jonsson, L. 2008. "Estimating the Economic Lifetime of Roads Using Replacement Data." VTI Working Paper 2008:5, Swedish National Road & Transport Research Institute, Solna, Sweden.

Ha-Duong, M., Grubb, M. J., and Hourcade, J.-C. 1997. "Influence of Socioeconomic Inertia and Uncertainty on Optimal CO_2 Emission Abatement." *Nature* 390: 270–73.

Hau, T. 1990. "Electronic Road Pricing: Developments in Hong Kong 1983–1989." *Journal of Transport Economics and Policy* 24: 203–14.

Hughes, G., Chinowsky, P., and Strzepek, K. 2010. "The Costs of Adapting to Climate Change for Infrastructure." Discussion Paper 2, the World Bank Economics of Adaptation to Climate Change Study, Washington, DC.

Hughes, J. E., Knittel, C. R., and Sperling, D. 2008. "Evidence of a Shift in the Short-Run Price Elasticity of Gasoline Demand." *Energy Journal* 29: 113–34.

IPCC (Intergovernmental Panel on Climate Change). 2000. *Good Practice Guide*. Paris: IPCC.

IPCC (Intergovernmental Panel on Climate Change)/UNEP (United Nations Environment Programme)/OECD (Organisation for Economic Co-operation and Development)/IEA (International Energy Agency). 1997. *Revised 1996 IPCC Guidelines for National Greenhouse Gas Inventories*. Paris: IPCC.

Kahn, M. 2006. *Green Cities: Urban Growth and the Environment*. Washington, DC: Brookings Institution Press.

Kinsella, Y., and McGuire, F. 2005. "Climate Change Uncertainty and the State Highway Network: A Moving Target." Conference paper. Transit New Zealand.

Leamer, E. 2007. "A Flat World, a Level Playing Field, a Small World after All, or None of the Above? A Review of Thomas L. Friedman's The World Is Flat." *Journal of Economic Literature* 45: 83–126.

Lecocq, F., Hourcade, J.-C., and Ha-Duong, M. 1998. "Decision Making under Uncertainty and Inertia Constraints: Sectoral Implications of the When Flexibility." *Energy Economics* 20 (5–6): 539–55.

McKinsey & Company. 2009. *Pathways to a Low-Carbon Economy. Version 2 of the Global Greenhouse Gas Abatement Cost Curve*.

National Research Council of the National Academies. 2008. "Potential Impacts of Climate Change on U.S. Transportation." Transportation Research Board Special Report 290, National Research Council of the National Academies, Washington DC.

OECD (Organisation for Economic Co-operation and Development)/ECMT (European Conference of Ministers of Transport) Transport Research Centre. 2007. *Transport Infrastructure Charges and Capacity Choice: Self-financing Road Maintenance and Construction*. Round Table Report 135. Paris: OECD.

OECD (Organisation for Economic Co-operation and Development)/IEA (International Energy Agency). 2009a. *Transport, Energy and CO_2. Moving Toward Sustainability*. Paris.

———. 2009b. *World Energy Outlook 2009*. Paris: IEA.

Parry, I. W. 2007. "Are the Costs of Reducing Greenhouse Gases from Passenger Vehicles Negative?" *Journal of Urban Economics* 62: 273–93.

Parry, M., Arnell, N., Berry, P., Dodman, D., Fankhauser, S., Hope, C., Kovats, S., Nicholls, R., Satterthwaite, D., Tiffin, R., and Wheeler, T. 2009. *Assessing the Costs of Adaptation to Climate Change: An Assessment of the Estimates of the UNFCCC and Other Recent Estimates*. London: International Institute for Environment and Development.

Polzin, S. E., and Chu, X. 2005. "A Closer Look at Public Transportation Mode Share Trends." *Journal of Transportation and Statistics* 8: 41–53.

Sachs, J., and The United Nations Millenium Project. 2005. *Investing in Development: A Practical Plan to Achieve the Millennium Development Goals*. London and Sterling: Earthscan.

Shalizi, Z., and F. Lecocq. 2009. "Climate Change and the Economics of Targeted Mitigation in Sectors with Long-lived Capital Stock." Policy Research Working Paper 5063, World Bank, Washington, DC.

Small, K. A., and van Dender, K. 2007. "Fuel Efficiency and Motor Vehicle Travel: The Declining Rebound Effect." *Energy Journal* 28: 25–51.

Sterner, T. 2007. "Fuel Taxes: An Important Instrument for Climate Policy." *Energy Policy* 35: 3194–202.

UNFCCC (United Nations Framework Convention on Climate Change). 2007. *Investment and Financial Flows to Address Climate Change.* Bonn, Germany: UNFCCC.

———. 2009. Report of the Conference of the Parties on its fifteenth session, held in Copenhagen from December 7–19, 2009. http://unfccc.int/resource/docs/2009/cop15/eng/11a01.pdf.

Weyant, J. P. 1993. "Costs of Reducing Global Carbon Emissions." *Journal of Economic Perspectives* 7: 27–46.

World Bank. 2009a. *Development and Climate Change. World Development Report 2010.* Washington, DC: World Bank.

———. 2009b. *Reshaping Economic Geography. World Development Report 2009.* Washington, DC: World Bank.

———. 2010a. *Royaume du Maroc. Adaptation du secteur du transport au changement climatique.* Washington, DC.

———. 2010b. *World Development Indicators 2010.* Washington, DC: World Bank.

World Economic Forum. 2010. *Global Competitiveness Report 2009–2010.* Geneva: World Economic Forum.

CHAPTER 2

Avoiding Future Disruption of Services

Recognizing that transportation is essential to growth and development, governments are increasingly concerned about how to grow or at least maintain this sector when emission reduction policies could increase costs and threaten services. Transport and climate change professionals have both focused on greenhouse gases (GHG), but too often they see their agendas as conflicting. This has made it hard for them to communicate about ways to work together to preserve and expand the economic benefits of transport services—through adaptation.

In all sectors adaptation to the physical impact of climate change constitutes "adjustment in natural or human systems, in response to actual or expected climatic stimuli or their effects, which moderate, harm or exploit beneficial opportunities" (World Bank 2010b). Adaptation thus describes all efforts, whether by bridge engineers, bus drivers, or urban planning agencies, to increase the resilience and reliability of transport in anticipation of climate change.

This chapter reviews how climate change is likely to affect transport operations and infrastructure, cost-effective measures for minimizing negative effects, and policies and decision frameworks in support of these measures. Most analytic work on climate change impact and adaptation has been done in high-income countries. This chapter takes those analyses, particularly that of the U.S. Transportation Research Board (NRC 2008) as a foundation, highlighting current and projected research findings and examples from developing countries.

Threats to Transport Infrastructure and Operations

Our climate is already changing (boxes 2.1 and 2.2), but projecting exactly how it will continue to change is difficult. Understanding what global climate models can and cannot tell us is central to understanding how to estimate and address local impacts.

Global and regional models can project broad climate trends over large temporal and geographic scales but cannot predict specific outcomes, especially

> **Box 2.1 Impact of Sea-Level Rise and Cyclones on Transport Infrastructure in Bangladesh**
>
> Typically, roads are partially damaged when surge inundation is less than one meter and totally destroyed when it exceeds one meter. If road networks are expanded by 25 percent growth between 2005 and 2050, geographic overlays of the road network and inundation zones indicate that—even without climate change—by 2050 3,998 km will be exposed to an inundation depth of less than one meter and 8,972 km to a depth of more than one meter. With climate change, these numbers will increase respectively to 10,466 and 10,553 km. Over a 10-year period, larger cyclones could add another 3,461 km of partially damaged roads and 2,205 km of destroyed roads. According to a 2007 damage loss assessment by Sidr, repair costs would be Taka 1 million for partial damage and Taka 2 million for partial and total destruction; bridge, culvert, and other damage would be 1.13 times the road damage. Combined damage costs by 2050 would thus be an additional $239.5 million. (The estimate of damage to roads, bridges, culverts, and the like is $173.6 million by 2050 without climate change, $413.1 million with climate change.) The estimated additional loss in a changing climate is $52.7 million.
>
> *Source:* Dasgupta and others 2010.

for shorter periods, such as a decade, or smaller geographic scales, such as a single metropolitan area. Further, while there is consensus on basic temperature indicators, it is much harder to estimate such climate features as surface water availability and extreme events. Even with finer-scale data or new observations from the next few decades, much uncertainty will remain.

Experience from a number of municipalities in high-income countries makes a case for looking at broad trends in assessing potential impacts and risks (Ligeti, Penney, and Wieditz 2007). Thus the impacts described below comprise a range of possibilities for a spectrum of areas. While planners are encouraged to seek detailed country-specific information to supplement this material, they should recognize that none of the projections are certain (Schneider and Kuntz-Duriseti 2002). (The end of this chapter addresses how to deal with uncertainty rather than shying away from it as an excuse for inaction.) Finally, all climate impacts must be considered in terms of other local features and changes.

Climate Changes Likely by Mid-Century

Higher average temperatures will bring more temperature extremes throughout the world, with more very hot days and heat waves. The 24-hour temperature range will also narrow because nighttime temperatures will increase more than daytime temperatures. There will be fewer very cold days. Warming will be greatest at the poles, where permafrost has already begun to melt, and ice covering the polar seas will shrink. Polar warming will be greatest in winter. Even in temperate zones, the timing of seasons will shift, with earlier spring thaws, later autumn freezes, and the potential for more freeze/thaw cycles. In the tropics, the hottest months will experience the most pronounced warming.

Box 2.2 The 1997–98 El Niño and Transport and Reconstruction in Kenya, Peru, and Ecuador

Climate change may already be altering the patterns of El Niño, although research has yet to confirm this.[a] In any case, El Niño weather extremes offer insight into the possible impact of severe weather caused by climate change. The particularly severe El Niño of 1997–98, felt around the globe, offers an example.

Kenya: The 1997–98 El Niño rains devastated the transportation sector. Floods and landslides destroyed several bridges and an estimated 100,000 km of roads. Damage was estimated at $670 million. Flooding disrupted aviation and shipping. Poor visibility and submerged navigational equipment and runways halted scheduled and chartered flights; flooded docks made it impossible to off-load merchandise from ships. Floodwaters, fallen trees, and collapsed buildings destroyed electrical equipment, interrupted electricity supplies, destroyed communication lines, and severely disabled underground cable channels and telecommunications. The energy sector did experience one positive benefit, however: hydroelectric dams were completely recharged, electricity production was enhanced.

Peru: The 1997–98 El Niño had a direct negative impact on Peru's highways and roads, which extend for 75,000 km (only a third of Peruvian highways are gravel or asphalt). Highways and roads carry 80 percent of Peru's merchandise. Transportation companies and merchants were hit hard by the highway system's vulnerability, but most affected were towns and villages, several of which were isolated by El Niño without adequate food or supplies.

Ecuador: The economic losses associated with the 1997–98 El Niño in Ecuador have been estimated at $2.9 billion, or about 15 percent of Ecuador's 1997 gross domestic product (GDP). Sixty percent of Ecuador's population was affected, with the coastal and southern provinces suffering most. Damage to manufacturing represented 53 percent of total damage, and damage to transport 28 percent. Ecuador's GDP growth rate in 1998 declined about 1.2 percent from the projection without El Niño. According to the National Institute for Census and Statistics, El Niño had a heavy impact on the country's coastal and island populations, which together make up 50 percent of Ecuador's inhabitants. Approximately 34 percent of those affected were younger than 15. Most of the flooded cities sustained damage to water supply, sewage, and infrastructure. Even though the affected urban population was larger, the rural populace suffered more. Flooding not only cut them off from the highways, bridges, and roads that are their lifelines to the cities but also destroyed their agricultural products, raising market prices.

Source: Adapted from Glantz 2001; see also CEPAL 1998.
a. Basic information on possible links between El Niño events and climate change is available from the Max Planck Institute for Meteorology: http://www.mpimet.mpg.de/en/aktuelles/presse/faq/das-el-nino-southern-oscillation-er so-phaenomen/beeinflussung-el-ninos-durch-den-anthropogenen-treibhauseffekt.html. Publications investigating the topic include Collins and others (2010); Collins and The CMIP Modelling Groups (2004); Paeth and others (2008); Philip and van Oldenborgh (2006); Trenberth and Hoar (1997).

Annual precipitation averages will shift. There will be a slight increase in global precipitation, but with enormous regional variability. Rainfall will likely diminish in continental interiors and increase in coastal areas. Nearly everywhere, rainfall will be more intense; that is, a given annual total is more likely to fall on fewer days, so that many places may experience both more dry spells and more floods. In addition to this increase in intra-annual variability, inter-annual variability will also increase—that is, there will be more extremely dry and extremely wet years—especially in areas strongly affected by El Niño and La Niña. More intense rainfall and more extreme swings between wet and dry, exacerbated by poor building practices, more impermeable paving, and deforestation, may increase mudslides and flash floods. And as the number of hot, dry spells increases, so too does the risk of wildfires and dust or sand storms.

The warmer atmosphere and accelerated hydrological cycle will bring more rain, wind, and snow storms. The intensity and possibly the frequency of tropical cyclones will increase. As more precipitation falls as rain rather than snow, winter replenishment of glaciers will decline and spring and summer melting will accelerate, eventually leading to the retreat or even disappearance of some glaciers. This will increase flooding during wetter, colder months and reduce water availability during drier, hotter months, when glacial melt is normally relied on to feed streams and rivers used for irrigation. The ocean will expand as it warms; the melting of mountain and polar glaciers will raise the sea level—at what rate is uncertain, but conservative estimates are about 60–80 cm, with more recent estimates at more than 71 or even two meters by century's end.[1] Upstream diversion of rivers for irrigation and hydropower, declining glaciers, and insufficient rainfall could reduce river flow, and reduced rainfall or population pressure could deplete underground water, both causing coastal subsidence. Subsidence combined with higher sea levels and increased storm intensity would expose many highly populated coastal areas to destructive storm surges.

The Effect on Transport in Developing Countries

Such changes in climate and hydrology have serious implications for transportation infrastructure, operations, and maintenance. This section discusses the impact on land transport (road, rail, metro, bridges, and pipelines); maritime transport (sea ports and inland rivers); and aviation. In a few cases, climate change will actually bring benefits—for example, opening transit routes in Arctic waters (although this will endanger sensitive ecosystems). However, most climate change will make it harder to provide safe, reliable transport, both because of its direct physical impact and because its uncertainty complicates long-term planning and daily decision making.

Climate change will also affect sectors linked to transport. Agricultural yields will decline in many places but could increase in higher latitudes. Dramatic changes in agriculture could accelerate migration from rural areas into cities, which, along with altering food trade patterns, would affect transport demand. Climate is a major determinant of tourism; if traditional ski areas become too warm, skiing could shift to either higher-latitude mountains or different environments altogether. Such indirect impacts on transport could be large at the local level. The discussion below, however, focuses on the direct impact of climate change on provision of transport and, to a lesser extent, demand for it.

Roads, Bridges, Rail, and Tunnels

Higher average temperatures and extreme heat can expand road surfaces and bridge joints, soften and deform paved surfaces, and buckle rail tracks (NRC 2008). Damaged and degraded pavement increases accidents, especially when it is rainy or foggy (for example, Huang and others 2008). Higher temperatures can interrupt bus, truck, and car use; engines can become overheated and air quality or pavement conditions can necessitate temporary limits on vehicle use. For example, in the Shymkent and Kyzylorda Oblasts in Kazakhstan, extreme heat combined with inadequate infrastructure has led to weight and travel restrictions on trucks in summertime when asphalt is softest (Nakat 2008). The number of days suitable for construction and maintenance might increase in colder areas, but the decrease in suitable days in countries like India or the Persian Gulf states could more than offset this.[2] During hot spells, individuals with the financial means and access may resort to using higher-emitting and congestion-causing cars rather than walking, cycling, or using public transit (GTZ 2009).

The reduction in very cold days will have a mixed impact. In some places, it will reduce the costs for removing snow and ice and create safer road conditions. In other places, particularly near seas and lakes, slightly warmer temperatures may actually *increase* the magnitude and thus the cost of snowfalls. Warmer winters will melt permafrost in Alaska, Canada, China, Mongolia, and the Russian Federation, as well as in Antarctica and parts of the Andes. Thawing may disrupt the settling process under rail lines and buildings, something already evident in some places, and compromise the integrity of oil and gas pipelines, threatening local safety and disrupting supplies across larger regions (Ebinger and others 2008; Nakat 2008). The ice roads used by the logging and mining industries, which may be the only routes to isolated communities, will become impassable for longer stretches. Warmer winters could mean more frequent freeze-thaw cycles in temperate areas, creating frost heaves[3] and potholes on roads and bridges, which in turn may require tighter weight restrictions and costly maintenance—more than half the stresses on Canadian roads result from freeze-thaw cycles (PIARC 2012).

More intense precipitation, which can trigger flash floods, landslides, erosion, and swollen rivers, will test physical infrastructure and the ability of operators to maintain safe and efficient service. When extreme rains punctuate long dry spells in places where desiccated soils and vegetation are less able to quickly absorb water, these effects are magnified. Intense rainfall also lengthens delays for road and rail traffic, limits vehicle speed, increases the risk of accidents per vehicle-km, and reduces mobility. Other risks include the hydraulic capacity of bridges being exceeded, destabilization of bridge foundations from scouring, and sediment blockage of culverts and other drainage systems. Extreme precipitation can also interfere with maintenance and construction, even as regular maintenance becomes more important to withstand the stresses of heat, freeze-thaw cycles, and standing water wearing down roads, bridges, and rail beds.

Floods are increasing in many places—Mozambique, Morocco, and Argentina, for instance—and can often be attributed to nonclimatic factors linked to land use, such as deforestation, slope destabilization, and, particularly in rapidly growing cities, expansion of paved areas and reduction of permeable surfaces. Without improvements in infrastructure and strategies for managing risk, intensified precipitation will only become more destructive. In October 2005, near Valigonda in Southern India, more than 100 people were killed when a train was derailed off bridge tracks that had been swept away by the overflow of water from a reservoir filled beyond capacity because of atypically heavy rains.[4]

Of course, more intense precipitation is a challenge not just to developing countries; nor does it always result in large-scale fatalities. The more common outcome may be harder-to-measure costs to transit-service users and businesses, as when the New York subway flooded in September 2004 and August 2007. The intense rains—about 75 mm per hour, or roughly double the quantity that the subway system is built to withstand—paralyzed the metropolitan area and resulted in at least one death. In the 2007 incident, flooding short-circuited essential electrical signals and switches so that none of the subway lines, which normally carry 7 million passengers daily, could run at full capacity during the morning rush hour.

Even in areas that experience more total precipitation, dry spells and droughts could increase and water availability and soil moisture could decline significantly, killing the natural or planted vegetation around roads and walkways that provides shade and protects against erosion. The combination of drought and intense heat also increases wildfire risk. Wildfires can easily destroy transportation infrastructure, even as firefighting crews become more dependent on functioning transport networks.

Storms that are more frequent, more intense, or both can cause major problems for road transport. Lack of preparedness for dealing with extreme snowfalls, which are likely to become larger or more frequent in some places,[5] can be costly. In January 2008, unexpectedly intense snowstorms in China paralyzed the train system just as migrant workers were trying to return home for the Chinese New Year. Millions were stranded. Worse, with the interruption of coal delivery, food and power could not reach suffering populations in the southern and central provinces (Pew Center on Global Climate Change 2010; World Bank 2010b).

Two years later, extreme snowfall on the east coast of the United States entirely shut down the economy of Washington, D.C., first in December 2009 and again in January 2010. Two such large snowstorms normally occur in the area about once every 25 years, not twice in two months.[6] Road conditions were so bad at one point that snow-plow trucks themselves were barred from driving. Estimated losses to private businesses vary widely; closure of the federal government cost taxpayers about $71 million a day.[7]

Tropical storms and cyclones, which according to some evidence are already growing more intense, may well become stronger and more frequent. Storms regularly set off land- and mudslides in mountainous Central America, devastating both people and infrastructure. For example, in late May and early June 2010, landslides and gushing rivers associated with tropical storm Agatha washed out numerous roads and bridges, impeding rescue efforts for the worst-hit areas. In 2005 Hurricane Katrina devastated New Orleans and severely disrupted transport connections: "Key railroad bridges were destroyed, requiring the rerouting of traffic and putting increased strain on other rail segments. Barge shipping was halted, as was export grain traffic out of the Port of New Orleans, the nation's largest export grain port. The pipeline network that gathers oil and natural gas from the Gulf was shut down, producing shortages of natural gas and petroleum products" (Grenzeback and Lukmann 2008).

Even in places that do not experience tropical storms, such as the Mediterranean coast of Africa, sea-level rises and storm surges threaten settlements and transport infrastructure. Morocco, for example, already experiences increasingly intense heat waves (a 1°–3° C increase since the 1970s) and droughts, as well as extreme rainfalls more often. This threatens the country's road pavement, rail tracks, bridges, drainage systems, and embankments, and the damage has already been costly. A flash flood in 2006 destroyed 15 km of the 20-km Tounfite-Agoudim road in the Atlas Mountains—repair costs were equal to half the initial investment. Low-lying Bangladesh, already extremely vulnerable to cyclones and flooding, is expected to suffer greatly from sea-level rise and more damaging storm surges (box 2.1).

Impact on Maritime Transport and Aviation

Maritime transport could be affected by changed water levels, more extreme precipitation and storms, higher temperatures, and in particular the opening of the Arctic because of ice melt (Gallivan, Bailey, and O'Rourke 2009). Lower water levels could plague many inland waterways, requiring stricter cargo weight limits, redesigned vessels, and costly and environmentally damaging dredging. Higher sea levels could reduce clearances under bridges near coasts, directly threatening port infrastructure and road and rail links. The combination of higher sea levels and more extreme coastal storms and precipitation is the greatest threat to ports from damage to bridges, piers, terminal buildings, ships, and cargo. Storms can also cause suspension of operations, reducing reliability and raising costs. Harbors may need to be dredged more often because of increased erosion and silting. By exceeding the capacity of drainage systems, intense rains and storms could cause fuel and industrial contaminants to leech into waterways.

The reduction of Arctic sea ice and the possible opening of new shipping routes represent the most dramatic impact of climate change on maritime transportation. Trans-Arctic shipping could reduce the distance traveled between northern Europe, northeastern Asia, and the northwest coast of North America by as much as 40 percent relative to traditional routes through the Panama or Suez Canal (which might see a decline in their share—though not necessarily the volume—of global shipping) (TRB 2008). Diminished sea ice, and eventually new routes, could create opportunities for new investment—for example, in different ship designs. However, an upsurge in traffic could threaten sensitive ecosystems already undergoing dramatic transformation because of climate change. Higher temperatures will affect paved surfaces at port facilities and increase cooling needs for warehousing and transporting goods.

Given its fuel intensity, the aviation sector is sure to be deeply affected by climate change mitigation policies. But beyond fuel, climate change has a direct effect on airport infrastructure, safety, and operations, particularly losses caused by delays. Threats to airport runways, towers, and signaling equipment are quite similar to those in ground transportation, especially the vulnerability of paved surfaces to heat and precipitation and inadequate drainage. Aviation-specific challenges include the impact of higher heat on lift-off, requiring longer runways, lighter loads, or better airplanes. Thawing permafrost and sinking runways already threaten small airports in isolated communities, although one benefit is the possible reduction in ice and snow removal costs. Airports in low-lying coastal zones are vulnerable to changes in sea levels. In fact, in Jakarta—where subsidence (from urban development and groundwater extraction) will make net sea-level rise particularly threatening—the international airport could be underwater before mid-century; flooding has already submerged the highway to the airport numerous times.[8]

At a colloquium in May 2010, the International Civil Aviation Organization warned of the threat of extreme weather to safety, noting that while technical standards have continued to rise, they are based on past climate probabilities and are not necessarily a guide to the future.[9] Sustaining gains in safety, particularly in developing countries, is extremely important. Less predictable or more extreme weather could increase delays, cancellations, and airport closures, which are costly to both operators and passengers. Climate change could affect the distribution of tourism and thus demand on certain routes. Travel to snowless ski destinations, drought or heat-stricken summer destinations, and places experiencing extreme weather is likely to decline. Dry spells can threaten visibility and safety by creating conditions ripe for wildfires and dust or sand storms. Climate change in the deserts of Iraq, causing die-off of vegetation and lower river flow, has produced dust storms that reach further and more intensely than usual into the Islamic Republic of Iran (Tajbakhsh, Moradi, and Mohamadi 2010). This has in many instances—and more often in the past 15 years—prevented aircraft from landing at the Ahwaz and Abadan airports. Flights have been forced to return to the departure airport or land elsewhere, wasting fuel and increasing costs for both airlines and passengers.

The Effect on Supply of—and Demand for—Transport

With more frequent, intense, and variable extreme weather events, the role of transport in minimizing disaster loss and enabling recovery becomes even more crucial—even as transport infrastructure and services themselves are increasingly threatened by climate extremes (box 2.2).

After a disaster, rescue workers and survivors must have a rapidly deployable communications network. But disasters in developing countries often occur where there is little or no infrastructure, or the disaster may have shut down what infrastructure there was. Without network redundancy, the first precious

Avoiding Future Disruption of Services

Box 2.3 Minimizing the Costs of Extreme Events: The Role of Transport

Extreme weather can result in both direct and indirect losses. Direct losses consist of the monetary value of physical assets destroyed or damaged, such as housing, infrastructure, crops, and plants. Indirect losses are the opportunity costs of reconstruction delays, including immobilized productive capacities (both machines and workers) and empty housing. Together direct and indirect losses account for actual losses. Poor logistics in developing countries multiply these losses.

One study defines total cost as the sum of direct and indirect losses. Another draws a relationship between direct costs and total costs through the empirical coefficient of the economic amplification ratio (EAR), defined as the ratio of the overall production loss (total costs) to the direct costs that are associated with an extreme event. The paper's non-equilibrium modeling shows strong nonlinearity with the capacity to conduct reconstruction after each disaster. Given short-term constraints on spending money productively after a disaster, there is a bifurcation value of direct losses beyond which total costs increase dramatically. Thus the EAR can be significantly higher than unity and it increases with direct costs.

Empirical studies of the aftermath of the 2004 and 2005 Florida hurricanes suggest that the surge in demand for reconstruction and repair along with supply shortages—in qualified workers, carrying capacities of reconstruction materials, and so on—pushes up prices for reconstruction (up to 60 percent in some regions) after an extreme event.

This all make the case for focusing on restoring transport infrastructure to minimize reconstruction delay opportunity costs and help production mechanisms return to optimal functioning.

Source: Hallegatte 2007, 2009.

---

hours must focus on restoring transit routes for affected populations. The functioning (or failure) of transportation networks after a disaster is a strong determinant of total damage, both direct and indirect, and the ultimate cost of recovery (box 2.3).

In many developing countries lack of strategic planning undermines infrastructure resilience—efforts are essentially reactive after a disaster. Perverse in road maintenance and construction incentives increase the cost of extreme events to taxpayers (Solberg, Hale, and Benavides 2003). Reactive strategies usually lead to the building of similarly inadequate infrastructure that has to be significantly refurbished every few years—a process known as the "reconstruction of vulnerability."

Why the Impact of Climate Change Is Different

Engineers, policymakers, and project designers may see nothing new in the impacts described. In making decisions that take into account climatic, hydrological, geological, and usage factors, they have always had to consult building and maintenance standards in choosing, for instance, how much clearance to allow below a bridge, how securely to attach a deck to a substructure to withstand high winds, how often to repave a surface, or whether to use riprap or extensive gabions to protect abutments from scour. They have always weighed probabilities and risks against costs and made locally appropriate choices based on a combination of physical factors, risk tolerance, and budget constraints. So what is all the fuss about? Why should investments not continue to be made as they always have been?

First, there is the increase in *variability*. Variability itself is not new. What *is* new is the projected *increase* in both intra- and interannual variability in temperature and precipitation. Greater intra-annual variability means that, even though total annual rainfall in a location may remain unchanged, rainfall that used to be spread out, say, 40/60 percent across two six-month periods may instead be clustered with 20 percent in one six-month period and 80 percent in the other. Thus, infrastructure and operational procedures will need to deal both with drier and with wetter conditions. This will very likely raise costs, for even if it were no more or less costly to build, maintain, and operate transport infrastructures in a dry climate or a wet climate, it *is* more costly to build, maintain, and operate assets to withstand both.

Interannual variability also complicates decision making, since it can be difficult to distinguish between a change in the mean trend and oscillation about a stable mean (Burton and Lim 2005). How can local authorities know if their region is really becoming drier on a multidecadal average, or if it is only that the variation around a stable mean has increased, with the past few dry years likely to be followed by a few wet years? Coming to the wrong conclusions, and relying on those conclusions when making investments in infrastructure intended to last for many decades, can be extremely costly. Changes in infrastructure maintenance and operations, though not easy to implement, might be achieved on a shorter time scale without enormous loss in sunk costs. But rebuilding—or in more extreme cases, entirely relocating transport facilities away from coasts vulnerable to sea-level rise—before the end of the intended life of the infrastructure would be very costly.

Even if transport providers did have the data and tools to analyze probabilities and respond accordingly, many private users of transportation do not. For example, variable rainfall might make driving more dangerous than predictable rainfall, even if actual average road conditions are unchanged. Car drivers tend to drive more slowly and carefully the day *after* a storm (Eisenberg 2004; Leigh 2009; Road Research Laboratory 1954). If rain yesterday is not a good predictor of rain tomorrow, then people are slowing down unnecessarily. More troubling, if clear skies today are an even less reliable predictor of the absence of fog or rain tomorrow, drivers will be even less likely to slow down when they should.

Second, climate change also introduces *deep uncertainty* about future climate, making current information and methods inadequate for decisions that have long-term implications. Future weather—be it tomorrow's forecast peak temperature or a seasonal estimate of rainfall—has always been uncertain. But past data have, until now, provided a guide to climate-sensitive decisions based on probabilities and averages. However, climate change invalidates past averages and probability distributions. And the real challenge is that the *new* probability distributions are unknown.

Climate has always varied, but in the past the variation has been within a fixed envelope, around a fixed mean. Infrastructure design and planning, insurance pricing, and numerous private decisions have long been based on stationarity, the idea that natural systems fluctuate within an unchanging envelope of variability (World Bank 2010b). With climate change, stationarity is dead (Milly and others 2008). Models of climate change cannot assign probabilities to the projections they generate—and certainly not at the fine temporal and geographic scale that transportation decision makers require. What was once uncertain but could be reasonably predicted with past data is now characterized by deep uncertainty—the phrase used when no underlying probability is known.

Drivers of Vulnerability and Resilience

The impact of climate change on transport will not be the same everywhere. Overall vulnerability is a function of both exposure to climate hazards and change and the sensitivities and adaptive capacity of the transport sector, broadly defined to include both providers and users (figure 2.1; IPCC 2001). Further, there are drivers of vulnerability, other than the climate itself, both within and outside the transport sector. There is intense debate and numerous studies on how to define and measure components of vulnerability and how to link them to related concepts even beyond the area of climate change (for example disaster risk reduction and social protection).[10] These debates are beyond the scope of this report, which will use the bare-bones Intergovernmental Panel on Climate Change (IPCC) framework commonly used by many sources, which is sufficient for understanding drivers of vulnerability.

The concept of exposure is straightforward: "it is determined by the type, magnitude, timing, and speed of climate events and variation to which a system is exposed (for example, changing onset of the rainy season, higher minimum winter temperatures, floods, storms, and heat waves)" (Fay, Ebinger, and Block 2010). However, it is difficult to characterize exposure, either quantitatively

Figure 2.1 Framework for Defining Vulnerability

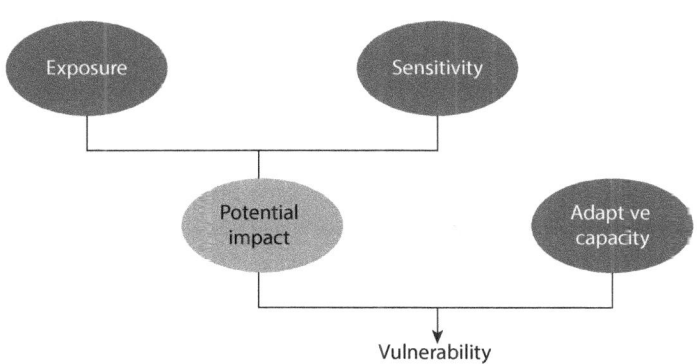

Source: IPCC 2001; graphic reproduced from Fay, Ebinger, and Block 2010.

or qualitatively, in a way that is useful to decision makers. Characterizing the exposure of a locality or a transport network depends ultimately on local capacity, which is not necessarily constant over time. But in all cases, qualitative understanding of current challenges and projected trends, however uncertain, will be the first step of several (boxes 2.4 and 2.5).

The sensitivity of a system comprises its structural characteristics. Some characteristics are more sensitive than others—for example, engineered dirt or gravel roads are more likely than are paved roads to become impassable during heavy rains—and poorly maintained assets of any type are more sensitive than better maintained assets. In addition to basic engineering specifications (for example, standard versus porous paved surfaces), location also matters. Settlements, and thus transport assets, are often concentrated in coastal zones, where climate hazards are particularly challenging.

An example of a system's sensitivity and exposure is a paved two-lane coastal road in a mountainous area. It could be exposed to sea-level rise; higher storm surges; hotter, longer, and more frequent heat waves; more frequent or more intense storms; and alternating dry spells and more intense rainfall. Sensitivity could include location on the coast or at the bottom of a slope, nearby slopes that are increasingly unstable because of deforestation and unplanned settlement, and poorly maintained drainage around the road that impedes the flow of water from the hillside to the sea. These variables combine to determine the potential impact

---

Box 2.4 Starting the Adaptation Process: Asking the Right Questions

It is recommended that transport officials, national and local, consider the following questions, developed by the Transportation Research Board:

- Which projected climate changes are most relevant for the region?
- How are climate change hazards likely to be manifested (for example, flooding and storm surge coupled with a rise in sea level)?
- Which transportation assets may be affected?
- How severe must a hazard be before action is required? Can thresholds be identified?
- How likely is it that a projected hazard will exceed the threshold? When and where?
- How much risk can be tolerated? In other words, what infrastructure performance level is tolerable?
- What level of investment (capital and operating) is needed to maintain different levels of service?
- Can acceptable performance standards for all modes of transportation be established?
- Are there critical levels of service needed to protect health and safety?
- Who is empowered to make these judgments and decisions?
- What are the risks of adverse impacts or consequences if no action is taken?
- If action is necessary, how will investment priorities be determined?
- Who will make the necessary investments, and how will they be funded?

Source: Reproduced from NRC 2008.

Box 2.5 Advancing the Adaptation Process: Assessing Risk and Defining a Strategy

A qualitative risk assessment requires the following steps:

1. Establish context and objectives. Formulate the issue and the scope of the assessment: define its objectives and the general context; identify climate scenarios; and define the affected geographic region and the stakeholders (government, sector, and community) or the targeted audience.
2. Inventory assets. Identify the components of the transportation infrastructure and their vulnerabilities, taking into account past challenges, both related and unrelated to climate.
3. Identify and analyze hazards. Identify hazards, especially what could happen with different climate scenarios. Structured brainstorming by stakeholders (for example, policymakers and experienced specialists, such as the "Structured What If Technique" (SWIFT), can help identify hazards.[a] Consider each, with any safeguards or controls, including policy and management responses, and assess the likelihood of various consequences given such controls. Determine the level of risk.[b]
4. Rank the risks. Screen out minor ones and prioritize major ones for further analysis. Describe the uncertainties of each risk and the sensitivity of the analysis to a variety of assumptions.
5. Identify and appraise options to manage risks. Identify climate conditions that represent benchmark levels of risk or thresholds between tolerable and intolerable risk.
6. Draft an adaptation plan. Prioritize the action plan based on options identified to manage risk, with a review of the costs and associated benefits of each. Discuss the risks of under-, over-, or maladaptation. Ensure that plans account for not only changing climate averages but also increased variability and extremes.
7. Take action. Decide whether to build on and update legal and regulatory frameworks, institutions, policies, strategies, and emergency and disaster management plans or to adopt new ones altogether. Determine current institutional capacity and what is needed to support implementation. Assess financing needs and sources. Identify data and information gaps and how to address them, such as through research and development.
8. Evaluate progress on the action plan. Establish monitoring and evaluation—a feedback loop—to periodically reevaluate risks and priorities as information becomes available or new events occur.

Sources: Fay, Ebinger, and Block 2010; TRB 2008
a. SWIFT screens hazards by considering deviations from business-as-usual operations, using checklists to support brainstorming. It allows for a systematic, team-oriented approach but relies heavily on the quality of the expert team. For more details, see http://rmd.anglia.ac.uk/uploads/docs/SWIFT.doc or HSE (2001).
b. Australian Government (2006); HSE (2001, 2006); New Zealand Climate Change Office (2004); and Willows and Connel (2003) provide good examples of risk matrices and their application.

---

of climate change on the road: intense rainfall could destabilize the slope, provoke mudslides, or even wash out the road; hot spells could soften and cause ruts in the pavement, making it less safe for drivers; and higher tides and increased buffeting by storm surge could greatly weaken the subgrade and destabilize the road.

How potential impacts translate into actual impacts depends not only on climate phenomena and sensitivity but also on the system's adaptive capacity—its resources for coping with impacts and mitigating damage. In the coastal road example, adaptive capacity could include the extent to which operators could close the road and reroute traffic with minimal delay; the capacity to foresee the need to maintain drainage and pavement surfaces, including the power to mobilize funding and ensure that the work gets done; and the ability of transport and land-use planning bodies to work together to ensure that new infrastructure is not sited in areas exposed to hazards.

As noted, nontransport factors such as poor drainage, deforestation, or bureaucratic blunders can increase transport vulnerability. While the adaptation options discussed below relate to the transport sector, an overarching recommendation is to consider risks and vulnerabilities, as well as opportunities for cooperation, beyond the sector so as to increase general economic, social, and transport resilience.

The exposure-sensitivity-adaptive capacity approach can help planners to identify combinations of factors that amplify or reduce the impact of climate change and to distinguish exogenous factors (exposure) from those amenable to local policy action (adaptive capacity—hence, future sensitivity) (Fay, Ebinger, and Block 2010). It can be applied to particular regions or cities, of which transport systems are just one component; to sectors; or to particular assets within one mode.

Preserving Resilient and Least-Cost Transport as the Climate Changes

With the many uncertainties of climate change, technologies, and policy regimes, there has been no clear agreement yet on how to adapt transport infrastructure to climate change. Priorities differ by country and there are diagnostic tools to identify these (boxes 2.4 and 2.5). There are, however, at least four recognized adaptation measures:

1. Raising engineering standards: infrastructure should be built more sturdily to make it more resilient to severe weather events.
2. Routine road maintenance, often neglected in developing countries (figure 2.2). Higher standards would require countries to invest more in roads and better maintain them. Without timely maintenance, road deterioration accelerates with time and severe weather.
3. Traffic rules, which should address such issues as speeding and overloading, both of which damage road surfaces, particularly under adverse weather conditions.
4. Broader adaptation measures in other sectors, such as urban planning, infrastructure location, creation of redundancy in logistics, accumulation of inventory, and preparation of disaster and emergency systems.

Standards and the Resilience of Transport Infrastructure

The nuts-and-bolts, engineering-centered approach to adaptation consists of components like building stronger bridges, paving dirt roads, increasing drainage system capacity, and building higher sea walls. New technologies and materials are

Figure 2.2 Deterioration of Paved Roads over Time

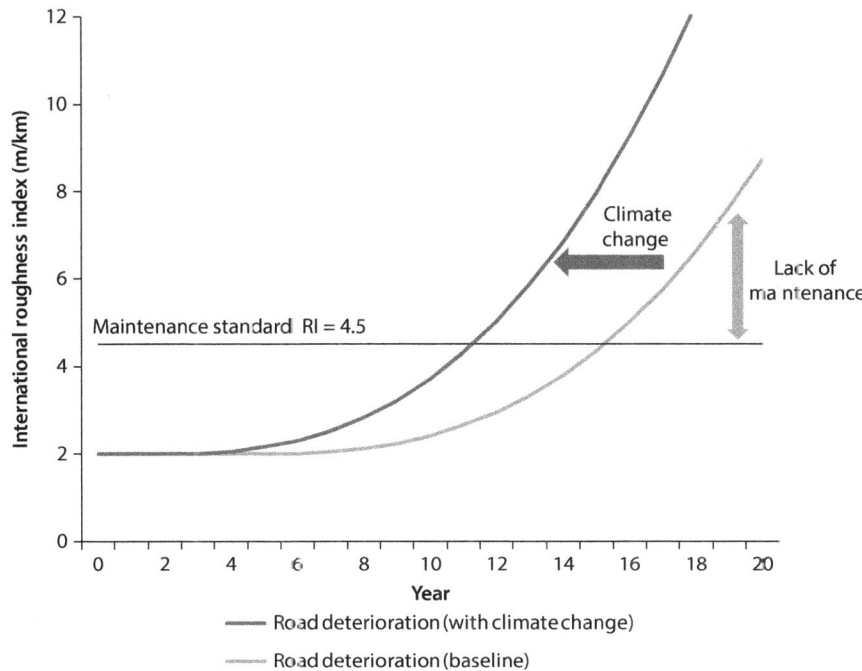

Source: Based on Harral and Faiz 1988.
Note: IRI = International Roughness Index.

necessary—for example, paving that can withstand extreme heat or allow drainage through its surface. Some technologies are still being studied, but advances in materials science (including nanotechnologies), sensors, computer processing, and communications could significantly alter infrastructure design and operation. Many known potentially helpful measures are not yet being applied.

Such proactive engineering measures, however, can be costly when they entail nonmarginal modification of infrastructure or result in "maladaptation"— measures that increase vulnerability. The greater the uncertainty about local climate, the greater the risk of maladaptation. Vulnerabilities and risks, therefore, must be carefully assessed before any building standards are revamped.

Roads with thicker pavements and better drainage are more resilient. Dirt and unsealed roads, though cheap, can lose surface to traffic and rainfall. In developing countries generally, more than half the roads are still unpaved; in Latin America, the Caribbean, and sub-Saharan Africa, only 15 percent of roads are paved (figure 2.3).

Higher-standard roads can reduce vulnerability and thus increase mobility and welfare, particularly in rural and remote areas. In Nepal, rural roads are operational only during the dry season. An estimated one-third of the nation's 24 million people live at least two hours walk from the nearest all-season road that has public transport (World Bank 2007). Although costly,[11] upgrading dry-season-only roads

Figure 2.3 Paved Roads by Region, 2005

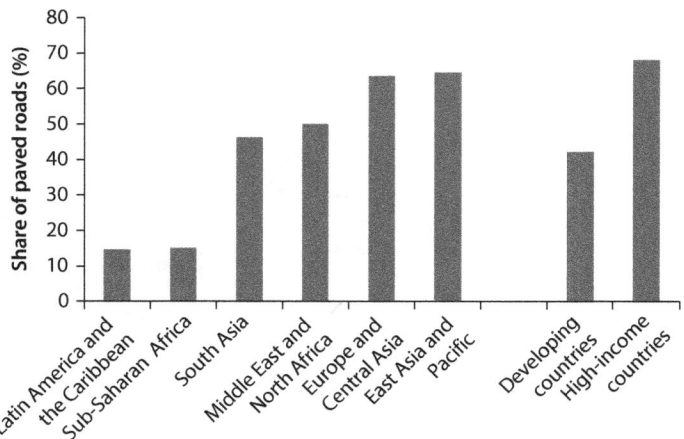

Source: World Bank 2010a.

to meet all-season standards with gravel and Otta seal, a low-cost paving option,[12] would increase both rural mobility and road resilience.[13]

Advanced technologies that would, for example enable airports, railways, and ports to withstand storms and blasts can improve resilience. In the Philippines, the number of accidents is closely related to the frequency of typhoons. Thousands of people are killed or injured in maritime accidents each year (JICA 2007).[14] Navigational aid facilities, such as lighthouses and lighted buoys, need to be upgraded. A promising technology being developed for rail systems is a gust prediction system using weather forecasting and Doppler radar (Kato and Hono 2009).

Another powerful recipe for increasing resilience is simple: do not build in harm's way. Transport infrastructure should be located based on accurate mapping of climate risks and vulnerabilities and incorporated into the broader land-use strategy (see below). For example, capacity aside, a culvert should at least be located so that "the flood waters are able to easily overtop the road near the culvert and re-enter the stream on the other side of the road causing only local damage to the road fill. Preferably the culvert should be at a low point in the vertical profile of the road ensuring all flood water is directed back into the channel and not allowed to run down the drainage ditches."[15] In other words, if all other design aspects fail, the right location will minimize disruption, destruction, and loss.

Realigning roads from flood-prone areas to high ground is another example. In Peru, El Niño caused massive flooding that submerged roads. In response, the government rebuilt the highway between the capital and the port city of Piura in the northeast on a higher embankment, rerouting it around a lagoon-prone area that had been completely submerged by the 1983 El Niño. Similarly, better road design as well as construction management in Ecuador could have avoided some of the 1997–98 El Niño damage (box 2.6; Solberg, Hale, and Benavides 2003).

Avoiding Future Disruption of Services

Box 2.6 Failures and Successes in Disaster Recoveries

Inadequate technical solutions to infrastructure failures: In Peru, highways cross a multitude of riverbeds that are normally dry but that in an El Niño year can channel avalanches of water and mud across the highways. In response, highway engineers have built pontoons across the riverbeds, but these still often overflow during an El Niño, eroding the highways. This explains television images during an El Niño showing a line of trucks traveling single file over severely eroded highways that have become a thin shred of asphalt.

When rebuilding leads to "reconstruction of vulnerabilities": In Ecuador, a section of highway of about 60 km from Quito to La Virgin Papallacta has often been washed out or made impassable. A major landslide in 2000 near Cuyuga closed the road for nearly a week. An audit by the Government of Ecuador Controller's Office found that the reconstruction and rehabilitation funds invested in this roadway over the years could easily have financed a high-quality, all-weather road. Problems included low-quality engineering, no contract supervision, and a faulty incentive scheme: the same construction firm fails to do maintenance but gets paid to clean up *after* the landslides and keep the road open.

A notable reconstruction success based on lessons well learned: In Peru, the 50 km stretch of highway that joins Piura with the port city of Paita is a triumph of forward thinking. The torrential rains of the 1983 El Niño created a lagoon that had completely submerged it, cutting off Piura from its supply route, causing famine and desolation. Later, the highway was rebuilt on a high embankment and rerouted around the lagoon-prone area. As a result, the highway stayed open during the 1998 El Niño.

Sources: Glantz 2001; Solberg, Hale, and Benavides 2003.

Though efforts to adapt technical standards to climate conditions have been slow, they are gaining momentum. Major disasters have prompted civil engineers and the construction industry to work to modify building codes and design standards. Although such a reactive strategy takes time, ultimately it should enhance infrastructure safety and reliability. Current design standards represent tradeoffs between performance and cost (TRB 2008). Some standards have already tried to account for the probability of extremely rare events. Building to higher standards must be weighed against additional costs—one reason adaptation of standards is slow.

Several high-income countries have already started to adapt standards to new climate conditions. Japan has introduced new pavement technology that increases resilience to heat waves (box 2.7). In response to increased precipitation Denmark has changed its drainage capacity. Other possible adjustments would be connecting bridge decks to deck piers so that storm-surge buoyant forces do not lift the decks off their supports or adding a safety margin to existing dikes against expected sea-level rise or extreme sea floods.

Upfront investment in higher standards can be cost-effective if the standards will reduce maintenance and operating costs. Severe weather may increase

Box 2.7 Standards Updating: Examples

Drainage systems in Denmark: extension of previous system: In Denmark increased precipitation and flooding overwhelmed drainage. In response, a new policy required a 30 percent increase in drainage capacity.

Use of new technologies: pavement coated with solar reflective technology: The Japanese have developed the innovative "Heat-Shield Pavement," a spray-on coating that increases reflectivity for near-infrared rays and lowers reflectivity for visible rays. A Heat-Shield surfacing albedo can be as high as 0.57, compared with 0.07 for conventional pavement. This technology also addresses asphalt surface temperature, which can peak in the summer at about 60°C. Coated with Heat Shield, slabs reach a surface temperature of only about 40°C.

Source: PIARC 2012.

---

the recurrent costs of maintaining low-standard bituminous-bound roads, for instance, and retrofitting is generally costly.

Maintenance and Operations and Vulnerability to Climate Change

Although higher standards and advanced technologies can increase the resilience of transport assets, developing countries must first commit to routine maintenance. In Africa, for instance, an estimated 20 percent of paved roads are in poor condition. Worse, an estimated 42 percent of unpaved roads, which are particularly vulnerable to precipitation and other severe weather, are poorly maintained (figure 2.4).

All roads deteriorate with time, but potholes or cracks accelerate deterioration by allowing water to infiltrate. Periodic maintenance is needed to keep roads smooth (figure 2.5). In Africa in the 1970s and 1980s, inadequate maintenance led to road loss estimated at $40–$45 billion. Adequate maintenance, in contrast, would have cost only $12 billion (Harral and Faiz 1988). In Ecuador, poor maintenance of highways, secondary roads, and bridges, exacerbated by noncompliance with regulations, contribute to El Niño damage. Enforcement of regulations was particularly low during the presidential campaign of 1996 and in the following troubled political period in early 1997.

Poor maintenance also undermines road safety. Rutting and potholes increase accidents (Huang and others 2008), as does the weather (Jung and others 2010). Precipitation reduces visibility. Water that accumulates in ruts and potholes—generally difficult to see when it is raining or dark—can cause hydroplaning. Slick pavements and adverse weather contribute to about one-fourth of all highway crashes in the United States (NRC 2008). Pavement-related road accidents increase by about 30 percent with rain (table 2.1; Huang and others 2008).

Nonroad transport sectors must also be properly operated and maintained. The lack of standard navigational aid systems in developing countries compromises the efficiency and safety of maritime operations. Many victims killed or injured

Figure 2.4 Africa: Roads in Poor Condition (Cross-Country Average Based on Latest Data)

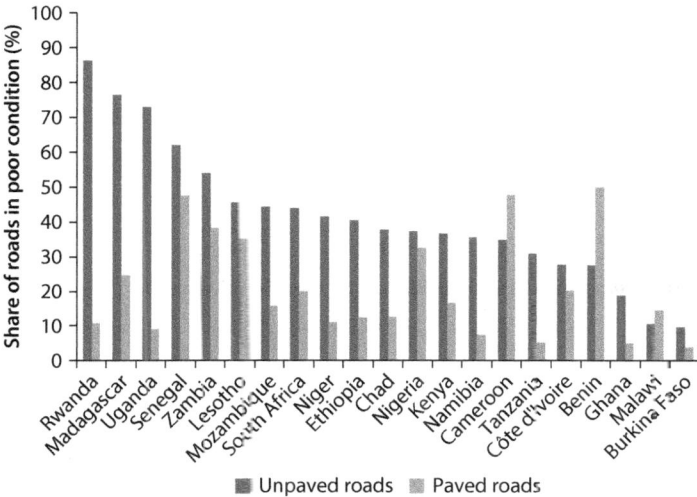

Source: AICD database.

Figure 2.5 Road Roughness and Maintenance Frequency over Time

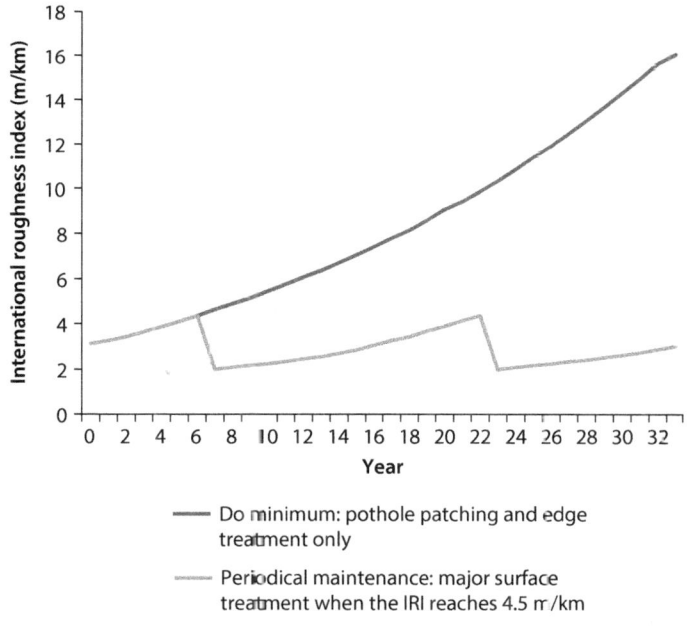

Source: Simulation based on HDM-4.

in maritime accidents could have been saved had ordinary infrastructure and equipment been in place. In the Philippines physical damage or poor maintenance shut down 112 of 419 lighthouses and lighted buoys before a maritime safe project was launched (JICA 2007). In Europe and Central Asia in the last two decades the extensive agrometeorological station networks developed during

Table 2.1 Effects of Pavement and Weather on Road Accidents

Weather condition	Estimated coefficient[a]	Implied effect of doubled rut depth (percent)[b]
Rainy	5.209***	29.8
Dry	0.050	0.3
Both	1.015	5.2

Source: Based on Huang and others 2008.
a. For each weather condition, a negative binomial regression is performed on average daily traffic and rut depth. The coefficient is associated with the rut depth.
b. It is assumed that rut depth increases from 0.05 inch, the sample average, to 0.1 inch.
Significance level: *** = 1 percent.

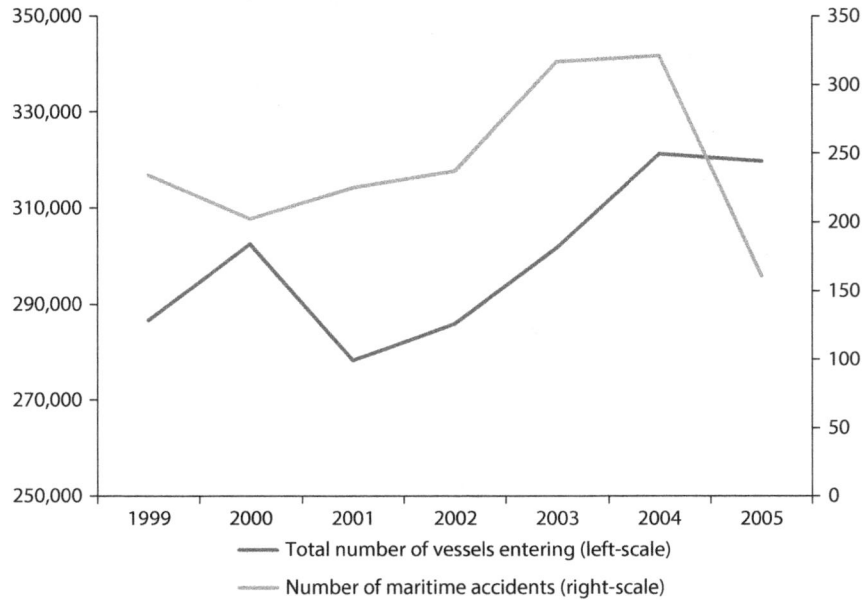

Figure 2.6 The Philippines: Vessels Entering and Maritime Accidents

Source: JICA 2007.

the Soviet era have deteriorated dramatically. While drought-prone Georgia once had 150 stations, today virtually all have ceased to function (Hancock, Tsirkunov, and Smetanina 2008).

The importance of maintaining infrastructure in developing countries rises with the demand for transport. In the Philippines, which consists of more than 7,100 islands, marine transportation is the second most important mode after roads. Although the number of vessels entering the country's ports increased about 10 percent between 1999 and 2005 (figure 2.6), maintenance of the country's navigational facilities has long been neglected.

Regulations, Traffic Rules, and Climate Change

Transport regulations must also adapt to climate change. Limiting speed is one way. Many countries already reduce speed limits when weather is severe, as in heavy rain or strong winds. Traffic accidents typically increase with speed limits

(Jung and others 2010), and precipitation substantially increases the risk of road collision and injury—in Canada risk by an estimated 45 percent (Andrey and others 2003). Lower speed limits also help preserve pavement. In Sweden, for example, estimates for pavement lifetime derive from speed limits and other traffic and road characteristics; the elasticity of pavement lifetime in Sweden is –0.001, a small but statistically significant number (Haraldsson 2007).

In general, good traffic regulations can prevent road deterioration. As noted earlier, in Kazakhstan, truck operations are restricted during the summer period to reduce road deterioration when the asphalt is soft (Nakat 2008). Controlling overload, a widespread problem, is also important in developing countries. In Eastern and Southern Africa, for instance, an estimated 10–50 percent of trucks are overloaded (table 2.2). Overloading damages road surfaces significantly because the equivalent standard axle load factor (ESALF)[16] is typically assumed to follow the fourth or higher power rule (Pinard 2010). In other words, if a truck is overloaded by 20 percent, its axle load factor approximately doubles using an increased load factor of 1.2 (Schneider and Kuntz-Duriseti 2002).

Overloading thus increases the axle load factor on roads exponentially accelerating deterioration (figure 2.7). Overloading by 20 percent shortens the life of roads by several years. The baseline maintenance strategy is to "do the minimum," meaning pothole patching and edge treatment, but more frequent road maintenance, including major structural overlays, is needed to maintain road surfaces at a reasonable level, for example, at the international roughness index of 4.5 m/km.

Regulations and operational procedures in other transport areas also need to adapt to climate conditions. Weather is a contributing factor in the approximately 10 yearly train derailments in Canada (Andrey and others 2003). About 40 percent of flights cancelled in the United States are weather-related, a percentage that has been increasing in recent years (figure 2.8). Operational regulations need to be updated because new equipment and advanced technologies are inefficient if they cannot be used in real-time operations. While more weather

Table 2.2 Reported Overloading, Southern African Development Community, 2004

Country	Percent of all vehicles
Botswana	10–25
Lesotho	20–35
Malawi	30–40
Mozambique	50
Namibia	20
South Africa	15–20
Swaziland	20–40
Tanzania	20–30
Zambia	40
Zimbabwe	5–10

Source: Pinard 2010.

Figure 2.7 Effect of Overloading on Road Roughness

Source: Simulation based on HDM-4.

Figure 2.8 Reasons for Flight Cancellations, United States

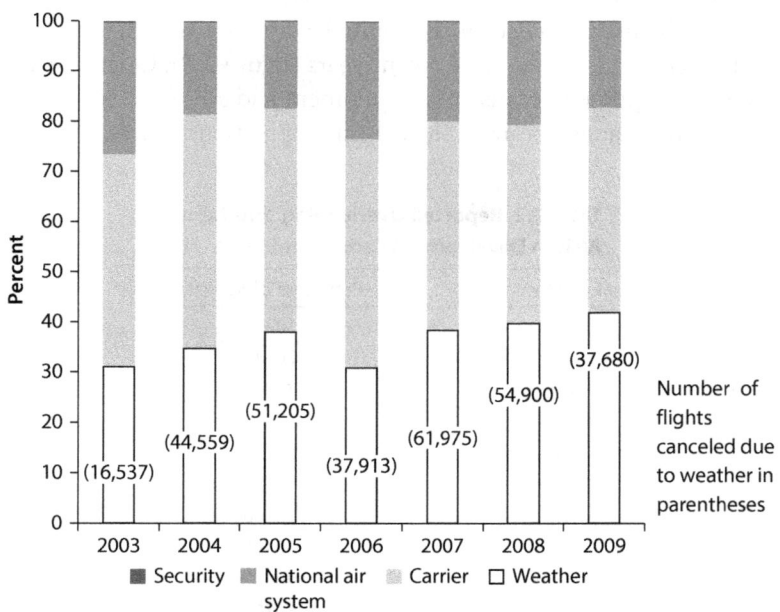

Source: Research and Innovative Technology Administration, U.S. Bureau of Transportation Statistics.

information is becoming available, there is no guarantee that it will be used promptly. A survey in three European and Central Asian countries found that 25–50 percent of respondents did not find out about severe weather until the day it occurred; the comparable figure for the United Kingdom was 6 percent. Equipment to convey station data to headquarters for analysis is often unreliable, labor-intensive, and expensive (Hancock, Tsirkunov, and Smetanina 2008). Integrating weather information and operations could make railway, maritime, and aviation operations more reliable.

Climate Resilience of the Economy as a Whole

An infrastructure network has to be considered as an integrated whole. "Network effects" (Economides 1993) involve both potential benefits from interconnectedness—as between trade, local development, and transportation speed—and critical interdependences that, if broken, could dramatically disrupt a regional economy. For example, if a crucial node or strategic link (Meyer 2007), such as a highway or a pipeline, were cut, there would be significant economic consequences for that region.

Box 2.8 Monitoring Corruption

Illegal side payments—often observed but not easy to verify—pad many contractors' budgets. When the contractor who offers the largest kickback wins the contract, competition on the basis of quality, price, and reliability is eliminated. In turn, poor quality means the project must be repaired or even redone, wasting time, money, and resources.

A remarkable experiment in reducing corruption in more than 600 Indonesian village road projects produced the following findings:

- By increasing the probability that it would audit a village from 4 to 100 percent, the central government audit agency reduced missing expenditures from 27.7 to 19.2 percent. If heavier punishment conditional on prosecution were to complement higher audit probabilities, this percentage could improve.
- Giving audit results to the public, who can then use them in making electoral choices, may be a useful complement to formal punishment.
- Grassroots monitoring is most effective with the distribution of private goods, such as subsidized food, education, or medical care, where individual citizens have a personal stake in ensuring that theft is minimized. When incentives to monitor are weaker, such as for public infrastructure projects, using professional auditors may be more effective.
- Grassroots monitoring programs must ensure that they are not captured by local elites.
- Auditors should be rotated often to avoid susceptibility to bribery. The best option may be to combine lower audit probability with heavier punishments.

Even if improved audits can reduce rent capture or bribery, this experiment suggests that there is no single, simple solution to this common problem.

Source: Olken 2007.

This suggests that such institutional aspects as land-use policies, procurement rules, disaster and emergency planning systems, hydrometeorological data collection and management, and circulation of information among transport sector ministries and administration services matter as much as technical issues. Close correlations between the maps of *hazard* (the exogenous probability of a potentially damaging phenomenon) and *vulnerability* (the controllable degree of loss resulting from such a phenomenon) disclose more institutional problems than technical or financial ones.

Creating Redundancy in Infrastructure and Logistic: Designing redundancies into a network means creating alternatives to key bridges or highway segments. Redundancy can diminish disruption to the population and the economy (GTZ 2009). Disaster risk management must also ensure accessibility to hospitals to avoid human loss and efficient rubble evacuation. There is much greater potential for creating redundancies in dense urban environments than in rural areas, which may require targeted preventive investments. Public transport could be considered a redundancy; for instance, during the floods in Manila in September 2009, elevated rail and metro transit proved more reliable than cars (box 2.9).

Creating redundancy in logistics, namely through inventory, could also increase the resilience of the economy to extreme events. Inventory costs represent a significant share of total logistics costs. For Japan, macrologistics costs represent some 10 percent of GDP, and inventory costs account for about 3 percent (table 2.3; OECD 2002). Obviously, holding more stock is costly enough that it could reduce an economy's competitiveness. Yet without

---

Box 2.9 Manila: Public Transport Resilience to Extreme Events

In September 2009 flash floods rendered major metro thoroughfares in Manila impassable. The Light Rail Transit (LRT) and the Metro Rail Transit (MRT) were alternatives for thousands of commuters. LRT Authority administrators were proud that their maintenance personnel kept LRT Lines 1 and 2 running efficiently and without disruption. The main problem was unavoidable congestion at LRT stations, but as a form of relief passenger fares were reduced. To accommodate the surge of passengers the number of trains was increased from 9 to 16.

Source: Philippine Star, September 28, 2009, http://www.philstar.com/metro/508853/stranded-commuters-turn-elevated-rails.

Table 2.3 Japan: Macro Logistics Costs

	Trillion JPY	Percentage of GDP
Logistics costs	47.1	9.5
Transport	30.5	6.2
Stock	14.5	2.9
Other (managerial)	2.1	0.4

Source: OECD 2002.
Note: GDP = gross domestic product.

some inventory an economy would suffer severely if its logistics were disrupted. There is thus a tradeoff between logistics efficiency and reliability.

Urban and Land-use Planning: The sensible principle of not building in harm's way could come up against politically sensitive land-use policies. These policies drive land prices and require cooperation among different, often opposing, interests: government and public decision makers, real estate developers, and the many people building informal settlements.[17] Transportation planning seldom considers likely climate change when locating facilities and developing land. The vulnerability of rapidly growing cities in developing countries increases without climate-proofing regulations.

Urban and land-use planning must answer questions like where to locate or relocate infrastructure at risk, and how to enhance the resilience of existing networks to climate. There are two main cases:

Construction of new transport infrastructure: That many developing countries do not currently have much transport infrastructure allows them, at least in theory, to locate new infrastructure out of harm's way. Climate-smart zoning, limited only by a country's ability to comply with it, would increase infrastructure resilience.

Relocation, rehabilitation, and retrofitting of infrastructure: Existing transport infrastructure, with marginal retrofits, might work with climate evolution but it might also be totally inadequate. In any case, "path dependency" prevents updating or relocating infrastructure overnight (see Dealing with Infrastructure Inertia in chapter 1). If relocation turns out to be impossible or too costly (as when a whole city is exposed to major climate risks), planners should focus on creating redundancies within the infrastructure that exists.

Although the strategic framework for urban and land-use policies is straightforward, institutional dysfunction and failure to enforce regulations are hurdles in many developing countries.

Disaster and Emergency Planning Systems: This section deals with setting up a strategic agenda to cope with emergency situations following disasters. Each phase of the disaster cycle—response, recovery, and reconstruction[18]—has a different set of priorities. The preventive building of redundancy into networks as part of a consistent disaster management plan is one option.

Response to the emergency: In this phase, which can last hours to weeks, the priority is to restore basic connectivity and communications and remove all barriers to relief. Redundancy is critical if main roads are impassible. The efficiency of response depends on the preparedness of local authorities.

Recovery: As most roads should be opened by this phase, recovery focuses not on transport infrastructure but on providing temporary housing and vital social and commercial activities.

Reconstruction: Transport networks are crucial here. If they have been damaged, the first emergency fix must be complemented by restoration that takes into account prior infrastructure vulnerabilities. Unfortunately, given resource shortages, decision makers in developing countries often choose what seems the cheapest solution, one that in fact benefits private companies at the expense of the public. The regulatory aspects are central here: Regulation deals with (i) upgrading building quality standards in the context of possible climate change; (ii) defining sound land-use regulation and urban codes; and (iii) modernizing procurement rules so that perverse incentives to favor cheap short-term infrastructure are translated into efficient incentives that result in long-lasting and robust works. The main goal of the reconstruction phase is to avoid creating new vulnerabilities.

An indefinite period of *preparedness* should follow reconstruction. Among other things, a consistent strategy should include early warning, relief supply, and emergency circulation plans that make the best use of existing networks.

Linking with other sectors: Ideally, transport adaptation should take into account the environment—the broader system that includes forestry, drainage, farming, and water management. For instance, bridge design should take into account both climate model predictions for increased precipitation and sedimentation from erosion amplified by land use.[19]

Good forestry practices—for example, no clear-cutting around infrastructure—can help prevent or soften the impact of extreme events. By contrast, upstream deforestation or informal irrigation channels that turn rainfall into flooding could worsen conditions. Deforestation combined with increased precipitation could shorten the recurrence of flooding, for instance, from an average of every 50 years to every 20 years. An integrated approach, however, battles the usual public policy sectoral focus and would require close coordination between very distinct actors and administrations.

Fundamentals of Transport Adaptation

A comprehensive approach to building resilience means that different stakeholders cooperate to define responsibilities, monitor building standards, enforce land-use regulations, manage uncertainties about climate information, and devise decision tools. Although strategic frameworks are well established, that is less true of practical mechanisms for achieving adaptation. The following section offers guidance in assessing climate information and decision-making tools.

Information

The robustness of transportation infrastructure has typically been calibrated using statistics for such climate variables as precipitation, wind speed, and temperature. Since climate change disturbs trends, past records are no longer reliable indicators. What is needed are updated information from cutting-edge climate modeling and new ways of thinking.

Unlike other sectors, such as agriculture, where stakeholders have long engaged with climate scientists to build mutual understanding, transport and climate specialists must still learn to communicate about how climate information might affect a specific project and what actions to take as a result. Further, local authorities must decide what variables are most important locally. Sometimes this will be obvious: land-locked countries need not consider sea-level rise, nor need low-elevation, low-latitude areas be concerned with changes in freeze/thaw cycles. But because the key variables are not always this obvious, there should be an initial general understanding about which variables need to be examined in detailed quantitative terms.[20]

Given the limits on the information available, a risk assessment approach should be both qualitative and quantitative to minimize the costs of engineering-based adaptation strategies and loss (box 2.10).

Besides raw climate information, sound strategy should map critical infrastructure links—kilometers of railroad tracks or roads, percentage of roads paved or gravel-surfaced, number of bridges or length of subway lines—as well as the physical and institutional context. (This has begun for Ethiopia.[21]) What is the landscape surrounding the asset? Who has jurisdiction over operations, maintenance, and design—both the original design and future retrofits? Are drainage systems integral? Are they managed by the roads authority or by the urban water and sanitation authority? What standards and manuals provide technical specifications? What is the intended design life? Has it already been, or is it likely to be, exceeded? What climate-related problems have already arisen? What non-climate-related problems?

Knowing the internal state of a structure is also important. Innovative technologies, such as nano-sensors, can monitor how during extreme events infrastructure reacts to water levels and currents, wave action, winds, and excessive temperatures.

Box 2.10 A Five-Step Risk-Assessment Approach to Infrastructure Design

1. Focus on infrastructure that has a long life (more than 40–50 years); infrastructure designed for a shorter life already has flexibility incorporated into the facility replacement schedule.
2. Identify geographic areas that are particularly sensitive to climate change, such as coastal or low-lying areas.
3. Assign a likely probability of environmental change to these sensitive areas to determine if such changes are likely over the useful life of the facility.
4. Create several designs based on different standards to account as needed for a changing environment. For each design estimate the cost, both replacement and economic of any disruption.
5. Apply the hazard probability to design components that will be affected by a changing environment. Estimate the likely costs of each in current dollars. Choose the design with the lowest net value cost.

The third step is particularly critical. The accuracy of the predicted probability of environmental change will depend on the reliability of the climate projections. Hence, planners must interpret results with caution, using corridors of values rather than single optimal values.

Source: Adapted from Meyer 2007.

Decision-Making Tools

Coping with a less predictable climate requires new decision-making tools tailored to manage deep uncertainty and reduce risks. Adaptive management should acknowledge the limitations of the information available and incorporate learning feedback loops.

Decision makers should be open to revising an investment or policy if new information becomes available. A key adaptive strategy therefore is to avoid locked-in technologies or land-use and siting decisions that can be costly to reverse if poorly adapted to future conditions, both climate and nonclimate (such as population growth).

Adaptive decision making means assessing the additional benefits of decisions that allow for fine-tuning or switching to an altogether different option. Additional benefits also accrue from decisions that incorporate options contingent on future states of nature (for example, building roads that can withstand temperature increases, or enacting climate-smart land-use policies for locating new infrastructure). Preserving future choices thus has a value per se, in addition to increasing the ability to adapt to new economic and climate contexts.

There are several practical approaches to increasing robustness and flexibility (Hallegatte 2009; World Bank 2010b):

- Pursuing *no-regret* investment and policy options, which provide benefits regardless of future climate changes
- Promoting *reversible* strategies, from easy-to-retrofit designs to structured application of an option-value framework that measures the costs associated with halting operations or making further investments while awaiting new information
- Incorporating *safety margins* that reduce vulnerabilities at manageable cost, which can include buying insurance, building redundancy into systems, or marginal design changes that can have a big impact at low or even no cost
- Identifying *soft* strategies when vulnerabilities are mainly caused by institutional failures
- Giving preference to strategies that *reduce decision-making time* by formalizing inclusion of feedback loops and periodic reassessment of initial policy and investment design
- Taking into account *conflicts and synergies* between isolated investments that should be covered by an integrated strategy; this is particularly important in the transport sector given barriers between modes and the very strong inertia of transport infrastructure (see chapter 1).

A structured tool for increasing adaptiveness and resilience is robust decision making. The Robust Decision-Making (RDM) framework[22] is a formalized approach to evaluating options that recognizes that traditional decision-making tools, such as the expected utility framework,[23] cannot cope with deep uncertainty. The expected utility framework requires that decision makers know the probability distribution of various climate phenomena and the likely losses or benefits from each—information fundamentally unknowable with a changing climate regime.

RDM, by contrast, is designed to cope with deep uncertainty where probability distributions of outcomes are unknown, when low-probability, high-impact events such as climate extremes are projected to increase at unknown speeds, intensities, and precise geographical distributions. Rather than asking the usual "What is the future likely to bring?" decision makers must ask "What actions should we take given that we do not know the future?"

RDM suggests a balancing not of expected utility and immunity to uncertainty under budget constraints but of various levels of "coverage" against uncertainty (analogous to insurance) given a society's threshold for acceptable versus unacceptable risk and its budget constraints. RDM may not offer complete protection from climate risks, but it does prepare decision makers to face uncertainty and helps them weigh the inevitable tradeoffs between cost of coverage and acceptable risks. Thus, rather than helping decision makers predict what will happen, RDM helps them to better define and select from available choices. In fact, RDM both reduces policy vulnerability and increases policy flexibility.

For transport, RDM could be most useful in guiding long-lived capital investments in new transport infrastructure when decision makers are confronted with both deep uncertainty and a wide array of options for location, capacity and other design features.[24] The aim would be to select not the traditionally "optimal" option but the option best suited to generate consensus among stakeholders, some with divergent views about the probability of various impacts, as well as to minimize the impact of adverse climate surprises.

Notes

1. The range published by the IPCC in the Fourth Assessment Report (IPCC 2007) is 18–59 cm. Because the IPCC strictly limits any claims that contributors consider too uncertain, the range excluded a potentially very large factor: ice sheet melting. Even at the time of publication, the IPCC numbers were widely considered to be underestimates. Subsequent estimates put the plausible range as easily crossing 1 m. An informal summary of the debate can be found at http://www.realclimate.org/index.php/archives/2010/03/ippc-sealevel-gate (accessed June 27, 2010). Major reports and peer-reviewed articles from the past few years include Allsor and others (2009); Copenhagen Climate Congress (2009); Deltacommissie (2008); Grinsted, Moore, and Jevrejeva (2010); Horton and others (2008); Pfeffer, Harper, and O'Neel (2008); Rahmstorf (2007); Scientific Committee on Antarctic Research (2009).

2. Kjellstrom, Holmer, and Lemke (2009); Nag and others (2009); NRC (2008); Dubai Municipality government news releases; ArabianBusiness.com various articles, for example http://www.arabianbusiness.com/press_releases/detail/19527.

3. Frost heave—cracking and uplift of portions of earth or pavement—occurs when water in the subgrade (or in the earth below) freezes and expands upward toward the surface.

4. There are many sources on this, including http://www.cnn.com/2005/WORLD/asiapcf/10/29/india.train/.

5. When cold-season temperatures are still below snow-versus-rain thresholds, moderate warming can actually intensify snowfalls by increasing the rate of evaporation and thus the concentration of water vapor in the air, setting up perfect conditions for a massive snowfall when the moist air collides with cold air. More detailed explanation of the potential for increased extreme snowfalls and evidence on the increased snows in the Great Lakes region of the United States are provided in Karl, Melillo, and Peterson (2009).
6. http://www.washingtonpost.com/wp-dyn/content/article/2010/02/11/AR2010021103895.html (accessed June 29, 2010); http://www.wunderground.com/blog/JeffMasters/comment.html?entrynum=1427 (accessed June 29, 2010).
7. http://abcnews.go.com/Politics/snow-storm-economics-winter-weather-stimulate-economy/story?id=9788401&page=3 (accessed June 29, 2010); http://voices.washingtonpost.com/federal-eye/2010/03/eye_opener_snow_days_cost_71m.html (accessed June 29, 2010).
8. Abidin and others (2009); Susandi and others (2007). Susandi PPT. http://www.eepsea.cc-sea.org/pages/ppt/C01_Susandi.pdf.
9. Air Transport World, "Climate Change May Impact Aviation Safety, ICAO warns." May 17, 2010. Accessed June 5, 2010. http://atwonline.com/eco-aviation/article/climate-change-may-impact-aviation-safety-icao-warns-0517.
10. For a review of the literature, good starting points are Füssel (2007); Janssen and Ostrom (2006).
11. Average road upgrading cost is estimated to increase by $3,688/km based on the original estimate of $18,173/km.
12. Project appraisal document, Nepal Rural Access Improvement and Decentralization Project (No. 31624-NP).
13. An interim survey of the project indicates that personal mobility increased by more than 20 percent and travel time plunged from 2.6 hours on average to 32 minutes (Project Paper on Nepal Rural Access Improvement and Decentralization Project, 2009 [No. 50766-NP]).
14. JBIC (2007); Ex-Post Evaluation Report on ODA Loan Projects FY2007.
15. World Bank 2010.
16. ESALF is defined by the number of applications of a standard 80kN dual-wheel single axle load that would cause the same amount of damage to a road as one application of the axle load being considered.
17. In many countries, public decision makers still consider climate change to be too long-term to be worthy of interest. Short-term political cycles do not match long-term climate policies, which only entail present costs
18. GFDRR/World Bank.
19. World Bank 2010, 62.
20. For example, see the variables chosen for Ethiopia (World Bank 2010, 30–31).
21. World Bank 2010, 39.
22. For a careful overview of RDM, see Lempert and McCollins (2007); Lempert and Schlessinger (2000).
23. Expected utility theory elaborates on the basic expected value framework by incorporating individual or social preferences (or tolerance) for risk. In a process based on

expected value alone, for each option the decision maker considers the *expected value* (the probability of the outcome associated with that option multiplied by the value, in monetary terms, of the outcome being realized, minus the known cost of pursing the option) and chooses the one with the highest expected value. For example, paving a gravel road costs more than maintaining it; if a flash flood that would wash out the gravel but not the paved road is not very likely, it would not be worth the extra expense of paving. In expected utility theory, the calculation is the same, except that for each option the decision maker considers the expected *utility* value of each option—wherein the probability is multiplied by the value in terms utility, which captures the decision maker's risk preferences. Decision makers who are risk-averse will be inclined to choose options that may have lower payoffs (or higher costs) but entail a lower probability of losses. (Monetary damages from a flood, once weighted by multiplying by the low probability of that flood, do not offset the additional cost of paving the road; however, the planner's attitude toward risk may be such that even the slim possibility of disaster is unacceptable, warranting the extra expense of paving.) It is essential to note that in both expected value and expected utility frameworks, the decision maker must know the probability distribution of the outcomes of choosing various options to assign an expected value or utility to each option.

24. So far, despite its promising new insights, this theoretical framework has yet to be applied to transport projects, though it has been used successfully for long-term water management decisions in California. See Groves, Wilkinson, and Lempert (2008) and Groves, Yates, and Tebaldi (2008).

References

AASHTO (American Association of State Highway and Transportation Officials). 2008. "Adaptation of Transportation Infrastructure to Global Climate Change (GCC): Implications for Design and Implementation." Mimeo, p. 4.

Abidin, H. Z., H. Andreas, I. Gumilar, M. Gamal, Y. Fukuda, and T. Deguchi. 2009. "Land Subsidence and Urban Development in Jakarta (Indonesia)." Paper presented at 7th FIG (International Federation of Surveyors) Regional Conference, "Spatial Data Serving People: Land Governance and the Environment – Building the Capacity," Hanoi, Vietnam, October 19–22.

Allison, I., N. L. Bindoff, R. A. Bindschadler, P. M. Cox, N. de Noblet, M. H. England, J. E. Francis, N. Gruber, A. M. Haywood, D. J. Karoly, G. Kaser, C. Le Quéré, T. M. Lenton, M. E. Mann, B. I. McNeil, A. J. Pitman, S. Rahmstorf, E. Rignot, H. J. Schellnhuber, S. H. Schneider, S. C. Sherwood, R. C. J. Somerville, K. Steffen, E. J. Steig, M. Visbeck, A. J. Weaver. 2009. *The Copenhagen Diagnosis, 2009: Updating the World on the Latest Climate Science*. Sydney: The University of New South Wales Climate Change Research Centre.

Andrey, Jean, Brian Mills, Courtney Jermyn, Brenda Jones, Mike Leahy, Ken McInnis, David Tammadge, Dan Unrau, Emily Vandermolen, Jessica Vandermolen, and Pete Whittington. 2003. "Collisions, Casualties, and Costs: Weathering the Elements on Canadian Roads." Research Paper Series No. 33, Institute for Catastrophic Loss Reduction. http://www.iclr.org/images/Collisions_Casualties_and_Costs.pdf.

Australian Government. 2006. "Climate Change Scenarios for Initial Assessment of Risk in Accordance with Risk Management Guidance." Prepared by Kevin Hennessy, Ian

Macadam, and Penny Whetton of the Commonwealth Scientific and Industrial Research Organisation (CSIRO) for the Australian Greenhouse Office, Department of the Environment and Heritage.

Battisti, D. S., and R. L. Naylor. 2009. "Historical Warnings of Future Food Insecurity with Unprecedented Seasonal Heat." *Science* 323 (5911): 240–44.

Burton, I., and B. Lim. 2005. "Achieving Adequate Adaptation in Agriculture." *Climatic Change* 70: 191–200.

CEPAL (Comisión Económica para América Latina y el Caribe). 1998. *Ecuador: Evaluación de los efectos socio-económicos del fenómeno de El Niño en 1997–1998.* Santiago: Comisión Económica para América Latina y el Caribe, 37–41.

Collins, M., S.-I. An, W. Cai, A. Ganachaud, E. Guilyardi, F.-F. Jin, M. Jochum, M. Lengaigne, S. Power, A. Timmermann, G. Vecchi, and A. Wittenberg. 2010. "The Impact of Global Warming on the Tropical Pacific Ocean and El Niño." *Nature Geoscience* 3: 391–97.

Collins, M., and The CMIP Modelling Groups. 2004. "El Niño- or La Niña-Like Climate Change?" *Climate Dynamics* 24 (1): 89–104.

Copenhagen Climate Congress. 2009. *Synthesis Report. Climate Change: Global Risks, Challenges, and Decisions.* Copenhagen: Copenhagen Climate Congress.

Dasgupta, S., M. Huq, Z. H. Khan, M. M. Z. Ahmed, N. Mukherjee, M. F. Khan, and K. Pandey. 2010. "Vulnerability of Bangladesh to Cyclones in a Changing Climate." World Bank Policy Research Working Paper 5280, Washington, DC.

Deltacommissie. 2008. *Working Together with Water: A Living Land Builds for Its Future.* The Netherlands: Deltacommissie.

Eisenberg, D. 2004. "The Mixed Effects of Precipitation on Traffic Crashes." *Accident Analysis and Prevention* 36 (4): 637–47.

Ebinger, Jane, Bjorn Hamso, Franz Gerner, Antonio Lim, and Ana Plecas. 2008. "Europe and Central Asia Region: How Resilient is the Energy Sector to Climate Change?" Background paper prepared for World Bank report, Washington, DC, World Bank.

Economides, N. 1996. "The Economics of Networks." *International Journal of Industrial Organization*. 14 (6): 673–99.

Fay, M., J. Ebinger, and R. I. Block, eds. 2010. *Adapting to Climate Change in Eastern Europe and Central Asia*. Washington, DC: World Bank.

Füssel, H-M. 2007. "Vulnerability: A Generally Applicable Conceptual Framework for Climate Change Research." *Global Environmental Change* 17 (2): 155–67.

Gallivan, F., K. Bailey, and L. O'Rourke. 2009. "Planning for Impacts of Climate Change at U.S. Ports." *Journal of the Transportation Research Board* 2100: 15–21.

GFDRR (Global Facility for Disaster Reduction and Recovery)/World Bank. *Disaster Reduction and Recovery. A Primer for Development Managers*.

Glantz, M. H., ed. 2001. *Once Burned, Twice Shy: Lessons Learned from the 1997–98 El Niño*. Tokyo: UN University Press.

Grenzeback, L. R., and A. Lukmann. 2008. "Case Study of the Transportation Sector's Response to and Recovery from Hurricanes Katrina and Rita." Background paper prepared for the National Research Council's Transportation Research Board. Cambridge Systematics, Inc. http://www.ardd.org/LIBRARY/DISASTER%20RECOVERY/Case_Study_Katrinatransportation.pdf.

Grinsted, A., J. C. Moore, and S. Jevrejeva. 2010. "Reconstructing Sea Level from Paleo and Projected Temperatures 200 to 2100 AD." *Climate Dynamics* 34 (4): 461–72.

Groves, D. G., M. Davis, R. Wilkinson, and R. J. Lempert. 2008. "Planning for Climate Change in the Inland Empire: Southern California." *Water Resources Impact* 10 (4): 14–17.

Groves, D. G., D. Yates, and C. Tebaldi. 2008. "Developing and Applying Uncertain Global Climate Change Projections for Regional Water Management Planning." *Water Resources Research* 44 (12): 1–16.

GTZ (Deutsche Gesellschaft für Technische Zusammenarbeit). 2009. *Adapting Transport in Developing Cities to Climate Change. Module 5f, Sustainable Transport: A Sourcebook for Policy-makers in Developing Cities.* Eschborn, Germany: GTZ.

Hallegatte, S. 2007. "Do Current Assessments Underestimate Future Damages from Climate Change?" *World Economics* 8: 131–46. http://www.world-economics-journal.com/Contents/ArticleOverview.aspx?ID=303.

———. 2009. "Strategies to Adapt to an Uncertain Climate Change." *Global Environmental Change* 19 (2): 240–47.

Hancock, L., V. Tsirkunov, and M. Smetanina. 2008. "Weather and Climate Services in Europe and Central Asia: A Regional Review." World Bank Working Paper 151, World Bank, Washington, DC

Haraldsson, M. 2007. "The Marginal Cost for Pavement Renewal—A Duration Analysis Approach." Swedish National Road & Transport Research Institute Working Papers 2007:8.

Harral, C. G, and A. Faiz. 1988. *Road Deterioration in Developing Countries: Causes and Remedies.* Washington, DC World Bank. http://www.rhd.gov.bd/Documents/ExternalPublications/WorldBank/TransSectPub/contents/documents/B29.pdf.

Horton, R., C. Herweijer, C. Rosenzweig, J. Liu, V. Gornitz, and A. C. Ruane. 2008. "Sea Level Rise Projections for Current Generation CGCMs Based on the Semi-Empirical Method." *Geophysical Research Letters* 35: L02715.

HSE (Health and Safety Executive). 2001. "Marine Risk Assessment." Offshore Technical Report 2001/063, prepared by Det Norske Veritas for HSE.

———. 2006. "Guidance on Risk Assessment for Offshore Installations." Offshore Information Sheet No. 3/2006

Huang, B., C. Y. Chan, X. Yan, and S. Richards. 2008. *Effects of Asphalt Pavement Conditions on Traffic Accidents in Tennessee Utilizing Pavement Management System (PMS).* Seed Grand Final Report, Southern Transportation Center, University of Tennessee, Knoxville, TN.

IPCC (Intergovernmental Panel on Climate Change). 2001. "Working Group II: Impacts, Adaptation, and Vulnerability." Technical Summary, Geneva, Switzerland.

———. 2007. "Summary for Policymakers." In *Climate Change 2007: The Physical Science Basis.* Contribution of Working Group I to the Fourth Assessment Report of the Intergovernmental Panel on Climate Change, edited by S. Solomom, D. Qin, M. Manning, Z. Chen, M. Marquis, K. B. Averyt, M. Tignor, and H. L. Miller. Cambridge, U.K.: Cambridge University Press.

Janssen, M., and E. Ostrom, eds. 2006. "Special Issue on Resilience, Vulnerability and Adaptation." *Global Environmental Change* 6 (3): 268–81.

JBIC (Japan Bank for International Cooperation). 2007. *Ex-Post Evaluation Report on ODA Loan Projects FY2007*. Tokyo.

JICA (Japan International Cooperation Agency). 2007. "Ex-Post Evaluation Report on ODA Loan Projects FY 2007." JICA, Tokyo. http://www.jica.go.jp/english/our_work/evaluation/oda_loan/post/2008/index.html.

Jung, M., M. Reichstein, P. Ciais, S. I. Seneviratne, J. Sheffield, M. L. Goulden, G. Bonan, A. Cescatti, J. Chen, R. de Jeu, A. J. Dolman, W. Eugster, D. Gerten, D. Gianelle, N. Gobron, J. Heinke, J. Kimball, B. E. Law, L. Montagnani, Q. Mu, B. Mueller, K. Oleson, D. Papale, A. D. Richardson, O. Roupsard, S. Running, E. Tomelleri, N. Viovy, U. Weber, C. Williams, E. Wood, S. Zaehle, and K. Zhang. 2010. "Recent Decline in the Global Land Evapotranspiration Trend due to Limited Moisture Supply." *Nature* 467: 951–54.

Karl, T., J. Melillo, and T. Peterson, eds. 2009. *Global Climate Change Impacts in the United States. U.S. Global Change Research Program*. New York: Cambridge University Press.

Kato, Wataru, and Yoshihiro Hono. 2009. "Research on the Use of Weather Radar in Train Operation Control." JR EAST Technical Review No.14, Disaster Prevention Research Laboratory Research and Development Center of JR East Group, East Japan Railway Culture Foundation. http://www.jreast.co.jp/e/development/tech/pdf_14/Tec-14-55-60eng.pdf.

Kjellstrom, T., I. Holmer, and B. Lemke. 2009. "Workplace Heat Stress, Health and Productivity an Increasing Challenge for Low and Middle-Income Countries during Climate Change." *Global Health Action* 2: doi:10.3402/gha.v2i0.2047.

Leigh, A. 2009. "Precipitation, Profits, and Pile-Ups." Discussion Paper DP629, The Australian National University Centre for Economic Policy Research, Canberra, Australia.

Lempert, R. J., and M. T. Collins. 2007. "Managing the Risk of Uncertain Threshold Responses: Comparison of Robust, Optimum, and Precautionary Approaches." *Risk Analysis* 27 (4): 1009–26.

Lempert, R., and M. Schlessinger. 2000. "Robust Strategies for Abating Climate Change." *Climatic Change* 45: 387–401.

Lenton, T. M., H. Held, E. Kriegler, J. W. Hall, W. Lucht, S. Rahmstorf, and H. J. Schellnhuber. 2008. "Tipping Elements in the Earth's Climate System." *Proceedings of the National Academy of Sciences* 105 (6): 1786–93.

Ligeti, E., J. Penney, and I. Wieditz. 2007. *Cities Preparing for Climate Change: A Study of Six Urban Regions*. Toronto: Clean Air Partnership.

Lobell, D. B., and C. B. Field. 2007. "Global Scale Climate-Crop Yield Relationships and the Impacts of Recent Warming." *Environmental Research Letters* 2: 1–7.

Meyer, M. D. 2007. "Design Standards for U.S. Transportation Infrastructure: The Implications of Climate Change." Background paper prepared for NRC.

Millennium Ecosystem Assessment. 2005. *Ecosystems and Human Well-Being: Synthesis Report*. Washington, DC: World Resources Institute.

Milly, P. C. D., J. Betancourt, M. Falkenmark, R. M. Hirsch, Z. W. Kundzewicz, D. P. Lettenmaier, and R. J. Stouffer. 2008. "Stationarity Is Dead. Whither Water Management?" *Science* 319: 573–74.

Mignone, B. K., R. H. Socolow, J. L. Sarmiento, and M. Oppenheimer. 2008. "Atmospheric Stabilization and the Timing of Carbon Mitigation." *Climatic Change* 88 (3–4): 251–65.

Nag, P. K., A. Nag, P. Sekhar, and S. Pandit. 2009. *Vulnerability to Heat Stress: Scenario in Western India*. WHO APW No. SO 08 AMS 6157206, National Institue of Occupational Health, Ahmedabad, India.

Nakat, Z. 2008. "Climate Change Adaptation in the Transport Sector: Impacts and Adaptation Options in the ECA Region." Background paper. Washington DC, World Bank.

New Zealand Climate Change Office. 2004. "Coastal Hazards and Climate Change: A Guidance Manual for Local Government in New Zealand." Wellington, New Zealand: Ministry for the Environment.

NRC (National Research Council). 2008. "Potential Impacts of Climate Change on U.S. Transportation." Special Report 290. The National Academies Press, Washington, DC.

OECD (Organisation for Economic Co-operation and Development). 2002. *Benchmarking Intermodal Freight Transport*. Paris: OECD.

Olken, B. A. 2007. "Monitoring Corruption: Evidence from a Field Experiment in Indonesia." *Journal of Political Economy* 115 (2): 200–49.

Paeth, H., A. Scholten, P. Friederichs, and A. Hense. 2008. "Uncertainties in Climate Change Prediction: El Niño-Southern Oscillation and Monsoons." *Global and Planetary Change* 60 (3–4): 265–88.

Parry, M., O. F. Canziani, J. P. Palutikof, and co-authors. 2007. "Technical Summary." In *Climate Change 2007: Impacts, Adaptation and Vulnerability*. Contribution of Working Group II to the Fourth Assessment Report of the Intergovernmental Panel on Climate Change, edited by M. Parry, O. F. Canziani, J. P. Palutikof, P. J. van der Linden, and C. E. Hansen, 23–78. Cambridge, U.K.: Cambridge University Press. http://www.ipcc.ch/pdf/assessment-report/ar4/wg2/ar4-wg2-ts.pdf.

Pew Center on Global Climate Change. 2010. Understanding Extreme Weather and Climate Impacts in China. (accessed May 15, 2010). http://www.pewclimate.org/chinaextremeweather_qa.

Pfeffer, W. T., J. T. Harper, and S. O'Neel. 2008. "Kinematic Constraints on Glacier Contributions to 21st-Century Sea-Level Rise." *Science* 321 (5894): 1340–43.

Philip, S. Y., and G. J. van Oldenborgh. 2006. "Shifts in ENSO Coupling Processes under Global Warming." *Geophysical Research Letters* 33: L11704.

PIARC. 2012. "Dealing with the Effects of Climate Change on Road Pavements." Technical Committee D.2 Road Pavements, World Road Association. http://www.piarc.org/en/order-library/16862-en-Dealing%20with%20the%20effects%2Cof%20climate%20change%20on%20road%20pavements.htm?catalog&catalog-size=general.

Pinard, M. I. 2010. "Overload Control Practices in EAstern and South Eastern Africa: Main Lesson Learned." Working Paper 91, World Bank, Washington, DC.

Rahmstorf, S. 2007. "A Semi-Empirical Approach to Projecting Future Sea-Level Rise." *Science* 315 (5810): 368–70.

Road Research Laboratory. 1954. "The Effect of Rainfall on the Number of Road Crashes in Great Britain." *Operational Research Quarterly* 5 (2): 50–54.

Schneider, S. H., and K. Kuntz-Duriseti. 2002. "Uncertainty and Climate Change Policy." In *Climate Change Policy: A Survey*, edited by S. H. Schneider, A. Rosencranz, and J. O. Niles, 53–88. Washington, DC: Island Press.

Scientific Committee on Antarctic Research. 2009. *SCAR Report on Antarctic Climate Change and the Environment*. Cambridge, U.K.: SCAR Scott Polar Research Institute.

Solberg, S., D. Hale, J. Benavides, 2003. "*Natural Disaster Management and the Road Network in Ecuador: Policy Issues and Recommendations.*" IDB 39838, Inter-American Development Bank, Washington, DC.

Susandi, Armi, Dwi Resti Pratiwi, Mamad Tamamadin, Miza Marta Fadila, Taora Violiza, Titania Suwarto, Saskya Saspavyana, Alliza Aulia, and Wulan Seizarwati. 2007. "Adaptive Behavior Assessment Based on Climate Change Event: Jakarta's Flood in 2007." Economy and Environment Program for Southeast Asia (EEPSEA). http://www.eepsea.net/pub/tr/Armi-Susandi-etal-Technical-Report.pdf.

Tajbakhsh, S., E. Moradi, and F. Mohamadi. 2010. "The Study of Impacts and Adaptations to Climate Change in a Aviation Case Study." Poster presentation at 18th Conference on Applied Climatology, Atlanta, GA, January 18. http://ams.confex.com/ams/90annual/techprogram/paper_165134.htm.

Trenberth, K., and T. Hoar. 1997. "El Niño and Climate Change." *Geophysical Research Letters* 24 (23): 3057–60.

Webster, P. J., G. J. Holland, J. A. Curry, and H. R. Chang. 2005. "Changes in Tropical Cyclone Number, Duration, and Intensity in a Warming Environment." *Science* 309 (5742): 1844–46.

Willows, Robert, and Richenda Connel, eds. 2003. "Climate Adaptation: Risk, Uncertainty and Decision-Making." UKCIP Technical Report. Oxford: United Kingdom Climate Impacts Programme.

World Bank. 2007. "Nepal: Managing Public Finances for a New Nepal, A Public Finance Management Review." Report 43384-NP, World Bank, Washington, DC. https://openknowledge.worldbank.org/bitstream/handle/10986/7745/433840ESW0P09710BOX327397B01PUBLIC1.pdf?sequence=1.

———. 2010. "Making Transport Climate Resilient." Country Report: Ethiopia. Consultant report prepared by COWI (Denmark) for World Bank. http://www.ppiaf.org/sites/ppiaf.org/files/publication/Ethiopia_Making-Transport-Climate-Resilient.pdf.

———. 2010a. *World Development Indicators 2010*. Washington, DC: World Bank.

———. 2010b. *World Development Report 2010: Development and Climate Change*. Washington, DC: World Bank.

CHAPTER 3

Integrating Sector-Wide Reforms for Mitigation

Transport accounts for 13 percent of total green house gas (GHG) emissions (IPCC 2007)[1] and is one of the fastest-growing sources. Without significant policy action, the increased mobility, motorization, and urbanization that accompany economic development will massively increase carbon emissions.

Some current policies could reduce energy intensity and curb transportation demand without compromising economic growth. But behavior and lifestyles are hard to change. Transport infrastructure is very long-lived. Success will require rapid intervention on many fronts.

Advances in engine fuel efficiency will, of course, pave the way, but new technology is not enough. Economic measures, such as pricing, regulation, and the availability of multimodal transportation systems, are also essential. Soft measures in infrastructure operations could also help—and rapidly. If they are to be effective, all these measures must be integrated into a coordinated sector-wide approach.

Urgent action is needed before economies become locked into high-carbon growth. In the United States, urban settlement patterns and interurban infrastructure established decades ago have led to today's high transport intensity (figure 3.1), making it difficult to expand mass transit and change behavior despite fossil-fuel price increases (see, for instance, Lecocq and Shalizi 2009).

This chapter discusses how to reconcile development with the need to curb emissions, looking at three sets of instruments. We first discuss new technologies and alternative fuels, limits to their potential in the short term, and their high cost. We then turn to supply-side measures and their limitations: without alternative modes, people have no choice but to rely on road transport. Finally, we look at demand-side policies, such as incentives. Ultimately, we argue that fuel taxation is the most effective and direct way to promote both energy efficiency and mass transportation.

Figure 3.1 Paths of Automobile Use

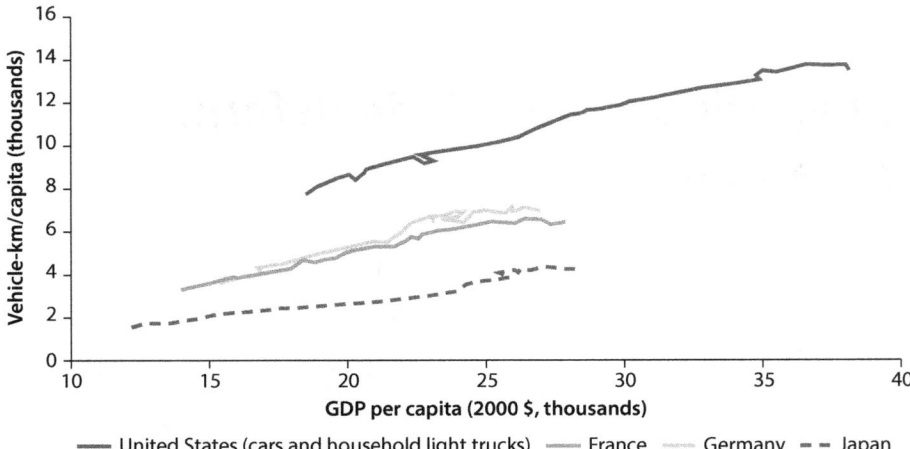

Source: World Bank 2010a.
Note: GDP = gross domestic product.

Technology: Necessary, Promising, but Still Far Off

New technologies are necessary for low-carbon growth, but they vary in their commercial readiness. New road, rail, and aviation engine technologies and biofuels still have relatively little potential for deep emission cuts because of their high cost, even when carbon prices are high (World Bank 2010a). Significant and accelerated technological development and diffusion are still needed.

Engine Efficiency and New Engine Technologies

Improving the efficiency of internal combustion engines is critical because they are expected to dominate the market for the near future. Cars and trucks account for about 67 percent of total transport emissions (figure 3.2) (World Bank 2008b). About 1 billion cars are now on the roads worldwide. Another 2.3 billion are likely to be added by 2050, mostly in developing countries (Chamon and others 2008) given the expected economic, motorization, and income growth there (World Bank 2010a), and most new cars will still rely on traditional internal combustion engines. Advanced low-carbon engine technologies, such as hybrids, comprise only a small percentage of the market in high-income countries and are very rare in developing countries.

Fuel Economy

Most improvements in fuel economy to date occurred before the mid-1980s (figure 3.3). U.S. fuel economy for passenger cars (sales volume weighted) dropped from 18 liters per 100 km (13 miles per gallon [mpg]) in 1978 to 8.3 liters per 100 km (28.3 mpg) in 2009; in Europe, it decreased from 10 liters per 100 km to 5.7–6.8 between 1975 and 2008.

Integrating Sector-Wide Reforms for Mitigation

Figure 3.2 World Transport CO_2 Emissions by Vehicle Type, 2000

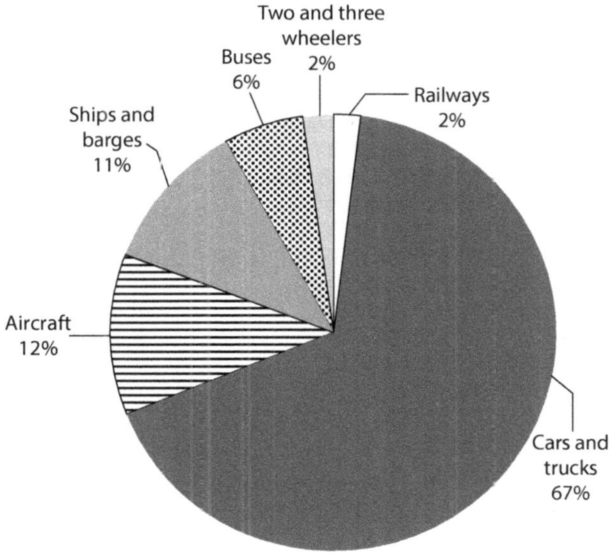

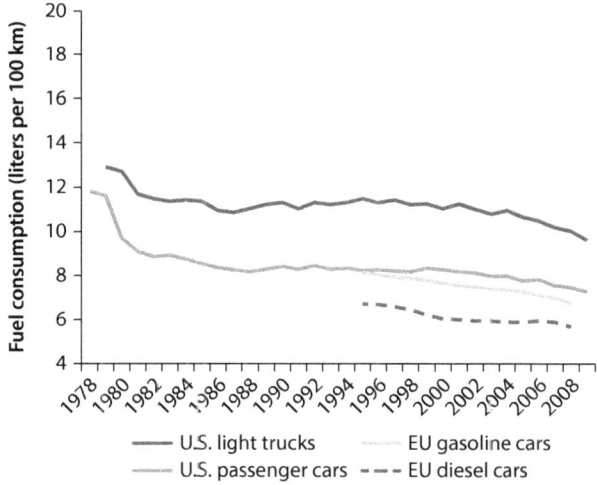

Source: WBCSD 2004.
Note: CO_2 = carbon dioxide.

Figure 3.3 Average Fuel Consumption, United States and European Union, 1978–2008

Sources: U.S. Department of Transportation; European Commission Environment.

The prevalence of diesel vehicles, which emit about 7 percent less carbon dioxide (CO_2) than gasoline vehicles, partly accounts for Europe's relatively high fuel efficiency.[2]

Some developing economies have therefore favored diesel over gasoline-powered cars, with diesel representing up to 90 percent of domestic markets (figure 3.4).

Figure 3.4 Diesel Share of Total Gasoline and Diesel Fuel Use

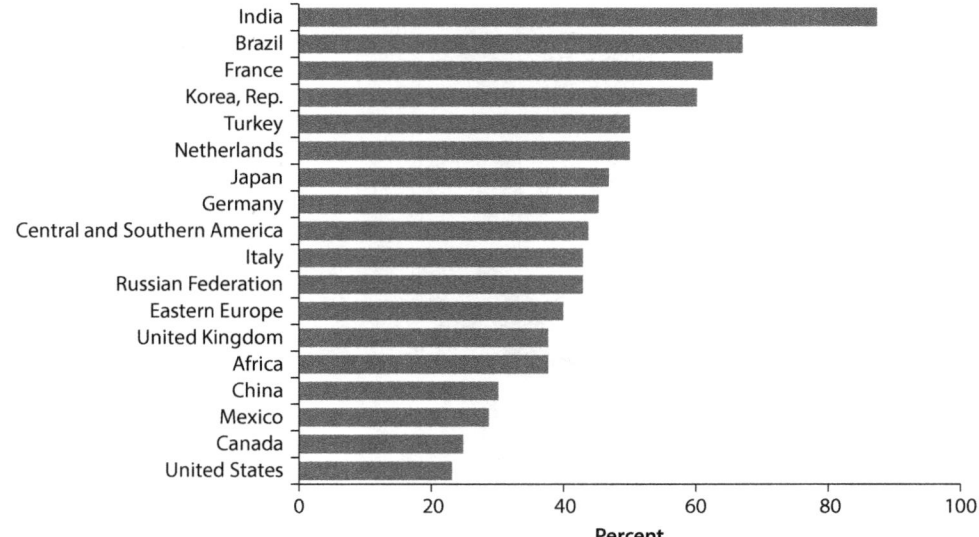

Source: OECD 2002a.

Table 3.1 Fuel Economy Standards for Passenger Cars, United States and European Union, and Japan

Year	United States	European Union	Japan
1995[a]	27.5 mpg (standard for 1995) (= 8.6 liter/100 km)	140 g/km (voluntary target by 2008) (= 6.1 liter/100 km)	6.4–21.2 km/liter (target by 2010) (= 4.7–15.6 liter/100 km)
2007[a]	27.5 mpg (standard for 2007) (= 8.6 liter/100 km)	120 g/km (expected by 2012) (= 5.2 liter/100 km)	7.4–22.5 km/liter (target by 2015) (= 4.4–13.5 liter/100 km)

Sources: Zachariadis 2006; U.S. Department of Transportation; European Commission Environment; METI 2006).
a. 1998 and 2009 for Europe.

Fuel economy standards also contribute to engine efficiency, although how much is debatable, especially relative to other interventions, such as fuel taxes. Standards differ by country (table 3.1). The U.S. Corporate Average Fuel Economy (CAFE) program introduced in 1975 requires automobile manufacturers to meet average fuel consumption targets. In 1995 Japan introduced standards to reduce fuel consumption by 19 percent and achieved the target by 2004.

A new target set in 2006 aims for another 23.5 percent reduction (METI 2006). In Europe improvements in fuel economy were largely a side effect of air pollutant regulations, although in 1998–99 car manufacturers agreed with the European Commission (EC) on a voluntary average emission target of 140 grams of CO_2/km for new cars—the 1995 average was 187 grams/km (Zachariadis 2006).

Hybrids

Low-carbon hybrid engines have great potential to reduce fuel input per vehicle-km but are still expensive (figure 3.5). For instance, the Toyota Prius, the best-selling of about 20 hybrid car models, uses 4.7 liters of fuel/100 km (50 mpg) but costs about $21,000. Hybrids have benefited from public programs:

Figure 3.5 Estimated Emissions Reduction by 2050 and Costs by Vehicle and Fuel Type

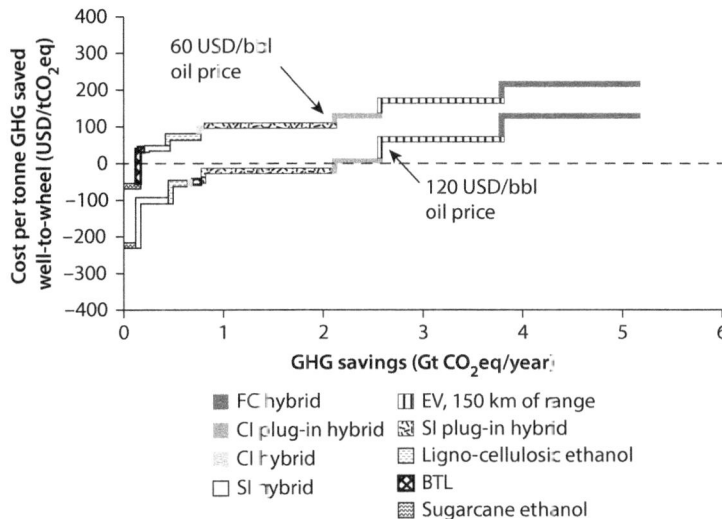

Source: OECD/IEA 2009, figure ES-3, p. 37.
Note: The curves indicate the marginal costs of different technologies and fuels in contributing to carbon dioxide (CO_2) reductions from light-duty vehicles in 2050. If low-carbon biofuels are used, the marginal costs could be negative, so that those technologies could generate net savings of CO_2 over their lifetimes. The figure shows that most technologies would be developed if oil prices are $120 a barrel and the carbon price is $130 per t$CO_2$eq, resulting in a savings of 5Gt CO_2eq a year. But at an oil price of $60 a barrel, more advanced technologies would not be tapped and emissions savings would be 3 Gigatonnes CO_2eq a year. BTL = biomass-to-liquids biodiesel, CI = compression ignition (diesel) vehicle, EV = electric vehicle, FC = fuel cell, "hybrid" refers to hybrid-electric vehicle, ICE = internal combustion engine vehicle, SI = spark ignition (gasoline) vehicle.

Table 3.2 Top Global Hybrid Vehicle Markets, 2009

	Hybrid sales	Total car sales (millions)	Hybrid share (percent)
United States	265,501	10.4	2.6
Japan	249,619	2.9	8.5
Canada	16,167	1.5	1.1
Netherlands	13,686	0.4	3.5
United Kingdom	13,661	2.0	0.7

Sources: hybridCARS 2010 (http://www.hybridcars.com/december-2009-dashboard/); Global Economic Research 2010; Japan Auto Dealers Association.

New York City aimed to replace all 13,000 taxis with hybrid cars by 2012, the equivalent of removing 32,000 cars from the road.[3] Boston, San Francisco and Seattle are also considering this approach.[4] Tax credits and subsidies are often offered as incentives to taxi or bus operators. For instance, the U.S. government allows hybrid buyers tax credits of up to $3,000 (Gao and Kitirattragarn 2008), and since 2002 the Japanese government has subsidized half the price differential between hybrids or electric cars and conventional vehicles.[5]

But hybrid vehicle use is still limited, especially in developing countries, and wider use will depend on lower prices. The 600,000 hybrid cars sold in 2009, mostly in the United States and Japan (table 3.2), are less than 2 percent of the 51 million cars sold worldwide (Global Economic Research 2010). With the price differential between a hybrid and a conventional car at 30–60 percent, it would take more than 10 years to pay back the additional cost of a hybrid if gas were $3 a gallon and average yearly mileage 15,000 miles. Ten years is a rather long investment period, particularly given technology and fuel price uncertainties.

Electric and Fuel Cell Cars

In recent years several major car manufacturers have begun to mass-produce electric cars. Electric cars emit no CO_2, but whether they reduce emissions depends on the carbon intensity of their electricity, which varies significantly and will continue to do so unless there is major intervention (figure 3.6). If their fuel efficiency does not improve, the advantage of electric cars will remain limited or disappear.

If electricity is reasonably efficient, the emission intensity of electric cars is significantly lower than that of conventional vehicles. A recent experiment in California illustrates the promising environmental benefits of electric school buses: CO_2 emissions were 3.5 kilograms (kg) per mile for a diesel bus and 0.8 kg for an electric bus. Replacing all 475,000 California school buses with electric buses could significantly reduce emissions.[6] Electric buses also reduce pollutants, emitting 93 percent less nitrogen oxide than diesels.[7]

Figure 3.6 GHG Intensity of Electricity Generation, by Region (IEA Baseline Scenario)

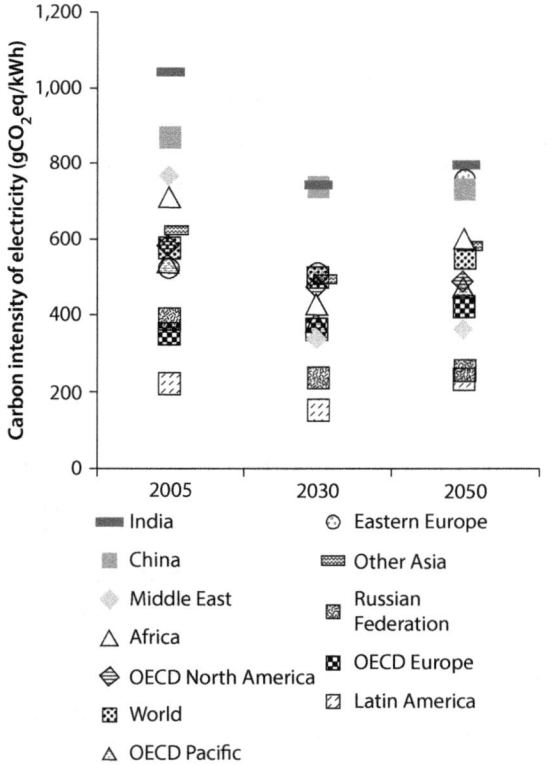

Source: OECD/IEA 2009, figure 2.11, p. 81.
Note: IEA = International Energy Agency, GHG = greenhouse gas, OECD = Organisation for Economic Co-Operation and Development.

However, electric cars currently cost at least $50,000, up to four times more than gasoline-powered vehicles. In the school bus project, electric buses cost more than one and a half times diesel buses.[8] The much lower operating costs—maintenance costs are lower and electricity costs one-fourth to one-tenth as much as conventional fossil fuel per km (even less if a battery is charged during off-peak hours)—are not enough to offset the high purchase price.

Electric cars will also need a whole new recharging infrastructure. Although electric cars can be charged through a normal household outlet, given the limited driving distance per battery charge there must also be public charge points. Without a minimum network in place, electric vehicle use will be limited. Some developed countries, such as France, Japan, the United Kingdom, and the United States, have begun building recharging stations, but current networks account for less than 1 percent of domestic gas stations.[9] Car manufacturers, power companies, electrical industries, car dealers, and regulators must collaborate to set up a network of charging stations that use standardized charger plugs and management systems.

Another constraint on electric vehicles is battery technology.[10] Batteries are still expensive—$6,000 for plug-in electric hybrids and $16,000–$20,000 for a fully electric vehicle (OECD/IEA 2009). In addition, the mass and volume of battery packs are still too large, and driving distance is limited by battery capacity. Most electric cars can travel fewer than 160 km on a single battery charge. Battery charging also takes 7–14 hours, depending on voltage. Safety is another concern, particularly for high-speed charger technology. Finally, a finite battery life of 5–10 years will necessitate regulations for environmentally safe disposal.

Despite these challenges, in certain conditions electric vehicles have advantages. School or public buses are one of the most promising examples. The driving distance of school buses is typically not long, and buses are usually only used for several hours a day. Thus, there would be time to charge batteries at school bus parking lots. Electric cars are also well suited for urbanites, who typically drive only short distances each day and could charge batteries at home at night. For longer distance travel, they could use mass transit, such as railways.

Fuel cells are attracting increasing attention. A number of materials, such as proton exchange membranes and solid oxide, can be used for fuel cells, though the focus has been on hydrogen (Transportation Research Board 2010) because it produces no atmospheric pollutants—water is its only byproduct. Although evolving, fuel-cell technology is still meeting commercial resistance because of its intensive use of expensive catalysts like platinum, the high cost of building hydrogen distribution networks, and the high temperatures and more-than-atmospheric pressures needed to operate it. Finally, current fuel-cell volume and weight need to be downscaled (National Academies 2002).

In addition, a significant amount of hydrogen has to be produced for fuel cell cars. This is problematic for mitigation. In general, fuel-cell technologies may still be too carbon-intensive even in the long run (figure 3.5). Current production depends on natural gas, coal, or grid electricity, creating significant upstream emissions. Frontier technologies using biomass may be able to reduce lifecycle emissions, but practical use still requires substantially more advanced technology (Transportation Research Board 2010).

Jet Engines

Air transport is fuel-intensive, accounting for 12 percent of total transport emissions. For example, a Boeing 747 flying at 900 km/hr uses one gallon of fuel every second. As with vehicle engines, aircraft technology is evolving. Over the past four decades, aviation fuel consumption has declined 60–70 percent with the development of high-bypass ratio engines and aerodynamic efficiency (figure 3.7) (IEA 2000; World Bank 2009a). The latest Boeing 747 is 20 percent more fuel efficient than the original model (table 3.3). Advanced materials such as aluminum alloys and composites that

Figure 3.7 Passenger Aircraft: CO_2 Normalized Energy Efficiency
megajoule/available seat km

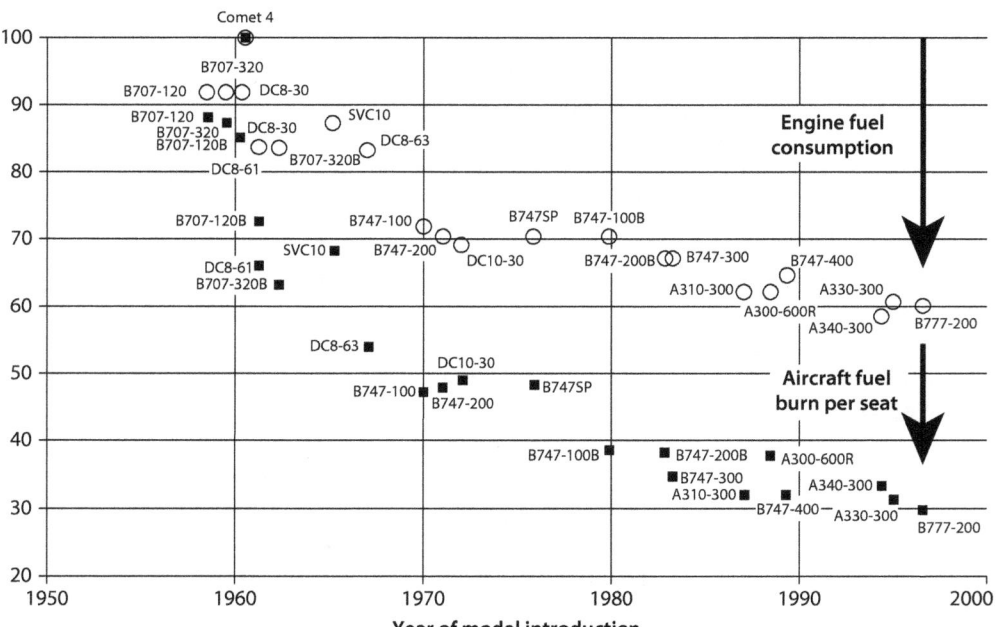

Sources: IPCC 1999; reproduced in World Bank 2009a.
Note: CO_2 = carbon dioxide. For each type of airplane, the circles refer to energy efficiency improvements in the engines and the squares ton improvements in airframes, such as winglets. Thus, the fuel efficiency of aircraft decreased from 80–90 MJ per available seat kilometer in 1960 to 30–40 MJ in the 1990s, about one-third from engine improvements and two-thirds from airframe improvements.

Table 3.3 Boeing 747 Average Fuel Efficiency

Model	Liters/hr
B747-100	14,645
B747-200/300	13,434
B747-400	11,865

Sources: U.S. Department of Transportation 2006; reproduced in World Bank 2009a.

reduce airframe weight have also improved fuel efficiency. A 1 percent reduction in the gross weight of an empty aircraft can reduce fuel consumption 25–75 percent.

Railway Technologies

Rail contributes as little as 2 percent of total transport emissions because railways are low-carbon emitters and rail networks are equivalent only to about 6 percent of global paved roads. In some major economies, however, railways account for about 9 percent of total passenger-km and 30 percent of total freight ton-km (figure 3.8; EC 2009).

Railways consume a significant amount of diesel fuel.[11] The United Nations Framework Convention on Climate Change estimates that industrialized countries consume 690,000 terajoule (TJ), 17,000 million liters for rail. This figure could double if developing countries, where diesel-powered locomotives are often outdated and highly polluting, are included (table 3.4) (UIC 2007). Developing countries may have more opportunities to reduce emissions through improved operations, which are often inefficient, than through new technologies.

Electrifying passenger railways within dense cities and between large cities could greatly reduce emissions. For instance, the EC has been tightening emission regulations for new railway engines since 2004. Railway electricity use could also be reduced through improved operations (see below) and less emission-intensive technologies (box 3.1).

Figure 3.8 Railway Traffic by Region

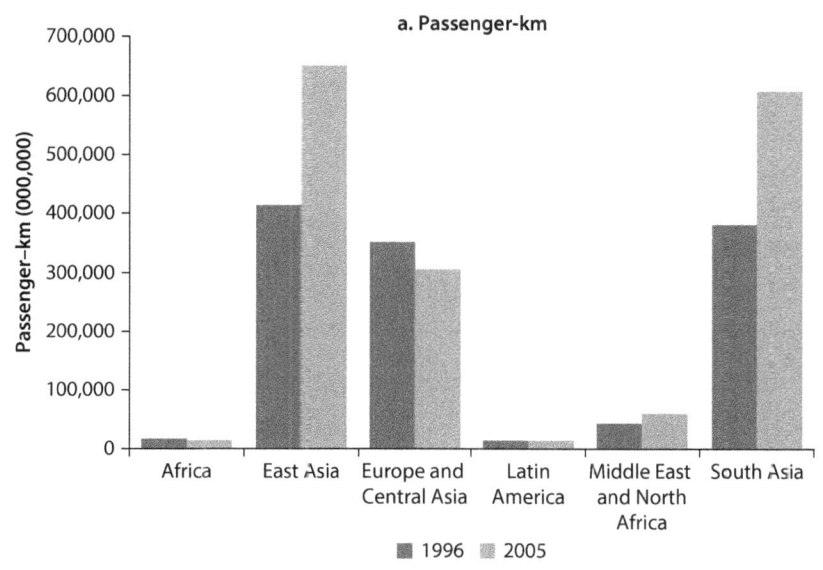

figure continues next page

Figure 3.8 Railway Traffic by Region *(continued)*

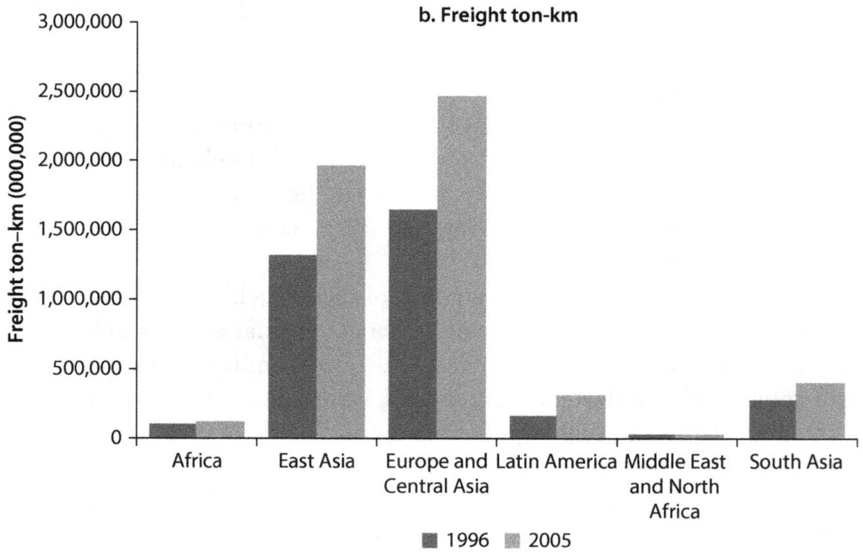

b. Freight ton-km

[Bar chart showing Freight ton-km (000,000) by region for 1996 and 2005: Africa, East Asia, Europe and Central Asia, Latin America, Middle East and North Africa, South Asia]

Source: Amos and Thompson 2007.

Table 3.4 Railway Diesel Fuel Consumption, Selected Countries

Country	Company/association	Fuel use (million liters)
United States	Association of American Railroads	16,655
Canada	Railway Association of Canada	2,209
India	Indian Railways	2,000
United Kingdom	Association of Train Operating Companies	600
Germany	DB	368
France	SNCF	238
United Kingdom	EWS (freight)	150
Latvia	Latvijas Dzelzcels	77
Romania	Romanian Railway Company for Freight Transportation	70
Switzerland	SBB	10
Netherlands	NS	6

Source: UIC 2007.

Box 3.1 Rail Companies: Energy Consumers but also Electricity Producers

JR East, a Japanese rail company serving 17 million passengers a day, can generate 3,500 GWh of electricity, 60 percent of the company's electricity consumption. This is roughly equivalent to the total consumption of Albania's 3 million people or Côte d'Ivoire's 20 million. Although the company generates a quarter of its electricity from hydropower, it still generates 1.1 million tCO_2 every year.

box continues next page

Box 3.1 Rail Companies: Energy Consumers but also Electricity Producers *(continued)*

Figure B.3.1 Energy Production Trends in Japanese Railways

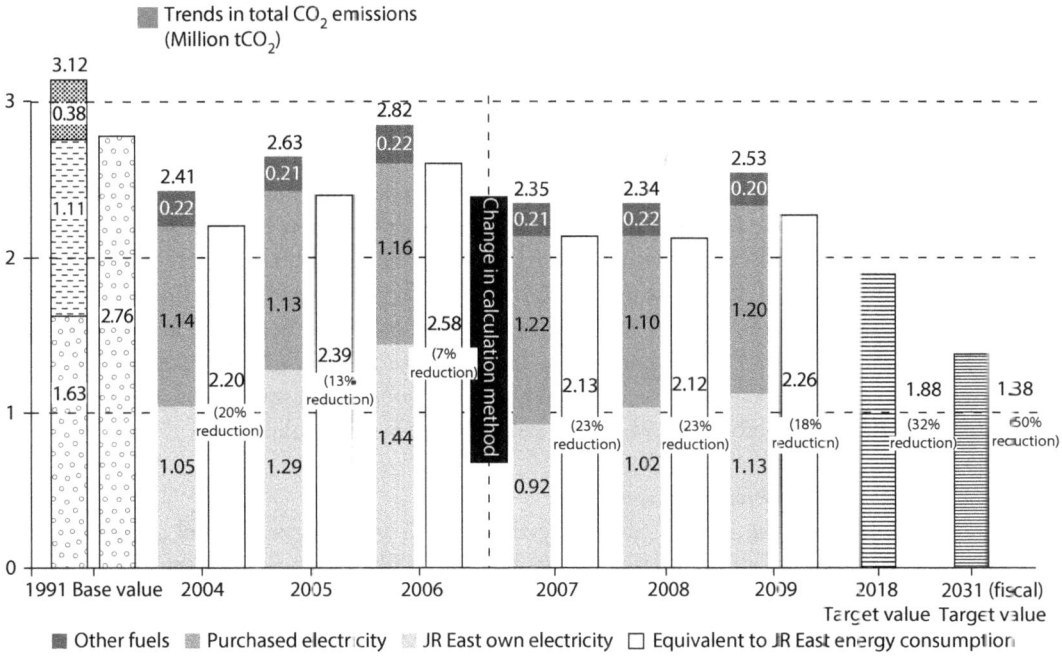

Source: JR East 2009. http://www.jreast.co.jp/e/environment/pdf_2009/p26_31.pdf.
Note: CO_2 = carbon dioxide.

Promise and Challenges of Biofuels

Biofuels could complement the modest technological advances in internal combustion engines. Ethanol is produced from food crops, such as sugarcane and maize, and biodiesel can be made from vegetable oil and animal fat. Both have the potential to lower hydrocarbon and carbon monoxide emissions. They are also sulfur-free. Higher octane biofuels allow ethanol-fueled vehicles to run on engines with a higher compression ratio, increasing engine efficiency.

However, the energy intensity of these first-generation biofuels may not be superior to pure gasoline. Ethanol contains about 33 percent less energy than gasoline and biodiesel up to 10 percent less. Total fuel economy, therefore, is expected to improve only a few percentage points (Kojima and Johnson 2005). Second, if accounting for lifecycle emissions, net emission savings from ethanol may not be large. Estimates differ substantially because of different assumptions and feedstock used (Croezen and others 2010). In Brazil the savings could reach about 90 percent, including fertilizer production and fuel manufacturing (Macedo and others 2004). But in general estimated CO_2 emission savings range from 6 to 28 percent when indirect land use change is taken into account (Croezen and others 2010). This would include the cost of expansion to new land for crops that were on land diverted to biofuel crops (Searchinger 2009).

Biofuel Market

The biofuel market is growing steadily. Many countries, among them Argentina, Australia, Brazil, Canada, China, Colombia, the European Union (EU), India, Indonesia, Malaysia, Mexico, Peru, the Philippines, South Africa, and the United States, have set biofuel targets (Kojima, Bacon and Bhattacharya 2010). However, the commercial viability of biofuels is questionable. On one hand, with increasing awareness of climate change, the public is more interested in biofuels. A recent survey shows that nearly half the respondents would pay at least 20 cents more per gallon (5.3 cents per liter) for ethanol fuel (figure 3.9); however, another study found that their willingness would depend on the greenness of the biofuel. While the premium for E10 (90 percent gasoline, 10 percent ethanol) is estimated at 12 cents per gallon, for E85 (15 percent gasoline, 85 percent ethanol) it would be 15 cents—30 percent more. In any case, the amounts people are willing to pay are far below the incremental cost of biofuel production, so that the government would have to give substantial support, both direct and indirect, for biofuels to become competitive with gasoline.

Biofuel Production Costs

Brazil and the United States are the world's two largest biofuel producers, but currently only Brazil has achieved commercially viable production (figure 3.10). While Brazil produces ethanol mainly from sugarcane and accounts for 42 percent of world ethanol fuel, the United States mainly uses maize to produce

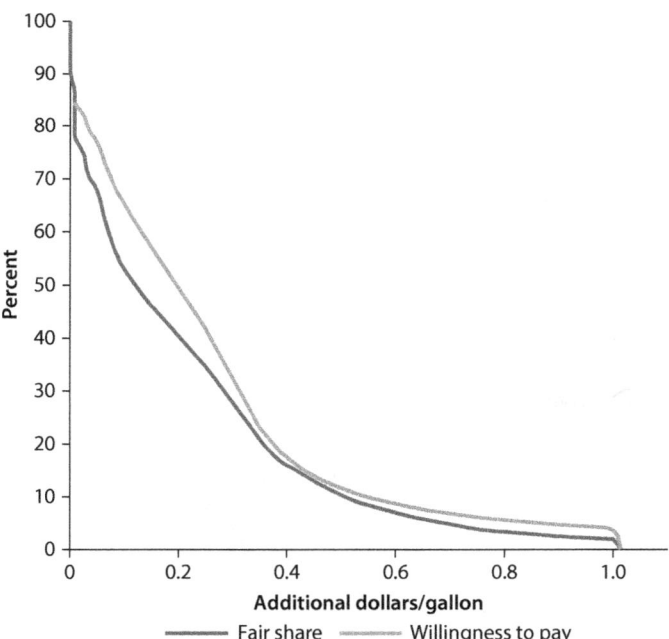

Figure 3.9 Willingness to Pay for Ethanol, United States

Source: Solomon and Johnson 2009.

Figure 3.10 Sugar Production Costs as an Input to Ethanol Production

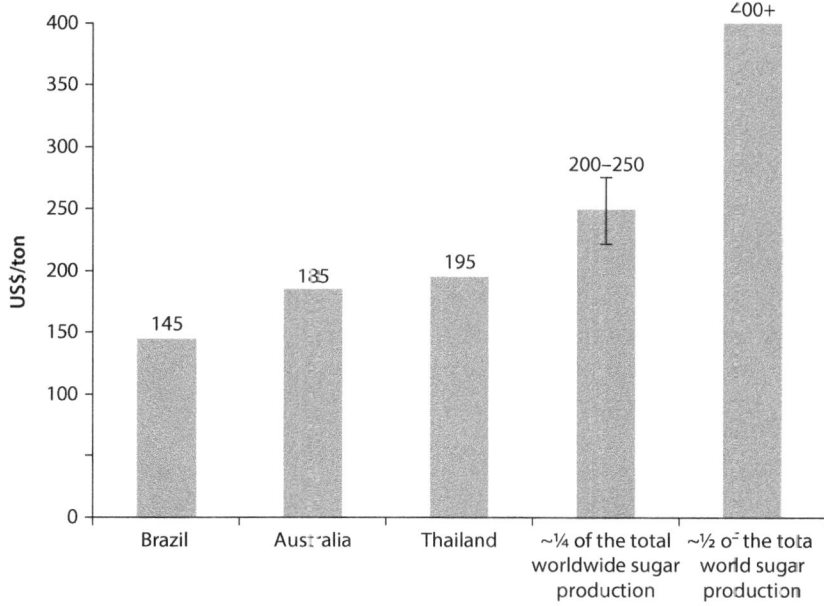

Sources: Macedo 2005; Nastari 2005; reproduced in Kojima and Johnson 2006.

46 percent of global ethanol fuel. The U.S. government subsidizes biofuel consumers and producers at a rate of about $1.44–$1.85 per gallon (38–49 cents per liter) of petroleum equivalent (World Bank 2008a). Brazil has supported its sugarcane-based ethanol industry for 30 years with a wide range of incentives, from price subsidies and tax exemptions to promotion of flexible-fuel vehicles (Kojima and Johnson 2005).

Crop-Based Biofuel Weaknesses

Beyond cost, first-generation biofuels have inherent disadvantages. First, the food crops from which they come often require considerable water, meaning there must be efficient water use, including good irrigation, and close coordination with other water users. Second, biofuel production often has environmentally adverse consequences, such as air emissions and waste water discharge. Finally, it increases feedstock prices, as was seen in the U.S. maize market in 2006. Without significant growth in the agricultural sector, balancing food security and crop-based biofuel production will be difficult (World Bank 2008a).

Potential and Challenges of Cellulosic Biofuels

Second-generation biofuels that use nonfood crops, such as agricultural residue (e.g., sugarcane waste) and timber and urban waste (e.g., waste paper and tree trimmings), are more compatible with food security and rarely compete for water resources. However, they are still in the initial stages of development, their commercial viability depends on significant economies of scale, and their use requires more efficient waste management systems.

Penetration of Compatible Vehicles

Biofuels require flexible-fuel vehicles that can run on any mixture of fuel ethanol and gasoline. But fleet turnover is generally slow, because vehicles last 10–15 years. In Brazil more than 9 million flexible-fuel vehicles are on the road, representing some 20 percent of the country's registered vehicles (Brazil Institute 2007). But it took 15 years after the launch of the National Alcohol Program in 1975 for 50 percent of the fuels used in flexible-fuel vehicles use to be biofuels. In the United States, where the government introduced CAFE credit incentives for the manufacture of alternative fuel vehicles in 1998, about 4 million flexible-fuel vehicles capable of using E85 are on the road (Kojima and Johnson 2005)—just 5 percent of the country's vehicles.

Biofuel-Related Infrastructure

Biofuel vehicles require a new network of refueling stations, hybrid mill and distillery complexes, and significant investment in feedstock delivery (Transportation Research Board 2010). Currently, there is a critical shortage of fuel stations. In Brazil 33,000 gas stations are selling ethanol alongside gasoline (Brazil Institute 2007), but in the United States there are only about 6,500 alternative refueling sites, of which only about 2,700 offer ethanol or biodiesel; in comparison, there are about 161,000 conventional refueling stations (U.S. Department of Energy 2010; NPN 2008). Incentives for flexible fuel cars have thus not been particularly effective. Potoglou and Kanaroglou found that Canadian consumers would not choose alternative-fuel vehicles unless fuels were available at more than 50 percent of existing stations.

Flexibility and Uncertainty

Technical flexibility is a robust strategy for dealing with climate change and commodity price uncertainty. Hybrid mills and distilleries could allow for easy switching between food and ethanol production. Fuel flexibility allows both producers and consumers to respond to a wider range of economic and climate conditions. For instance, in Brazil an ethanol mandate allows the fuel blending proportion to vary between 20 and 25 percent. In March 2006 after world sugar prices reached a historic high the government reduced the proportion from 25 to 20 percent; raised it several months later to 23 percent; raised it to 25 percent in July 2007; and reduced it back to 20 percent in February 2010 (Kojima, Bacon, and Bhattacharya 2010).

Transforming Infrastructure to Low-Carbon Assets

Given the considerable uncertainties related to engine and alternative fuel technologies, alternative transportation in the form of mass transit is needed. Once high-carbon transport infrastructure is in place, people adapt their lifestyles to it; travel patterns become locked in.

A recent study in São Paulo shows that expanding road capacity by 20 percent would speed up car travel by 13 percent, which would improve vehicle fuel efficiency. But increased speeds could encourage more car use, so that fuel consumption would increase 5 percent and CO_2 emissions 3 percent (Anas and Timilsina 2009b). Similarly, road expansion in the periphery of Beijing would increase private car use; improvements in city mass transit would reduce it. But because more buses could worsen city congestion, total emissions in that case would decline by only a few percent.

Alternative modes alone do not guarantee emissions reduction. In principle, transport emissions, especially from cars, could be reduced by supply-side measures such as increasing alternative transport options, improving current infrastructure energy efficiency, or connecting different transport modes more effectively. Using available transport assets more effectively is just as important, especially in developing countries where a number of measures could enhance efficiency. Finally, different transport modes should be connected so that people can use them flexibly and efficiently, without taking unnecessary detours. This demands a much broader city management approach, including land-use and transport planning policies.

Supplying Alternative Transport Modes

The modal structure of transport plays an important role in determining carbon emissions, particularly when car ownership is relatively low (box 3.2). Shifting from passenger vehicles to mass transit can significantly reduce emissions (table 3.5). An average public bus emits only half as much CO_2 equivalent per passenger-km as a small petrol-fueled car. Railways, especially between cities that are far apart, are even more ecofriendly. Light-rail emissions are less than or at most equal to average bus emissions. Subways also seem to be less polluting, though this depends on passenger occupancy. For large vehicles, such as public buses, compressed natural gas (CNG) and liquefied petroleum gas (LPG) have an advantage over diesel (Defra 2009). Since the late 1990s, 30 major cities in China have implemented the National Clean Vehicle Action program to use more CNG and LPG for public transportation. More than 80 percent of taxis in Shanghai and 50 percent of buses in Beijing use CNG or LPG (Hou and others 2002; Zhao 2006).

The relevance of particular transport modes depends on city size, density, and other geographic factors. For rapidly growing, densely populated large cities, rapid transit and light rail transit can be best. In Bangkok, for instance, an elevated 23.5-km rapid mass transit system, Skytrain, was constructed in 1999 to relieve congestion. As of 2008 the system was transporting 460,000 passengers a day (Mandri-Perrott 2010). Another mass transit system, MRT (mass rapid transit) Blue Line, that went into service in 2004 was used in 2007 by more than 170,000 customers a day. Road traffic was reduced along the Blue Line, although only marginally for several reasons (JBIC 2008). Manila's LRT1 has been a major public transportation mode since it was commissioned in 1985. LRT1 carries about 300,000 people a day. In Tunis, the 32-kilometer LRT (Light Rail Transit), in operation since 1985, was carrying some 294,000 people per day in 2002 (Godard 2007).

Box 3.2 How Multimodality Affects Emissions: ASIF Decomposition

ASIF decomposition, defined below, is useful for analyzing the links between transport, fuel consumption, and carbon dioxide (CO_2) emissions. In this approach, A stands for CO_2 emissions (CO_2 tons) equal to the product of transport activity (passenger-km or ton-km); S for modal structure (the share of each activity by transport mode); I for modal energy intensity (energy use per unit of passenger or freight travel by mode); and F for emission rate (CO_2 emissions per unit of energy consumed).

$$\text{Emission} = \text{Passenger km} \cdot \frac{\text{VMT}}{\text{Passenger km}} \cdot \frac{\text{Fuel consumption}}{\text{VTM}} \cdot \frac{\text{Emissions}}{\text{Fuel Consumption}}$$

(Activity) (Structure) (Intensity) (Fuel carbon intensity)

In developed countries, ASIF is an important determinant of emissions (table B3.2.1). In Australia, for instance, passenger transport emissions increased by about 61 percent between 1973 and 1995. Even in Japan, which has extensive mass transit, the modal shift to road increased passenger transport emissions by 25 percent, though much of this could be attributed to the country's rapid economic growth and increased travel. Meanwhile, in most countries the energy intensity effect, which measures a change in carbon emitted per passenger-km, has been insignificant.

There has been a significant modal switch from rail and marine shipment to road in recent decades, reflecting a demand for flexibility and frequency in freight transport and the poor quality of rail services. In developed countries the shift significantly increased transport emissions. However, rail still offers a comparative advantage for long-distance freight and bulk cargo. Coordinating intermodal transportation systems can enhance competitiveness and reduce emissions.

Table B3.2.1 ASIF Decomposition, Selected Developed Countries, 1973–95 (1973 = 100)

	Travel				Freight			
	United States	Japan	Australia	Sweden	United States	Japan	Australia	Sweden
Emissions	119	226	174	136	163	157	172	105
Activity effect	148	189	190	124	162	137	166	106
Structure effect	101	125	161	101	124	140	116	104
Intensity effect	78	97	93	110	89	85	61	95
Fuel mix effect	100	101	99	99	101	105	103	100

Source: OECD/IEA 2000.

An increase in the number of rapid transit or LRT passengers can reduce emissions, though of course not all passengers are former users of more polluting transport, such as cars and taxis. The majority of passengers in the Bangkok MRT Blue Line, for example, were former bus users (table 3.6). Nevertheless, over the next 30 years, increased passenger rail use could save some 1.7 million tons of CO_2, as well as reduce such other pollutants as sulfur dioxide (SO_2) and nitrous oxide (NO_2) (table 3.7).

Table 3.5 Average CO_2 Emission Factors by Vehicle Type, United Kingdom

Vehicle type	gCO_2 equivalent per kilometer	gCO_2 equivalent per passenger-km
Petrol car		
Small	151.8	—
Medium	187.7	—
Large	260.6	—
Diesel car		
Small	127.1	—
Medium	158.0	—
Large	215.4	—
LPG or CNG car		
Medium	188.3	—
Large	260.7	—
Average bus		
Local	1,014.7	111.5
London	1,122.9	83.9
Railway		
International	—	17.8
National	—	61.1
Light rail	—	84.0
London metro	—	78.6

Source: Defra 2009.
Note: — = not available, CO_2 = carbon dioxide, CNG = compressed natural gas, LPG = liquefied petroleum gas. Average passenger occupancy is assumed to be 9.1 for local buses and 13.4 for London buses.

Table 3.6 Transport Modes Used before the MRT Blue Line Opened in Bangkok

Mode	Percent	Mode	Percent
Bus	51.0	Motorcycle	5.5
Car	14.2	Van	3.7
Taxi	12.9	Walking	3.5
Mass transit system (BTS)	8.6	Boat	0.7

Source: JBIC 2008.
Note: MRT = mass rapid transit.

Table 3.7 Estimated Emissions Reduction by the MRT Blue Line in Bangkok
tons

Fiscal year	Global benefits			Local benefits		
	CO_2	SO_2	NO_2	CO_2	SO_2	NO_2
2004	28,600	27.3	60.5	23,100	0.4	25.6
2005	32,200	32.2	68.0	26,000	0.4	28.8
.						
.						
.						
2033	74,700	71.1	158.0	60,200	0.9	66.6
Total	1,736,000	1,680	3,727	1,422,000	21.5	1,575

Source: JICA 2008.
Note: CO_2 = carbon dioxide, MRT = mass rapid transit, NO_2 = nitrous dioxide, SO_2 = sulfur dioxide.

However, there are enormous costs associated with heavy rail systems. Very high passenger density is needed to justify the investment, and many projects have overestimated demand. For instance, the estimated ridership of the Skytrain in Bangkok was 600,000–700,000, but initial ridership was only 150,000 (Mandri-Perrott 2010). Similarly, the original estimate for the Blue Line was 250,000–430,000 passengers (JBIC 2008). The LRT1 in Manila envisaged 560,000 passengers a day, but the actual number is about half. Reasons for this vary, from mispricing to lack of coordination with other transport policies.

High-speed rail is another alternative. For instance, a Eurostar journey is estimated to emit on average one-tenth the CO_2 emissions of an equivalent airline flight.[12] It also saves considerable time for long-distance travelers. In Sweden high-speed trains are the fastest mode of transportation for distances of 100–600 km. For shorter distances, cars are better, and for even longer distances, air has a comparative advantage (figure 3.11). As economies grow, so too does demand for high-speed transportation (box 3.3). High-speed rail technology has responded to this demand, increasing maximum speeds from 200 km/hr to 515 over the past three decades (figure 3.12). However, because high-speed rail is extremely costly, it may be relevant for only a few developing countries with a critical mass of potential users, such as

Figure 3.11 Long Distance Travel Time, Sweden

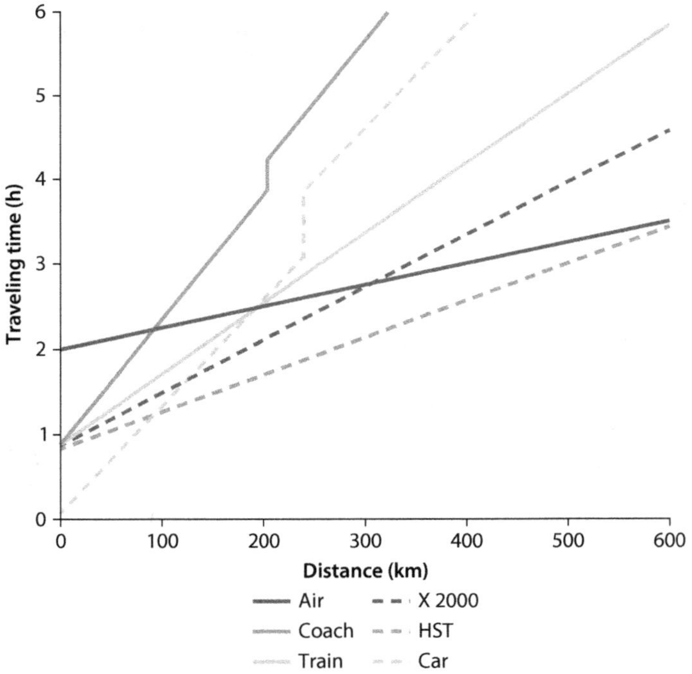

Source: Froidh 2008.
Note: The X2000 is a tilting train introduced in 1990 on the Stockholm-Gothenburg main line. HST = high-speed train.

Box 3.3 Demand for High-Speed Rail

Demand for high-speed transportation rises with income as the perceived opportunity costs of travel time increase. Thus in Europe introduction of high-speed trains increases passenger rail demand by 8 percent (Couto and Graham 2008). In Spain the time elasticity of demand for intercity trains is estimated at 2.5, so that a 10 percent reduction in travel time would increase demand by 25 percent (Martin and Nombela 2007). People also appreciate the higher frequency and shorter access time of rail compared to air, particularly for business travel (Gonzalez-Savignat 2004).

Figure 3.12 Maximum Speed of High-Speed Trains

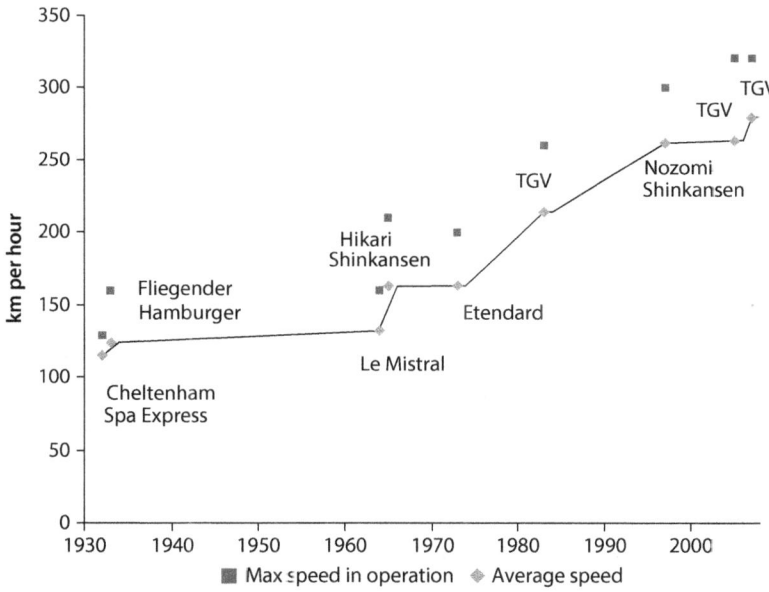

Source: Free Encyclopedia Wikipedia: "Land Speed Record for Rail Vehicles."

China, Brazil, and the Russian Federation (figure 3.13). China is building a 300-km/hr train from Beijing to Tianjin and planning a 1,300-km line between Beijing and Shanghai. Vietnam is also looking at high-speed rail between its two largest cities, Hanoi and Ho Chi Minh, a distance of about 1,700 km.

Bus rapid transit may be a more attractive option in small and medium cities, especially where dense corridors are developing. Although it may generate slightly more emissions than rapid transit, it is much cheaper to build (table 3.5). Many cities now have exclusive or separate bus lanes in main corridors. Dublin, Ireland, established Quality Bus Corridors for city buses in peak hours, enabling buses to travel 20 percent faster than before and bringing about a 20 percent

Figure 3.13 High-Speed Rail Construction Costs

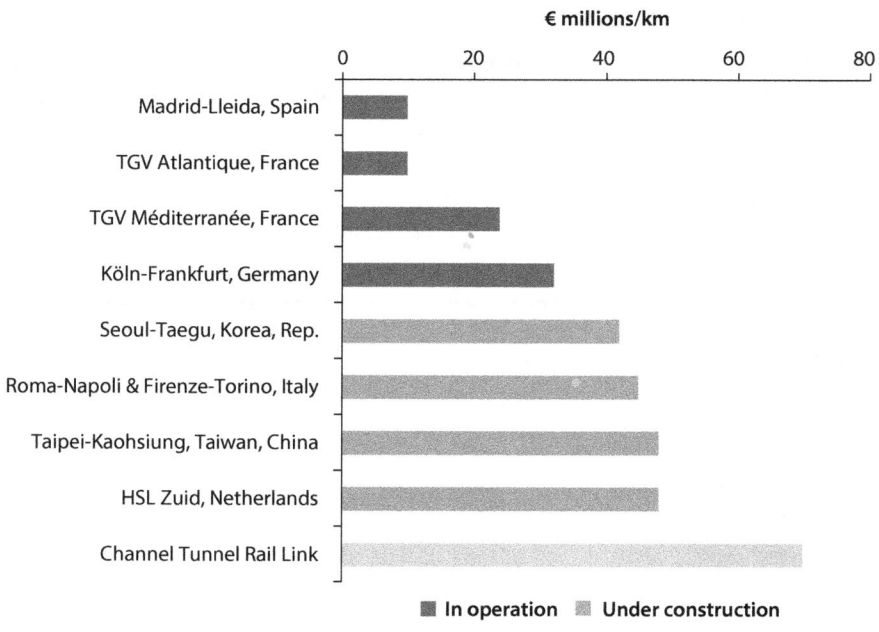

Source: Hughes 2006. http://www.jreast.co.jp/e/development/tech/pdf_8/Tec-07-42-51eng.pdf.

increase in the share of bus transportation (OECD 2002b). Curitiba, Brazil, has successfully implemented an integrated transit and land-use strategy using high-speed bus systems. Combined with land-use regulations, it has permitted Curitiba to boast one of the world's highest rates of urban mass transit use: 70 percent of the urban population, an increase of 62% since the transit network's inception in 1974.

In Bogota, Colombia, public bus fares had been set above competitive levels, leading to excess competition and inefficient, fragmented operations. Bus rapid transit, TransMilenio, was substituted for the old bus system and currently supplies 20 percent of daily trips in Bogota, serving 1 million passengers daily. Average public transit travel speeds increased from 15 km/hr to 27, and accidents on service corridors decreased 79 percent (NBRTI 2006). With innovative pricing and land use measures, the system aims to carry 80 percent of the city's population by 2015 (Echeverry and others 2005).

Whether bus rapid transit actually reduces emissions depends on the number of passengers and how efficiently it is operated. Without high passenger occupancy, exclusive bus lanes that crowd out other vehicles could increase congestion elsewhere. Proper route planning and other transport measures are important to achieving high occupancy (see below). Successful bus rapid transit systems also need to link with feeder transportation. In Bogota about 50 percent of TransMilenio passengers connect from other bus

Integrating Sector-Wide Reforms for Mitigation

Table 3.8 Average CO_2 Emission Factors, Road and Rail Freight, United Kingdom

Transport mode	gCO_2 equivalent per passenger-km
Road freight	120.4
Rigid	234.3
Trailer	86.0
Rail freight	78.6

Source: Defra 2009.
Note: CO_2 = carbon dioxide.

systems, and roughly half use the feeder system that belongs to TransMilenio. The rest use traditional bus systems, which are energy inefficient and pollutive (NBRTI 2006). Without efficient and coordinated operations, hard infrastructure development does not always reduce emissions.

Substituting rail for road freight holds great potential for reducing emissions. Diesel rail, for instance, generates only one-third as many emissions per ton-km freight as a trailer truck, although the net effect depends on the load factor and the size and type of truck, trailer or rigid (table 3.8). In the United States, using rail rather than truck could reduce emissions by about two-thirds per ton-mile of freight transported (Transportation Research Board 2010).

However, because freight demand is for more frequent and flexible transport, it may be difficult for rail to maintain its share of total freight transportation. In some countries privatization and other reforms have revitalized rail freight operations, but in many developing countries freight rail is marginalized. It may be worth reinvesting in freight rail infrastructure to take advantage of its capacity to significantly reduce not only emissions but also trade, transportation, and logistics costs.

Wiser Use of Transport Infrastructure

Wiser use of existing infrastructure can reduce both emissions and trade and transportation costs. The efficiency gains are likely to be significant in developing countries where infrastructure tends to be poorly maintained and inefficiently operated. Soft measures are normally cheaper and quicker to implement than hard. Four examples relate to public buses, air, railways, and logistics.

Optimizing Public Bus Operations

Energy efficiency in public bus operations can be improved dramatically. In Mexico, for instance, bus system optimization could greatly abate emissions (figure 3.14). Restructuring redundant feeder routes and improving bus stops, traffic signals, public information, and the vehicles themselves could reduce emissions by 31.5 megatons (Mt) of CO_2 equivalent/yr (Johnson and others 2010). Switching from diesel to compressed CNG could complement such measures.

Figure 3.14 Marginal Emissions Abatement Costs in Mexico

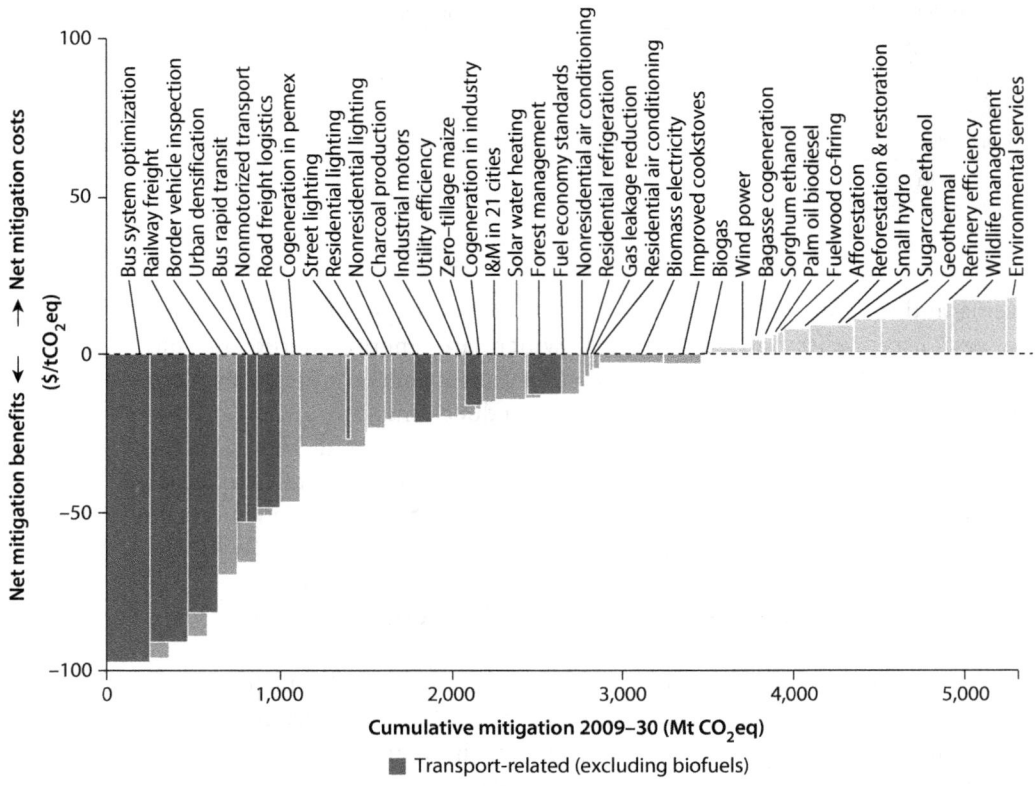

Source: Johnson and others 2010.
Note: CO_2 = carbon dioxide, I&M = inspection and maintenance.

Optimizing Air Traffic

Jet fuel consumption could be reduced by shorter routes, better taxiing, and continuous descent of aircraft (OECD/IEA 2009). Several airlines have initiated a pilot program to conserve jet fuel that includes single-engine taxiing on departure and arrival, continuous climb and descent, and a tailored arrival. Through this program a B767 flight from Miami to Paris saved about 1,500 lbs of fuel—about 2.5 percent of total fuel consumption between the two cities.[13] A B747 flight from Paris to Miami could save two to three tons of fuel and six to nine tons of CO_2 emissions. One company estimated that total savings on all transatlantic flights could add up to 43,000 tons of fuel a year (ATW Online 2010), reducing costs by about $40 million and CO_2 emissions by about 135,000 tons. These measures not only reduce emissions but also improve air carrier competitiveness, particularly if international fuel prices remain high (figure 3.15). While cost concerns should motivate airlines to undertake these measures, governments can help by publicizing best practices.

Figure 3.15 Average Jet Fuel Prices

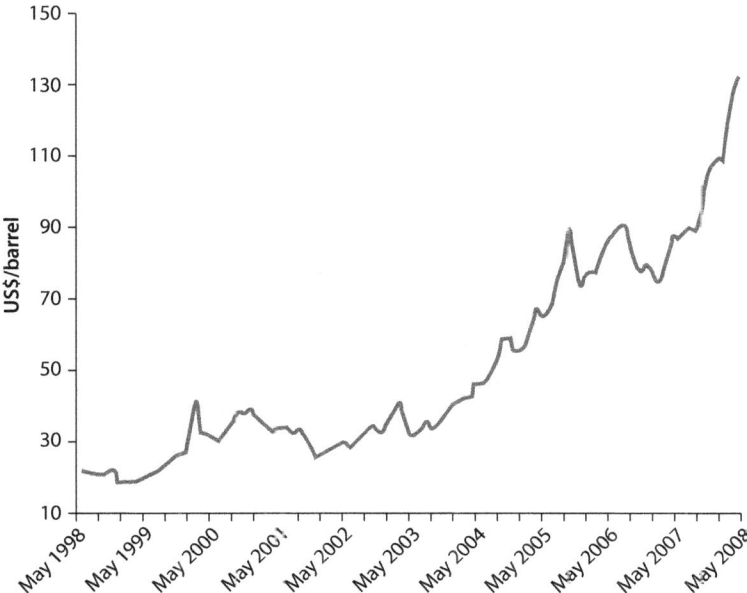

Sources: Air Transport Association; reproduced by World Bank 2009a.

Modernization of Rail Assets and Operations

Despite the increasing importance of bulk freight, railways in developing countries are often poorly maintained. The expected life of locomotives is more than 40 years. Upgrading and modernizing locomotives and important lines would increase rail capacity and mitigate emissions by attracting more freight from roads and retaining more current rail users. In the Ukraine, transporting freight by road produces more than triple the amount of emissions as moving it by rail. A railway modernization project could facilitate a move toward this more fuel-efficient mode. For every million ton-km shifted from truck to rail or retained by rail, 53–55 million tons of CO_2 could be saved (World Bank 2010c).

Better rail operations could also improve national competitiveness and economic growth. With high-quality services, freight rail could support bulk exports and imports. In Ghana, because of the poor quality of rail services, cacao beans travel by truck, where they are more likely to be damaged (JBIC 2006).

Subsidies may be needed for rail freight. Road transport is already heavily subsidized because roads are publicly financed and usually used without charge. The United Kingdom partially subsidizes capital investments in rail: since 1975 the government has spent £185 million to support about 250 projects (OECD 2002b). This not only improves railway operational efficiency but also reduces overall transportation costs.

Improvements in Logistics

An estimated 2,800 megatons of CO_2, 5.5 percent of total emissions, are produced by the logistics and transport sector (figure 3.16). Large-scale, consolidated freight transportation is often more efficient and generates fewer emissions than the fragmented small-volume operations that are dominant in developing countries. Trade-related transport costs for landlocked countries are 50 percent higher than for coastal countries (Arvis 2005). One of the reasons for high trade costs is inefficiency in freight operations. Up to 60 percent of truck trips in developing countries are done while empty, compared with 26 percent in the United Kingdom (McKinnon and Ge 2006). Not surprisingly, the higher the empty rate, the higher the freight cost and emission intensity (figure 3.17; Londono-Kent 2009). More efficient routing and higher load factors should help reduce fuel intensity.[14] Transshipment load centers, multimodal facilities, and logistic services are critical.

A study in Odense, Denmark, showed that establishing a city logistics terminal could decrease total freight transport by 2 percent and energy consumption and CO_2 emissions by 15 percent. Copenhagen has adopted a similar system (OECD 2002b). In the United Kingdom the freight industry improved efficiency markedly through better route planning and reducing empty-vehicle travel. Improved truck specifications reduced fuel consumption 20 percent for 1988–1998. An added benefit is that manufacturers were able to reduce their stocks 20 percent, and wholesale and retail sectors saved £11 billion.

Figure 3.16 Emissions from Logistics Activities

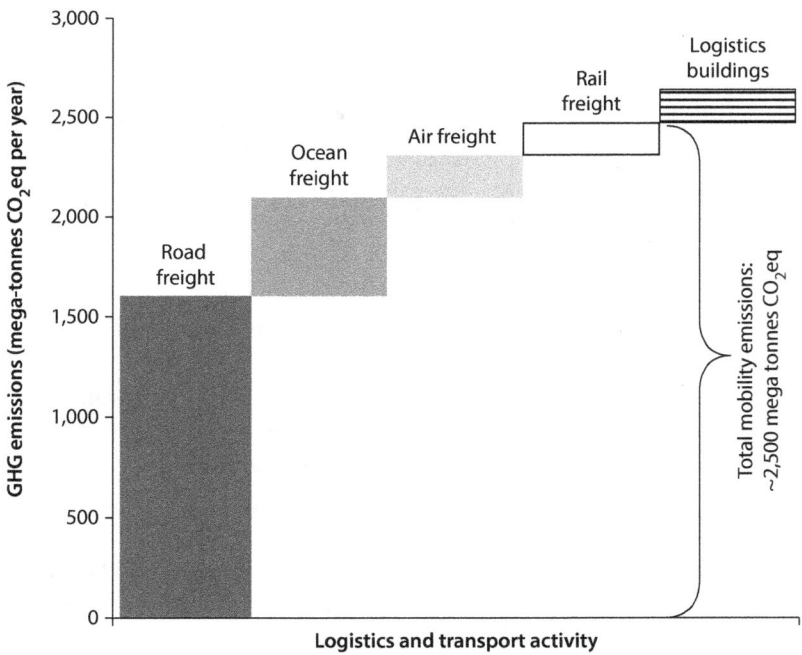

Source: World Economic Forum 2009.
Note: CO_2 = carbon dioxide, GHG = greenhouse gas.

Integrating Sector-Wide Reforms for Mitigation 99

Figure 3.17 Average Freight Cost and Empty Trip Rate

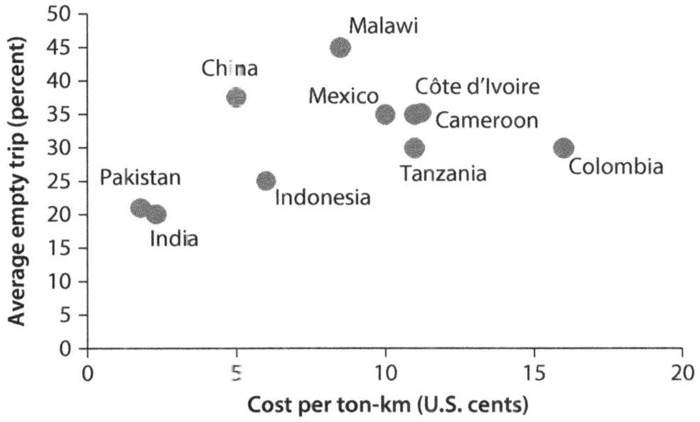

[Scatter plot showing Average empty trip (percent) on y-axis (0–50) vs Cost per ton-km (U.S. cents) on x-axis (0–20). Data points: Pakistan (~2, 22), India (~2, 20), China (~6, 38), Indonesia (~6, 25), Malawi (~8, 45), Mexico (~10, 35), Tanzania (~10, 30), Côte d'Ivoire (~11, 36), Cameroon (~11, 34), Colombia (~16, 30).]

Source: Based on Londono-Kent 2009.

Box 3.4 Building Greener Transport Infrastructure

Street lighting. Streetlights operate for 9–12 hours every day. Bulbs last a year, fixtures more than 10 years. In the City of Rizhao in China, most traffic signals and street and park lights are powered by solar cells (Suzuki and others 2009). Mexico aims to replace all street lights with energy-efficient high-pressure sodium lamps in the next two decades, which would reduce emissions by 0.9 Mt CO_2 equivalent a year (Johnson and others 2010).

Greener rail stations. A commuter train station in Tokyo reduced its energy use 30 percent by introducing automatic on-off systems and LED displays and equalizing the levels of illumination on platforms (JR East 2009).

Greener and carbon-neutral airports. Although technically falling within the commercial building rather than transport sector, an airport can be made more carbon-neutral by combining energy-efficient building technologies, airport design, and air traffic operation. In Brazil, for instance, the first energy-efficiency contract was awarded to Tancredo Neves/Confins International Airport in Belo Horizonte in 1999. Contractor proposals had to include not only costs but also a technical work plan, including energy-saving measures. The price and technical proposals were weighted roughly equally in the evaluation (Poole 2008; Singh and others 2010). A five-year contract will save 1 million Brazilian reals to the economy annually (INFRAERO 2006). Other airports, among them Gander International Airport in Canada, are promoting the idea of carbon neutrality.

Better Connecting Transport Infrastructure

Having good intermodal connectivity and good integration between transport corridors and feeder systems is crucial to the success of alternative infrastructure. Connectivity is challenging because the demand for transport is dynamic and depends on numerous factors. Transport infrastructure must therefore be analyzed within the broader context of urbanization and economic development.

Compact Cities

A compact city can be designed through complementary land-use and urban planning. Denser cities are generally more energy efficient and less polluting, with lower vehicle miles (figure 3.18). Thus, European and Japanese car drivers travel 30–50 percent fewer vehicle km than those in the United States (table 3.9; World Bank 2010a, 2010b).

Regulations can lead to more compact cities. In Curitiba, Brazil, land use and mobility planning were integrated, with the city's radial (axial) layout designed to divert traffic from downtown. (Three-fourths of city residents use a highly efficient bus system.) The industrial center was built close to the city center to minimize commuting (World Bank 2010a). In Demark, Norway, and the United

Figure 3.18 Individual Transport Emissions and Population Density

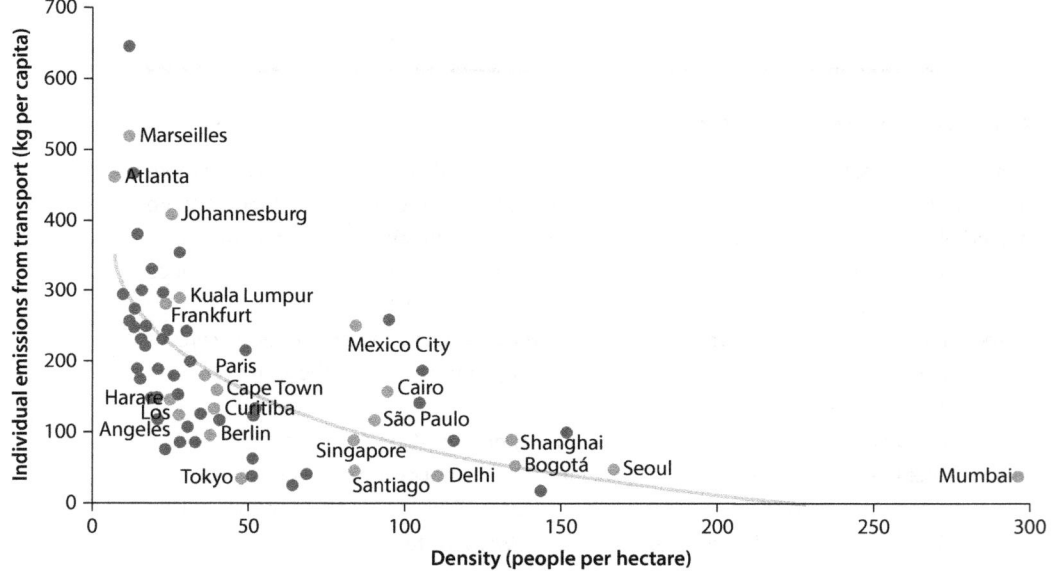

Source: World Bank 2010a.
Note: The figure does not correct for income because a regression of transport emissions on density and income reveals that density, not income, is a key factor. Data are for 1995.

Table 3.9 Average Vehicle-km Traveled, Selected Urban Areas

	Los Angeles[a]	London[b]	Tokyo[c]
Vehicle-km traveled (millions)	63,020	25,401	25,487
Population (millions)	9.85	7.62	6.45
Passenger cars registered (millions)	5.86	2.57	3.21
Passenger-km traveled per capita	6,399	3,334	3,954
Passenger-km traveled per vehicle	10,755	9,897	7,948

a. Los Angeles County.
b. Greater London.
c. Tokyo Prefecture.

Kingdom to ensure that shopping can be done locally, large shopping centers cannot be built outside city centers (OECD 2002b).

Evidence indicates that people will go without cars if there are good transport connections to their homes. German data show that demand for cars decreases significantly with good access to shopping centers, cinemas, and theaters (Woldeamanuel and others 2009). In the United States, car ownership decreases with the distance to the nearest bus stop (Kim and Kim 2004). In Hamilton, Canada, the number of cars per household decreases as the number of bus stops within 500 meters of residences increases (Potoglou and Kanaroglou 2008). But if household members work more than 6 km from their dwelling, they are more likely to own one or more cars.

Intermodal Connections for Passengers. It is important to connect complementary mass transit systems because time spent in transit matters to people (Cervero, Golub, and Nee 2007; Holmgren 2007; Takeuchi, Cropper, and Bento 2007; Anas and Timilsina 2009a, 2009b). The lack of feeder transportation to the Bangkok Skytrain was a factor in its disappointing initial ridership (Mandri-Perrott 2010). The MRT Blue Line, on the other hand, had feeder buses and commercial facilities around its stations. However, with the delay of other mass transit projects, such as the Red Line, the number of passengers remains stagnant (TBIC 2008).

Only 14 percent of Bangkok MRT Blue Line riders are former car users. The park-and-ride facilities at seven stations have been underused. Price incentives, such as discounts for park-and-ride and bus-train transfer passengers, could address this problem. However, a park-and-ride facility could also increase vehicle travel and emissions. For instance, driving distances increased in Osaka, Japan, when a park-and-ride system was built outside the city center, pushing down estimated net CO_2 emissions reductions to only 1,400 kg/month (OECD 2002a). A combination of policies should address the issue of intermodal facilities for road users.

Nonmotorized Modes. Integrating walking and cycling with mass transit is essential to making a city compact. Such nonmotorized modes, along with low-carbon two- or three-wheel motorized vehicles, have a clear advantage in mitigating emissions, are an important alternative within cities, and are still dominant in individual transportation in developing countries (table 3.10). In Dhaka, Jakarta, and Shanghai, nonmotorized modes account for more than 40 percent

Table 3.10 Trip Purpose by Bicycle
Percent

Trip purpose	Accra	Delhi	Leon	Lima
Commuting	31	72	44	46.2
Business/goods transport	4	10	—	4.5
School	8	14	Little	25.2
Shopping	24	2	High	10.5
Leisure	33	2	Little	6.8

Source: I-ce 2000.
Note: — = not available.

Figure 3.19 Modal Share, Selected Cities in Asia

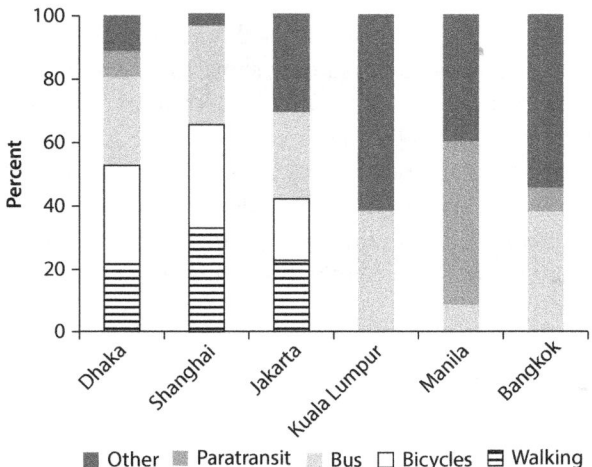

Sources: International Road Federation 1998; reproduced by I-ce 2000.

of total trips (figure 3.19). In Africa walking still predominates in urban areas; in Nairobi and Dar es Salaam half the trips are entirely on foot (I-ce 2000). The use of nonmotorized modes may decline with economic growth, but even in developed countries, they can still represent a significant share of travel if they are well integrated with other transport modes, as in the Netherlands and Denmark (IEA 2000). In addition, new nonmotorized tools are being developed. In China for instance, the electric bicycle (E-bike) is becoming more popular; the market has grown to 21 million in the past decade (World Bank 2009a).

Nonmotorized Modes and Pedestrian Safety

A particular challenge is ensuring the safety of pedestrians and bicyclists, who comprise the majority of road fatalities (table 3.11). Establishing and improving sidewalks and nonmotorized transport bridges can do so cost-effectively (table 3.12) (I-ce 2000).

Intermodal Freight Connections

Although rail freight can reduce emissions by two-thirds or more, the limited extent of railway networks constrain freight mobility. In Ghana, for example, demand for freight transit to neighboring countries, such as Burkina Faso, Niger, and Mali, jumped in 2002 because of political disorder in Côte d'Ivoire, but most freight was carried by truck because of the lack of intermodal facilities, such as storage and handling equipment, at the north end of Ghana's rail network in Kumasi (JBIC 2006). Thus a significant opportunity to take advantage of railways was missed. Combining more than one transport mode can increase rail attractiveness and improve freight energy efficiency. In Japan, for example, total energy expended for door-to-door 20-km freight transport was lowest when rail was

Table 3.11 Road Users Killed, by Transport Mode, as a Percentage of Total Fatalities

City (year)	Pedestrian	Bicyclist	Motor-cyclist	Car driver	Other
Delhi (1994)	42	14	27	12	5
Thailand (1987)	47	6	36	12	—
Kathmandu	43	9	13	36	—
Bandung (1990)	33	7	42	15	3

Source: I-ce 2000.
Note: — = not available.

Table 3.12 Costs and Benefits, Selected Nonmotorized Modes

Test interventions	Total benefits	Benefit components	Total cost	Cost components	B/C ratio
Walk way improvement along corridor in Morogoro	14,400 USD (per year)	Saving travel time	18,000 USD 4,200 USD (per year)	Repair culverts Walkway construct Build bridges	3.4
Raised zebra-crossing in Dar es Salaam and Morogoro	4,350 USD (per year)	Avoidance cost of accidents	4,500 USD per zebra-crossing 1,000 USD (per year)	Raised zebra-crossing	1.45
NMT bridge in Dar es Salaam	6,000 USD (per year)	Saving travel time	11,000 USD per bridge 1,500 USD (per year)	Bridge Cost reduction because community participation	4

Source: SSATP 2005.
Note: B/C = benefit/cost.

Table 3.13 Energy Consumption, Door-to-Door Transportation
kilocalorie/km

Transport mode	100 km	200 km	500 km
Truck only	444	417	396
Intermodal: rail short feeder	398	363	305
Rail only	557	436	363

Source: OECD 2002c.

combined with short-feeder road transport. Truck or rail alone would not be as energy-efficient (table 3.13; OECD 2002c).

Regional Integration of Transport Infrastructure

There can be both institutional and physical barriers to good transport connectivity between countries. Institutional barriers include excessive border tolls (legal or illegal) that induce travelers and freight to detour to roads that are longer but quicker to travel. For example, there are two corridors between Greece and Hungary: Corridor X is 405 km with 13 tolls; Corridor IV is 450 km but with only 7 tolls (table 3.14; map 3.1). Before the former Yugoslav Republic of Macedonia improved Corridor X, much freight was diverted to Corridor IV, which is 10 percent longer but does not require crossing non-EU borders and has fewer toll plazas.

Table 3.14 Corridors between Thessaloniki, Greece, and Nish, Serbia, Compared

	Length (km)	Number of tolls	Number of border crossings
Corridor X	405	13	2
Corridor IV	440	7	2

Sources: World Bank (2009a); Country Economic Memorandum for FYR Macedonia.

Map 3.1 Corridor IV (Thessaloniki–Sofia–Hungary) and Corridor X (Thessaloniki–Skopje–Belgrade–Hungary)

Source: World Bank 2007.

Physical barriers include few or no border-crossing corridors, necessitating detours. For instance, in South East Europe, Corridor VIII could facilitate East-West traffic (Corridor VIII Secretariat 2007) except that rail sections are missing (map 3.2). Sometimes institutional barriers are the problem. In South Africa and Mozambique, for example, the Maputo Development Corridor created after

Map 3.2 Rail Sections, Durres-Skopje-Sofia, along Corridor VIII

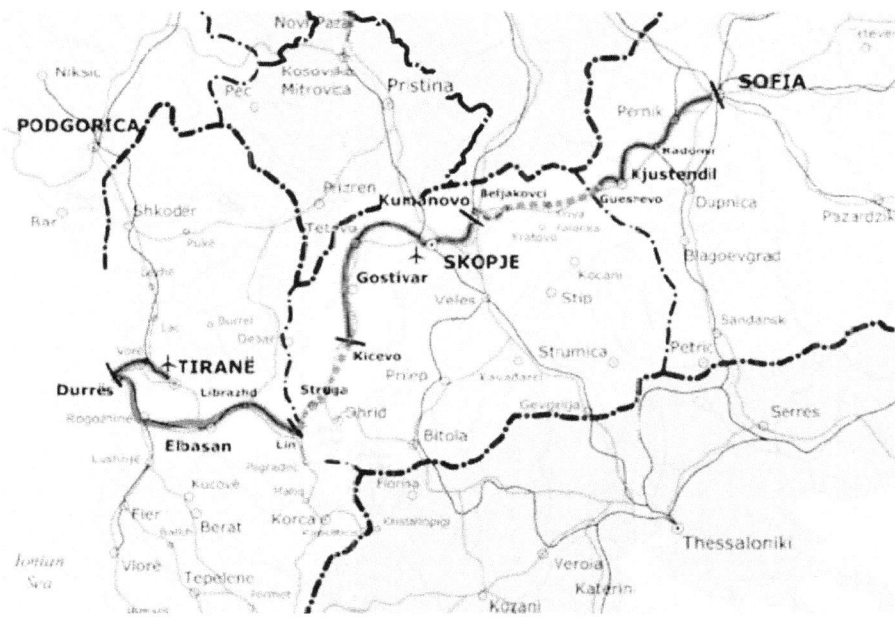

Source: World Bank reproduction based on Corridor VIII Secretariat (2007, figure 11, p. 46).

1995 extends from South Africa's northern landlocked provinces to Maputo's deepwater port, but border-crossing costs and delays divert freight to Durban through a corridor 25 percent longer (World Bank 2009b).[15]

Demand-Side Transport Policies for Mitigation

Pricing Incentives

In addition to technology and infrastructure, pricing is not only critical to reducing emissions, it is more effective than regulations.

The price of car use relative to alternative mass transit is central. Price can be adjusted in various ways, for example through the cost of fuel and other aspects of car use and through mass transit fares. In developing countries the price of driving seems low compared with developed countries (table 3.15). Among selected major cities, Tokyo's cost of driving is highest relative to mass transit use because of low rapid transit fares and high gas prices. New York also has high mass transit use because the cost of parking is high. By contrast, in three selected cities in developing countries, the the cost of driving is only 1.21–4.15 times higher than mass transit, and is much lower than in developed countries. In those cities parking rates are too generous and mass transit fares set relatively high to cover investment costs quickly.

Changing the relative price depends on institutional feasibility, consumer response, and political acceptability. There are a wide range of policy options, each with advantages and disadvantages (table 3.16).[16] Fuel pricing is the best

Table 3.15 Relative Costs of Driving and Mass Transit in Selected Cities

City	Rapid transit	Bus	Parking	Gasoline (US$/liter)	Range of relative costs of driving to public transit[a]
Washington, DC	$1.75–$4.70	$1.45	$5–$10/hour, $15–$20/day	0.56	5.37–8.77
New York	$2.25	$2.25	$10/hour; $25–$30/day	0.56	6.75
London	£4.00–£10.80	£2.00	£4–£5/hour; £25–£30/day	1.44	2.46–5.24
Tokyo	¥160–¥300	¥200	¥600/hour; ¥2,000–¥2,500/day	1.42	5.19–7.20
Bangkok	16 Baht–41 Baht	7 Baht–8 Baht	40 Baht/hour	0.87	1.21–2.48
Manila[b]	Php12–Php15	Php9 up to first 5 km + Php1.85 per additional km	Php100/day	0.91	3.87–4.25
New Delhi	Rs. 8–Rs. 29	Rs. 2–Rs. 10	Rs. 20 up to 10 hours; Rs. 40 for 10 hours or more	1.09	1.91–4.13

Sources: Based on data from Washington Metropolitan Area Transit Authority; Metropolitan Transportation Authority; Transport for London; Tokyo Metro; Toei Bus; Bangkok Metro Public Company, Ltd.; Bangkok Mass Transit Authority; Light Rail Transit Authority; Land Transportation Franchising and Regulatory Board; Delhi Metro Rail Corporation, Ltd.; Delhi Transport Corporation; and GTZ International Fuel Prices (2009).
a. Public transit assumes a combination of rapid transit and bus. Driving cost is the sum of a daily parking rate and gasoline costs for 10 km of driving (or 0.7 liters of petrol).
b. For calculating the relative price, a bus ride of 10 km is assumed.

Table 3.16 Effectiveness of Major Price Policies in Reducing Transport Emissions

Policy	Reducing vehicle miles traveled	Increasing fuel economy
Best policy option		
Fuel pricing	Effective	Effective
Alternative policies		
If charging on mileage traveled Toll road pricing	Effective	Not effective
If charging on individual car use Cordon pricing Parking prices	Partly effective	Not effective
If charging on car ownership Registration/inspection fees	Not effective	Partly effective
If subsidizing new car ownership Cash for clunkers program	Not effective	Effective
If subsidizing alternatives Lower mass transit fares	Effective	Not effective

option for reducing emissions. However, while less effective at reducing emissions, other policies have other desirable outcomes. For instance, road use charges raise the marginal cost of car travel, thus reducing congestion by discouraging people from driving.

Fuel Pricing: Best Policy Option

Fuel pricing is unique in its ability to both discourage people from using cars and increase fuel economy. First, higher fuel prices normally correlate with low car use over the long run (figure 3.20; OECD/IEA 2004). Second, high prices should

Figure 3.20 Passenger Car Travel, Fuel Economy, and Average Fuel Prices, 1998

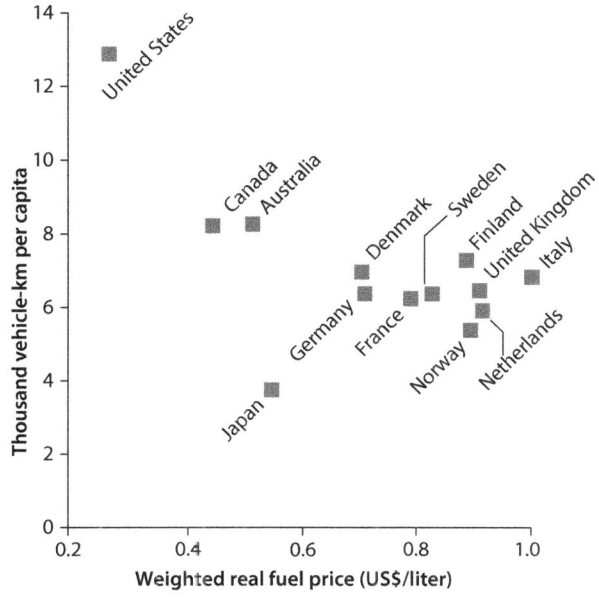

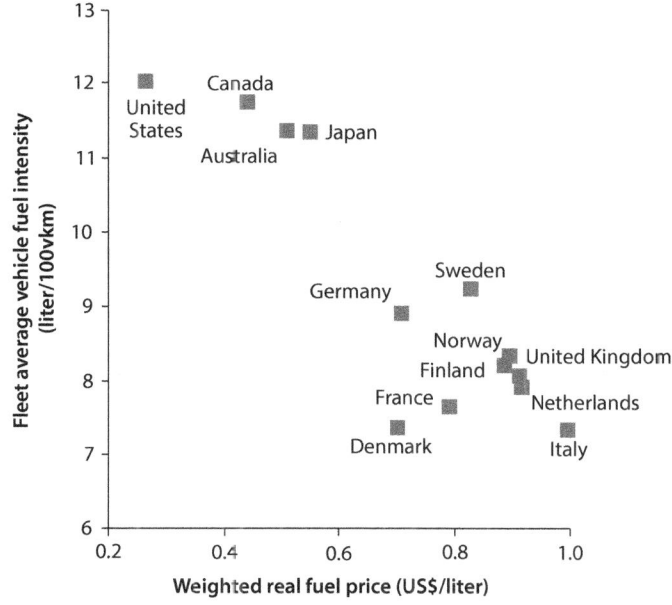

Source: OECD/IEA 2004.

induce people to buy more fuel-efficient vehicles, thus reducing vehicle-fuel intensity (figure 3.21).

Fuel taxes vary significantly by country (Delucchi 2007; Chamon, Mauro and Okawa 2008; figure 3.22). The 20 developing countries that most subsidize energy spent some $310 billion on subsidies in 2007 (World Bank 2010a). From an environmental standpoint, these subsidies should be replaced with a fuel tax, but that is politically difficult (OECD 2000; Clerides and Zachariadis 2008) because it could affect the economy negatively. Certainly, low fuel prices help domestic businesses and citizens in the short run, but they also are financially unsustainable, reduce competitiveness, and harm long-term growth.

How much and how quickly consumers respond to fuel price changes depends on the price elasticity of demand. Estimates of price elasticity vary

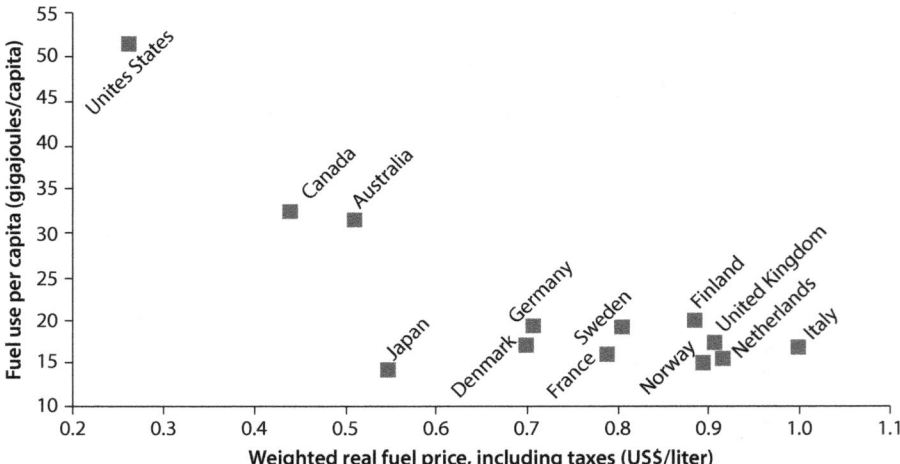

Figure 3.21 Passenger Car Use and Average Fuel Prices, 1998

Source: OECD/IEA 2004.

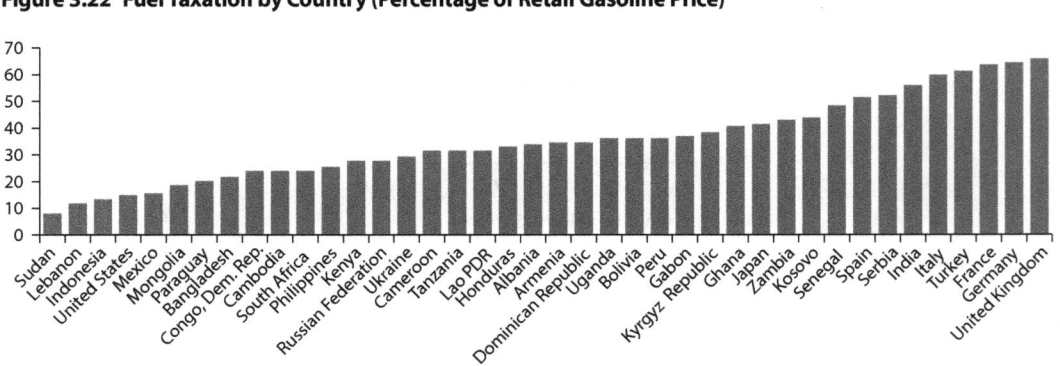

Figure 3.22 Fuel Taxation by Country (Percentage of Retail Gasoline Price)

Source: Chamon and others 2008.

widely and depend on the functional form used, the estimation technique, the period of estimation, and the country. The literature indicates that the price elasticity of automobile fuel demand would range from –0.03 to –0.4 in the short run and –0.6 to –1.1 in the long run (Chamon and others 2008; Hughes and others 2008; World Bank 2010). Highly volatile prices affect fuel consumption, as they did during the oil crises in the late 1980s (figure 3.23). Although price elasticity was surprisingly low in the United States in the early 2000s (Hughes and others 2008), it has increased since 2005 (Park and Zhao 2010). Expecting fuel prices to remain high, consumers have begun to change their behavior.

Low price elasticity may result from a strong "rebound effect," in which as fuel economy improves and the cost of driving declines, people drive more. This can partly offset fuel reductions associated with higher prices. One study estimated the short-run rebound effects at 4.5 percent and the long-run effects at 22.2 percent (Small and van Dender 2007); another reported even larger rebound effects of 58 percent (Frondel and others 2008).

Behavioral inertia also helps keep price elasticity low; it takes time to change people's preferences and perceptions. Price elasticity has been particularly low in the United States, where fuel prices historically have been low (Hughes and others 2008). There about half the passenger cars are sport-utility vehicles (SUVs), pick-up trucks, or four-wheel-drives, whereas in Europe nearly 90 percent of passenger cars are four- or two-door sedans (OECD 2002a).

Figure 3.23 Fuel Taxation (Percentage of Retail Gasoline Price), 1970–2009

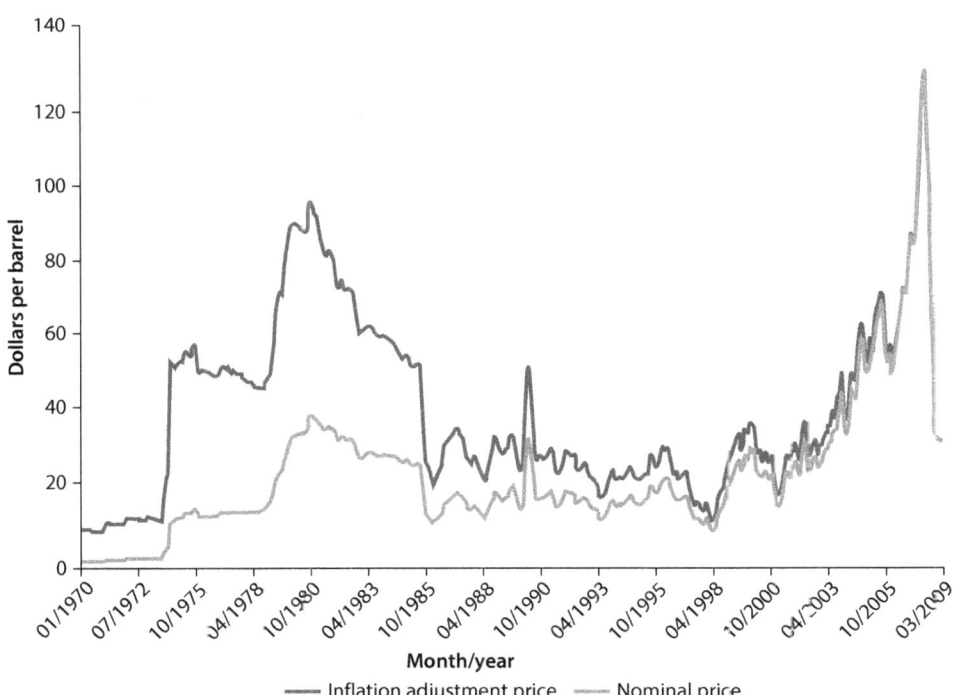

Source: http://tonto.eia.doe.gov/country/timeline/oil_chronology.cfm.

In the United Kingdom and Germany, where fuel prices historically have been two to three times higher than the United States, price elasticities are also about twice as high (Frondel and others 2008; Bonilla and Foxon 2009; Frondel and Vance 2010). European economies also offer more transport options, meaning fuel prices can be more elastic because people can more easily switch to other means of travel. One popular option is to subsidize cleaner and renewable energy sources. In many countries, diesel fuel is consistently cheaper than gasoline (GTZ 2009). This encourages the use of diesel-powered vehicles, which with appropriate filters are less polluting. Biofuels need to be 20–30 percent cheaper than gasoline because their energy content is lower than that of gasoline (Kojima and Johnson 2005), but subsidizing biofuels simply adds to their development cost.

Road User Pricing

Road user pricing is the second-best solution. Toll roads and cordon pricing are typical examples. Road pricing is less effective than fuel pricing because road charges do not affect consumer choice of vehicle unless charges are based on vehicle emission class. Road pricing is, however, more effective than other vehicle-based charges because it closely—though not perfectly—relates to fuel consumption and thus emissions. This is distinct from car ownership charges, which are not linked to driving distances or the amount of fuel used.

Tolls, which are charged according to miles traveled, are more effective than cordon pricing, which charges for entry into an area and lacks the link between pricing and emissions. But cordon pricing can reduce congestion.

Although road pricing generates extra revenue, it is still not in wide use, although at least 46 countries do operate toll facilities. In the United States there are 277 toll roads, bridges, and tunnels. They total about 5,000 miles, but that is only 2 percent of total roads and 5 percent of federal-aid highways. Toll revenue accounts for less than 10 percent of total highway funding, though in some countries, such as Indonesia, Mexico, and Argentina, highways are nearly 100 percent tolled (NSTIFC 2009). In general, however, there are still plenty of opportunities globally to charge road users, especially those driving on highways and at peak times.

Historically, road pricing—both tolls and cordon pricing—has been highly effective in urban areas in reducing not only congestion but also emissions. Road user charges discourage people from driving on toll roads or through toll zones. When the Republic of Korea introduced congestion charges at the southern edge of Seoul, traffic declined by 11 percent within two years, and speed increased by 50 percent (OECD 2002a). In 1975 Singapore introduced the Area Licensing Scheme, the first comprehensive road pricing scheme anywhere. People had to pay an area license fee of $3 or $1.25 a day to enter the central business district during peak hours. The results: the number of vehicles entering the restricted zone declined by 73 percent, and average speed in that zone increased 10–20 percent (World Bank 1978). The decreased traffic and congestion clearly mitigated emissions.

Road pricing can target polluting vehicles specifically by differentiating tolls according to vehicle type. For cordon pricing, Milan, Italy, introduced Ecopass, which in 2008 began charging heavily polluting vehicles to reduce congestion and emissions. It was expected to reduce incoming traffic by 10 percent (Prasad and others 2009; Rotaris and others 2010). In 2008 London introduced the Low Emission Zone to deter old, polluting vehicles from driving in the area. Trucks over 12 tons were targeted first, with other vehicles to be restricted over time (Prasad and others 2009).

One disadvantage of road pricing is that it may divert traffic to toll-free or unrestricted roads. Narrowly targeted road pricing or poorly coordinated transport policies can be a problem. In Singapore the number of vehicles entering the restricted zone did decline, but the ring road outside the city became more congested (World Bank 1978). London's cordon pricing—among other reasons—has increased passenger car congestion, though the speed of public transport has increased (NSTIFC 2009). In Bangkok poor coordination has increased emissions and pollutants in the expressway network development project. An 11.5-km, six-lane metropolitan highway from Ramindra to Rama IX IC commissioned in 1996 is carrying less than half the forecast 108,000 vehicles a day. In this case, the government built another six-lane public side road in conjunction with the expressway that was toll-free. More and more people chose the toll-free road, thus limiting the positive effects of road pricing. Emissions and pollutants did not decline significantly (JBIC 2003).

Advanced technologies, such as electronic toll collection systems and the global positioning system, can make road pricing more effective.[17] Singapore replaced the initial Area Licensing Scheme with a more advanced mechanism, Electric Road Pricing Scheme, which is an automatic toll collection system. The price to enter the central business district is optimized by a time-of-use system that varies price according to the time of day, thus better managing traffic flow and speed (OECD 2002b). Using a satellite global positioning system, Germany charges trucks heavier than 12 tons in certain mileage and vehicle emission classes. Initial evidence indicates that direct user charges increase efficiency in the heavy vehicle industry (NSTIFC 2009). Developing countries could adopt these advanced technologies if they become cheaper and more prevalent.

Parking Policies and Effective Urban Land Use

Initiating or raising parking rates in urban areas is another way to raise the cost of car use, although it has no bearing on the distance people drive. The experience of Perth, Australia, is interesting: in 1998 it replaced traditional license fees for residential car ownership with charges on all nonresidential parking in the Perth Parking Management Area. It used the revenues to provide free public transport in the city center (OECD 2002b).

Parking policies also help promote effective urban land use. Most urban streets have one or two parking lanes that typically take up 20–30 percent of their width. In developed countries roads account for about 20 percent of total urbanized areas. Parking policies are not always enforceable, however, thus aggravating city traffic congestion. Thus, a significant portion of urban areas is devoted to on-street parking, with serious implications for urban planning (Litman 2005).

Parking charges help reduce car use. In Singapore's city center, monthly parking fees were increased by 30–50 percent, which, along with other measures, significantly reduced traffic (World Bank 1978). In Copenhagen in 1990 and 1991 new parking fees were introduced in most of the city's public parking areas. The number of cars parked dropped 25 percent, and traffic to and from the area declined 10 percent. The 1997 Lloyd District program in Portland, Oregon, that introduced on-street parking charges reduced drive-alone commuter traffic by 7 percent (OECD 2002b).

Parking availability also affects household decisions about car ownership and use. Parking costs are the most important determinant of car use in the Seoul metropolitan area (Sohn and Yun 2009). Households are less likely to own cars if they have difficulty parking them (Woldeamanuel and others 2009). By contrast, if parking spaces are provided at work, car use and demand for fuel increase (Cervero, Golub, and Nee 2007; Frondel and Vance 2010).

Successful parking policies need the participation of both the public and the private sector. In Singapore private operators were required to set the same fees as public parking areas (World Bank 1978). Parking cash-out is another option: in the United States this allows employees to exchange their parking space for its cash equivalent and use alternative transportation (OECD 2002b).

Charges on Individual Car Ownership and Car-Maker Competitiveness
Another option is charging taxes and fees, such as annual and one-off charges on car purchase, registration, and inspection. However, that may not be enough to reduce car use and emissions. Moreover, without other policy measures, these charges may motivate car owners to travel more in the belief that expensive ownership costs have already been sunk—especially when fuel demand is inelastic. Higher sales taxes and new registration fees may also discourage people from replacing old cars with new fuel-efficient cars (OECD 2000).

Emission-based charges and car scrapping programs could lead to more low-carbon vehicles and make the industry more competitive. If they do not adopt low-carbon technologies, car companies will eventually lose market share. In 2009 about 600,000 hybrid cars were sold globally, most of them the Toyota Prius. More and more manufacturers have begun to produce hybrid and electric vehicles. Major vehicle industries are concentrated in developed countries and some emerging economies, such as Brazil, China, India, and South Africa. Since it is important that developing countries introduce low-carbon technologies quickly, multinationals should promote international technology transfers.

Emission-Based Vehicle Taxation
In 2001 the United Kingdom introduced an excise duty for new cars based on CO_2 emissions. Cars are assigned to one of four categories, and the category determines the duty (OECD 2002a). Many countries already tax heavy vehicles and trucks more than light. In the United States a 12 percent federal sales tax on

trucks and trailers weighing more than 33,000 lbs generates more than $2.5 billion annual revenue (NSTIFC 2009).

Car Scrapping Programs

Subsidies for fuel-efficient vehicles, including a sales tax exemption, are another powerful tool (Potoglou and Kanaroglou 2007). As in other developed countries, such as France and Norway, the United States recently implemented the Car Allowance Rebate System (CARS) or "cash for clunkers" program, which paid up to $4,500 for each energy-inefficient car (18 or fewer mpg) that was replaced with a more efficient one. The price incentives worked; the number of consumers applying for the program was much higher than expected. In all, $3 billion was allocated for trade-ins of 690,000 vehicles. In France the 1994 vehicle retirement program offered a 5,000-franc subsidy, which shortened the average duration of car holding by 3.3 years (Yamamoto and others 2004). In Spain two cash-for-clunker programs in 1994 and 1995 promoted diesel engines. The replacement of any vehicle more than 7 or 10 years old earned €600; in the 1990s the market share of diesel-powered cars gradually increased from 13 to 50 percent (Miravete and Moral 2009).

Car-scrapping programs, however, are limited by their high cost. In recent U.S. experience, only 30 percent of total passenger cars were traded in, at a cost of $3 billion. Car scrapping thus cannot be the only solution for fleet turnover.

Alternative Mass Transit Pricing

Lowering mass transit prices increases the relative price of car use and thus induces more people to use public transportation. The price elasticity of public transport demand is generally about –0.3 but can vary considerably from almost zero to more than one (Holmgren 2007). The price elasticity of bus rapid transit demand is estimated at –0.26 based on data from 44 bus systems around the world (Hensher and Golob 2008). In Spain price elasticity is –0.61 for train and –0.49 for bus (Martin and Nombela 2007). In Bangkok it is much higher, –2.2 to –2.5, because buses are more popular, with 40 percent of households using buses only (Dissanayake and Morikawa 2010). In Beijing price elasticity is low, –0.01 to –0.12, and depends on income; in other words, the lower the income share of transport expenditure, the lower the price elasticity. The rich continue to use their cars regardless of public transit fare changes (Anas and Timilsina 2009a).

The relative prices of public transit systems also affect consumer choice. In Mumbai reducing bus fares had more impact on modal shift than reducing rail prices. The cost of traveling by rail is much cheaper than bus. While the one-way rail cost of commuting 20 km is Rs. 90 per month, less than Rs. 4 per day, the bus fare for 20 km is about Rs. 20 per day. Price elasticities are thus estimated at –0.35 to –0.45 for bus and –0.07 to –0.08 for rail (Takeuchi and others 2007). In contrast, in São Paulo rapid transit and trains were found to be better able to attract passengers by lowering prices[18]; buses were price-inelastic because the majority of households had little alternative but to use public buses and trolleys at the time

Box 3.5 Information and Consumer Vehicle Choice

Reasons for vehicle choice are complex because they are affected by economic, social, cultural, and psychological factors. Car safety and fuel economy are important determinants (Dreyfus and Viscusi 1995), but people tend to discount future fuel prices and buy cars based on size, speed, and appearance rather than fuel economy (World Bank 2010a). It has been found that car ownership and use are closely related to "symbolic" and "convenience" motives (Sohn and Yun 2009) and may be affected by neighbors' behavior. Thus, the more people use new vehicle technologies, the more others will follow (Mau and others 2008; Axsen and others 2009).

In addition to financial incentives, people need information Coad and others (2009). People are not always familiar with low-carbon vehicle options (figure B3.5.1; Anable and others 2006, prepared for the U.K. Department for Transport). To raise public awareness, Singapore launched the Climate Change Awareness Program in 2006, showing the public simple ways to save energy and money and reduce emissions. The Philippines has implemented similar programs (Prasad and others 2009). Eco-labeling can significantly affect consumer vehicle choice, although psychological factors and prior choices are also important. In 2005 the United Kingdom introduced a new green car label in connection with the Vehicle Excise Duty rating (Anable and others 2006). The U.S. Environmental Protection Agency also provides two emission ratings: the Air Pollution Score and the Greenhouse Gas Score (Teisl and others 2008).

Nonmonetary incentives can help. For instance, people in California—the largest hybrid car market in the United States—buy hybrid cars so that they can use high-occupancy vehicle (HOV) lanes when driving alone (Sangkapichai and Saphores 2009). Californians are twice as likely to purchase a hybrid car as are New Yorkers (table B3.5.1). While incentives clearly work, however, traffic conditions, local socioeconomic conditions, and consumer behavior can affect them. In Hamilton, Canada, the effect of HOV lanes is insignificant because such lanes are not common in that country (Potoglou and Kanaroglou 2007).

Figure B3.5.1 The United Kingdom Respondents Familiar with New Vehicle Technologies

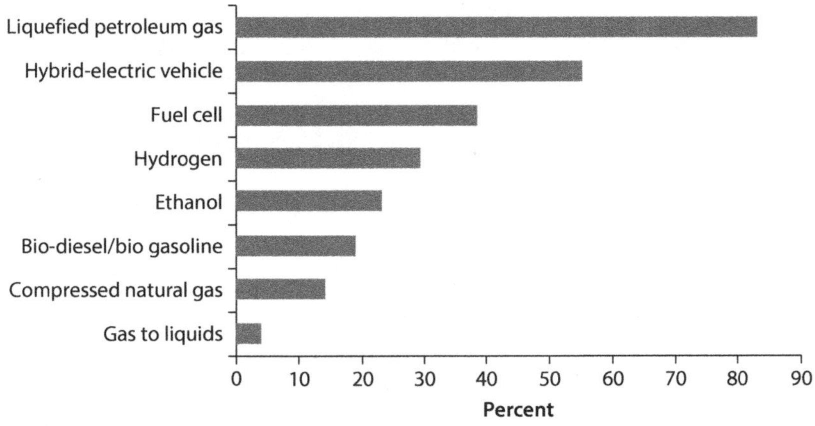

Source: United Kingdom Department of Transport 2006.

box continues next page

Box 3.5 Information and Consumer Vehicle Choice *(continued)*

Table B3.5.1 Hybrid Markets in the United States

Top five U.S. hybrid markets	(a) New hybrids purchased (December 2009)	(b) 2008 Population (millions)	(a)/(b) (percent)	2008 median household income (US$)
California	55,553	37.0	0.150	61,021
New York	15,348	19.5	0.079	56,033
Florida	14,949	18.5	0.081	47,778
Texas	14,632	24.8	0.059	50,043
New Jersey	11,367	8.7	0.131	70,378

Sources: U.S. Census Bureau; hybridCARS.

of the survey in 1987 (Swait and Eskeland 1995). A later study in São Paulo found that public transit fares had more influence on people's modal choice: a 1 percent reduction in public transit fares could reduce car use by 4–32 percent (Arias and Timilsina 2009b). In that case, the rich seemed more responsive because cars were not an option for the poor regardless of public transit fares.

An integrated transit and parking system may be especially effective. Bremen, Germany, achieved high public transit use by ensuring that transit prices were never greater than car use plus parking charges. Half of all trips into the city center are on mass transit and one-quarter on bikes (OECD 2002b). In developing countries mass transit is more expensive than in developed countries.

In addition to pricing, service is important. If passenger comfort level is low, the effect of pricing is limited. People prefer air-conditioned rapid transit over a crowded bus without air conditioning. Travel time is also part of service quality. In Gran Canaria, Spain, demand for buses is more sensitive for those who found the experience less comfortable (Espino 2007). People who are not satisfied with service are more likely to be price-sensitive; if prices go up, they shift to alternative modes.[19] In the United States public transport demand is highly elastic to service quality—about 1.05 (Holmgren 2007). The German Mobility Panel data indicate that household car ownership would decrease significantly if there were access to good quality urban rail (Woldeamanuel and others 2009).

Importance of Regulations for Emissions Mitigation

Price incentives, though important, cannot predict emission reduction. People may not choose to purchase fuel-efficient vehicles or use alternative mass transit, regardless of supply and pricing. Fuel taxes and road pricing can be difficult to implement because of political sensitivities (OECD 2000; Clerides and Zachariadis 2008). In such cases, direct quantitative intervention may make more sense, although among other drawbacks it can be more expensive. Regulations should be considered complementary to pricing incentives.

There are at least four regulatory approaches to capping car emissions (table 3.17): (1) setting fuel economy standards at the production level;

Table 3.17 Major Quantitative Regulations for Emissions Mitigation

	Vehicle energy intensity	Number of vehicles	Driving behavior
Fuel economy standards/used car import policy/inspection and maintenance programs	Effective		
Private car ownership restriction		Effective	
Conditioning on road use		Partly effective	
Road traffic rules and regulations			Effective

Figure 3.24 U.S. Fuel Economy Standards and Actual Performance

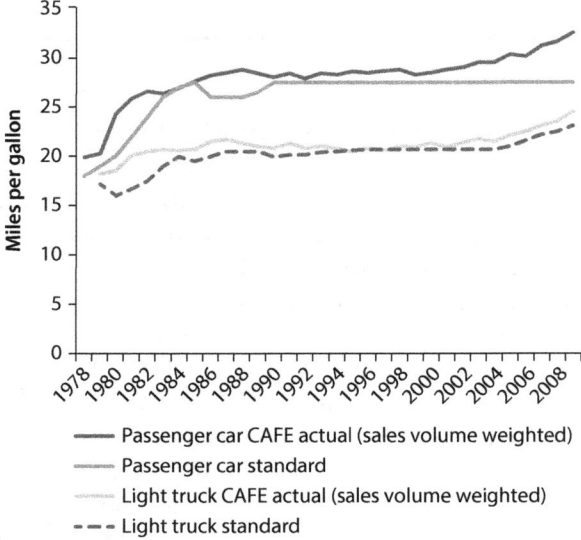

— Passenger car CAFE actual (sales volume weighted)
— Passenger car standard
— Light truck CAFE actual (sales volume weighted)
--- Light truck standard

Note: CAFE = Corporate Average Fuel Economy.

a corollary to this would be periodic emissions inspections, which would be especially important in developing countries; (2) restricting the number of cars on the road; while rare, this is obviously a very strong measure; (3) imposing road-use conditions to reduce traffic volume—high-occupancy vehicle (HOV) lanes are an example; (4) change driving behavior.

Choice of Regulatory Interventions

Fuel Economy Standards for New Vehicles. The U.S. CAFE standards introduced in 1975 aim to reduce new vehicle fuel consumption. Over the past 30 years, fuel economy has improved from 20 mpg to 32 for passenger cars (figure 3.24). If they fail to achieve the standards, manufacturers pay a considerable penalty ($50 per car for each mpg below the standard; OECD 2002a). In 1995 Japan introduced standards to reduce new car fuel consumption by 19 percent, which it had achieved by 2004; its new reduction goal is 23.5 percent (METI 2006; Clerides and Zachariadis 2008). In Europe there is no regulation of fuel consumption, but in 1998 and 1999 car manufacturers agreed on a voluntary emission target of 140 grams of CO_2 per km for new cars, compared with a 1995 average of 187 grams. This was intended to be extended to 120 by 2012 (Zachariadis 2006).[20]

Trade and Inspection Policies for Imported Used Cars

For most developing countries, trade policies and inspection of imported used cars are more important than regulating the fuel economy of new vehicles. The global used car market is huge, estimated at more than 5.5 million (OECD/IEA 2009). Japan alone exported 380,000 used cars around the world, though the United States exported only 120,000 (Pelletiere and Reinert 2006). In addition, the global used-car component industry is significant, estimated at about $60 billion. Some countries prohibit used cars for safety and environmental reasons. Others allow only old cars to avoid competition with domestic new car dealers (table 3.18). But imported used cars may be cleaner than a developing country's fleet of older vehicles (OECD 2004; Timilsina and Dulal 2009). Because the average lifetimes of new vehicles may be short in some countries, such as Japan, trade liberalization could introduce more fuel-efficient vehicles into other domestic markets.

Border vehicle inspection is critical. In general, older cars emit more CO_2 and other pollutants. In California 10-year-old vehicles emit about twice as many pollutants as the newest cars (figure 3.25). Until recently, Mexico imported more

Table 3.18 Prohibitions on Imported Used Cars and Tires

	Motor vehicles	Tires
Argentina		X
Bolivia	X	
Brazil	X	
Brunei	X	
Canada	X	
Chile	X	
Dominican Republic	X	
Ecuador	X	X
Egypt, Arab Rep.	X	
Ghana	X	
India	X	
Maldives	X	
Mozambique		X
Nicaragua	X	
Nigeria	X	
Peru	X	X
Salvador	X	
Thailand	X	
Venezuela, RB	X	X

Source: OECD 2004.

Figure 3.25 Total Vehicle Emissions by Base Year

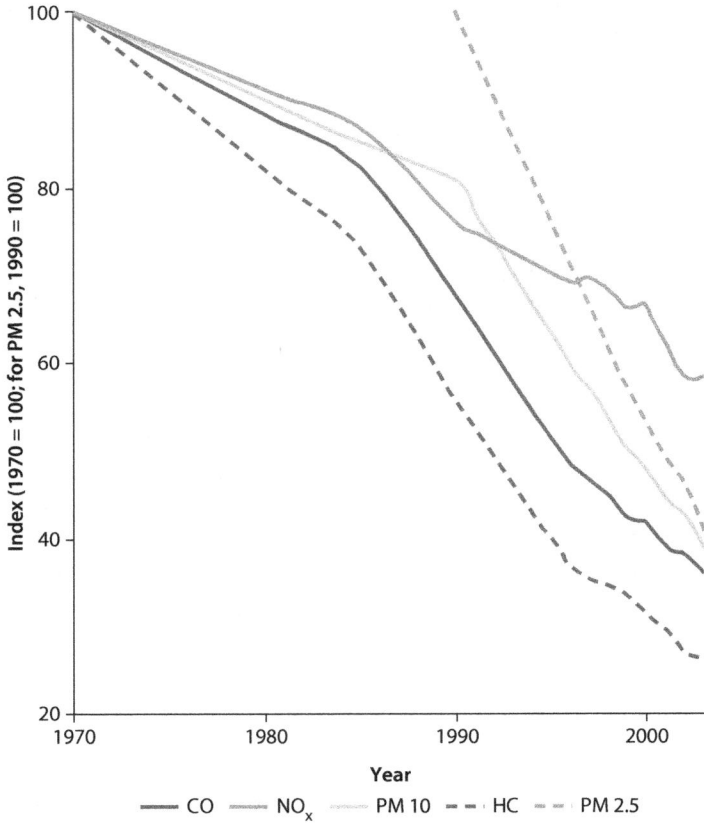

Source: Parry and others 2007.
Note: CO_2 = carbon dioxide, HC = hydrocarbons, PM = particular matter, NO_x = nitrogen oxide.

than a million used cars annually, many of them 10–15 years old. In 2006 about 20 percent of these cars exceeded the 2 percent CO_2 threshold. Reinforcing border vehicle inspections could reduce 11.2 Mt of CO_2 equivalent every year (Johnson and others 2010).

Inspection and Maintenance Programs

Most developing countries have yet to introduce fuel economy standards, although many have emission standards (Timilsina and Dulal 2009). China, for instance, adopted European emission standards in 1999 that required all new light-duty vehicles to meet Euro I standards by 2000 and Euro II standards by 2004 (Zhao 2006).

It is debatable whether inspection and maintenance programs are effective in controlling emissions. They entail high compliance costs for car owners, including time spent on the inspection and for repairs (Merrell and others 1999), but a well-designed inspection and monitoring program can be effective (Yamamoto and others 2004; Ribeiro and Abreu 2008). Enhanced inspection and maintenance in Southern California is expected to reduce light-duty vehicle emissions by 14–28 percent (Eisinger 2005). Despite some disadvantages (see below), consumers should be motivated to switch to fuel-efficient cars, and overall vehicle energy inefficiency should eventually improve.[21]

Restrictions on Private Car Ownership

This is a direct measure to control the number of vehicles on the road. In 1990 Singapore introduced a vehicle registration quota; each year the government fixes the maximum number of vehicles to be newly registered. The right to register is put out to tender among people who want to buy a new car. The initial quota system divided vehicles into seven categories (table 3.19). In 1999 categories one and two were merged, as were three and four. Each category has a premium value determined by a sealed-bid, uniform-price auction (see Tan 2001 for further detail). The system is thus a strong quantitative intervention with a quasi-market mechanism. Supply and demand determine the premium. Before the 1999 recategorization, premiums tended to be larger for luxury than for smaller cars, consistent with reducing emissions. However, after recategorization, the premiums of the two new categories, renamed A and B (figure 3.26), converged. Nonetheless, the quota system has successfully controlled the growth of cars on the road.

Conditioning on Road Use

Automobile-restricted zones are a strong quantitative regulation, but public transport and bicycle paths must also be available. Aalborg, a city of 120,000 in northern Denmark, closed roads in the city center, introduced energy-efficient buses, and extended pedestrian areas and bicycle paths. Car traffic was reduced by an estimated 750,000 km annually (OECD 2002b).

Highway HOV lanes reserved for public buses, carpools, and vehicles with two or more occupants are common in North America and some European countries. On the San Francisco-Oakland Bay Bridge, four HOV lanes carry two-thirds of travelers, with 18 mixed-flow lanes carrying the other third.[22] About 60 percent of respondents to a carpool survey cited the availability of HOV lanes as important to their decision to carpool (OECD 2002b). HOV lanes also have revenue potential. In recent years, excess capacity on HOV lanes has been sold to solo drivers who want to use the express lanes (high-occupancy

Table 3.19 Vehicle Classification of Singapore's Quota System

Category 1: Small cars with engine capacity of 1,000 c.c. and below;
Category 2: Medium-sized cars with engine capacity of 1,001 to 1,600 ex., and taxis;
Category 3: Large cars with engine capacity of 1,601 to 2,000 c.c;
Category 4: Luxury cars with engine capacity of 2,001 c.c. and above;
Category 5: Goods vehicles and buses;
Category 6: Motorcycles and scooters; and
Category 7: "Open."

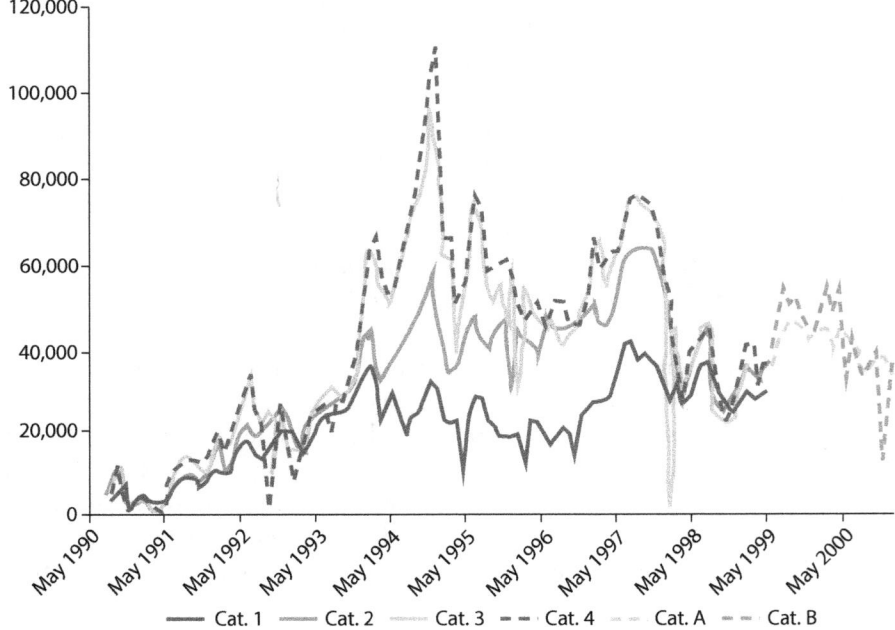

Figure 3.26 Singapore: Quota Premiums for Passenger Cars

Source: Tan 2001.

toll—HOT—lanes), as in the vehicle registration quota system. A pilot project in San Diego, California, found that people were willing to pay a fee of $0.50–$8 per trip, possibly generating more than a million dollars a year. Several states have converted HOV lanes to HOT lanes (NSTIFC 2009).

Enforcement of Traffic Regulations

Regulations should be adopted and enforced that address certain driving activities, such as overloading, that increase emissions. In India the primary long-distance goods carrier is a two-axle, nine-ton truck, which is often overloaded with 14–20 tons, especially on outward-bound trips (World Bank/ESMAP 2002). Overloaded trucks not only emit more CO_2 they also wear down road surfaces. In 2005 Albania eliminated a user charge for three-axle trucks because multi-axle trucks damage pavements less than overloaded two-axle trucks do (World Bank 2006).

Emissions increase with traffic speeds (figure 3.27). In the United States, for every one mile-per-hour reduction, a heavy truck traveling at 60–65 miles per hour can improve fuel efficiency by 0.8 percent (OECD/IEA 2009). A study in Japan found that if environmental externalities are taken into account, current speed limits on national highways in rural areas are 10 km/hr higher than the socially optimal limit (Thanesuen and others 2006).

Speed limits are also conducive to safety. Traffic accidents are usually associated with speed limits (Houston and others 1995; Scuffham 2003; also see

Figure 3.27 Fuel Consumption and CO_2 Emissions per Vehicle-km

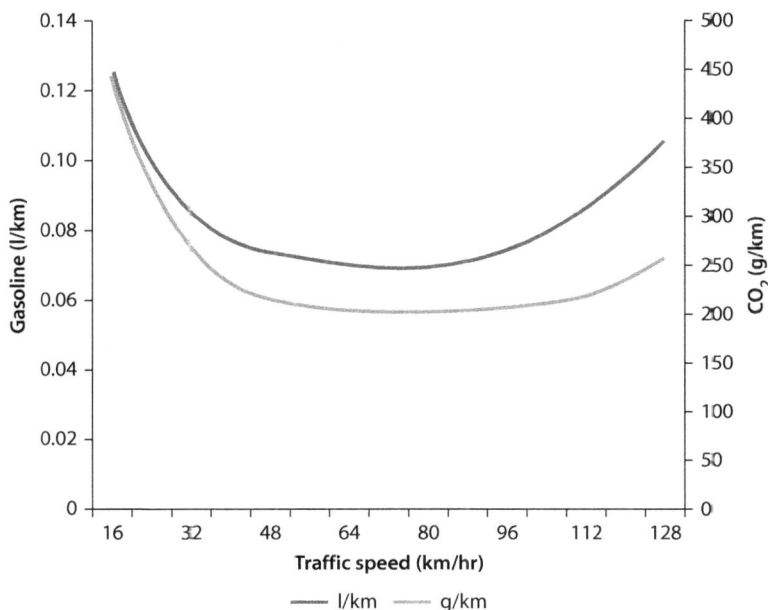

Source: Anas and Timilsina 2009a.
Note: CO_2 = carbon dioxide.

the next section for further details). The elasticity of total fatal accidents may exceed unity: a 1 percent increase in the speed limit increases fatal accidents by more than 1 percent (see the next section). Enforcing speed limits not only reduces emissions, it also saves lives.

Drawbacks of Hard Regulation

Regulatory measures can increase the certainty of emissions reduction because they impose emission ceilings regardless of consumer preferences. However, past approaches have faced four difficulties: mistargeting, misquantification, enforceability, and costs of implementation.

Mistargeting

Good regulations have to be targeted correctly, leaving no room for them to be bypassed. This is not always easy. An example is the U.S. dual CAFE standards, which have a fairly modest fuel standard for "light trucks." The problem is that household cars, such as SUVs and minivans, also fall into this category. Although the standards were slightly tightened in 2004 and in 2006 (Transportation Research Board 2010), manufacturers' efforts to improve fuel economy are diluted by consumer preference for large vehicles with greater acceleration and towing capacity (National Academies 2002)—half the U.S. passenger cars now fall in this category. In the next two decades, however, energy efficiency is expected to improve by 50 percent (NSTIFC 2009).

Targeting also fails when traffic bypasses a regulated area. After Switzerland imposed a stringent limit of 28 tons on all trucks traveling through the country and required that heavy freight be carried by rail rather than road, much of the international road freight traffic simply went through neighboring countries instead (OECD 2002a). There is always the risk that regulations will be bypassed.

Misquantification

How stringent should a regulation be? The U.S. CAFE standard for light trucks may be too loose, but regulations that are too stringent can cause other business and efficiency problems. The U.S. CAFE experience, for example, raises the issue of safety. The uniform down-weighting of the fleet, including both heavy SUVs and smaller light trucks, means these vehicles are not required to have as much occupant protection as heavier vehicles. Aggressive downsizing in the late 1970s and early 1980s may have contributed to more traffic fatalities in the early 1990s (National Academies 2002).[23] Mandating a nationwide uniform speed can result in higher than optimal speeds in some areas and lower than optimal in others (Lave and Elias 1997; Thanesuen and others 2006). In the United States, underused HOV lanes can be seen as pushing solo-occupancy vehicles into mixed-flow lanes.

Enforceability

Having a regulation does not ensure that it will be enforced. Not all drivers obey speed limits and other traffic rules. Enforcement is particularly difficult when governance is poor and regulatory capacity minimal, as in developing countries. In Bogota, although operators are required to scrap old buses that were operating in TransMilenio corridors, some continue to use them on routes not served by TransMilenio (Echeverry and others 2005). Thus, allocating road space to dedicated bus lanes can aggravate congestion and air pollution in other corridors if too few car drivers are induced to switch to mass transit (World Bank 2010b).

Enforcing inspection and maintenance requirements can also be a problem. Emissions inspection for imported used cars in Mexico has been imperfect (Johnson and others 2010), and the Californian Smog Check program failed to lower emissions in the 1980s: about a third of cars tested roadside had excessive emissions, whether they drove within or outside the program region. It was thought that inspection stations may have been unreliable or corrupt (Glazer and others 1995). In Nepal 31–81 percent of gas-fueled vehicles failed the roadside emissions test, and diesel cars failed at an even higher rate, 64–90 percent. Why? Because many drivers pass the formal emissions inspection by making temporary engine adjustments, reverting afterward to pre-inspection conditions (Faiz and others 2006; Timilsina and Dulal 2009). In India, where all vehicles must have a valid certificate of pollution-under-control, compliance has never exceeded 23 percent (Pandey 2006). Traffic violations are another common problem: In Albania it was estimated that about 40 percent of trucks were overloaded before the heavy-user charges for multi-axle trucks were eliminated (World Bank 2006).

Of particular note, many environmental regulations related to land use, transit operations, nonmotorized facilities, and parking are local or regional. Thus, if government at these levels is not effective, regulation does not work well, particularly in developing countries.

Costs of Implementation

The regulatory approach can be more costly than other options, such as price incentives. For instance, the cost of imposing 10 percent lower CAFE standards is estimated at $3.6 billion, $228 per vehicle, raising prices for consumers and decreasing profits for producers (Austin and Dinan 2005). Inspection programs can also be costly. While fuel taxes are automatically collected at the gas pump, inspections also cost people time. The U.S. inspection program is estimated to cost $1,032 million a year, consisting of $479 million in drivers' time and travel costs and $553 million in inspection costs (proxied by total inspection fees; Merrell and others 1999).

Enforcing traffic rules can also be costly. There is an argument that strict speed regulation uses up too much highway patrol resources and could compromise other aspects of traffic safety. In fact, a study shows that fatality rates dropped by 3.4–5.1 percent when the U.S. government allowed states to increase speed limits from 55 mph to 65 in 1987. This has been interpreted to mean that the nationwide 55 mph speed limit was too costly to implement and overused fiscal resources (Lave and Elias 1997). The costs cannot be ignored when regulations are being enacted.

Box 3.6 Policy Options Compared

There is a wide range of policy options available, and the implementation cost of each varies, as does its enforceability. Also, any policy may change consumer behavior. This comparison is thus based on a complex set of factors.

In comparing fuel taxes with fuel economy standards, one study estimates that a 3-mpg improvement in U.S. Corporate Average Fuel Economy (CAFE) standards would impose welfare losses of about $4 billion to save 5.2 billion gallons of gas annually (Kleit 2004). The implied carbon price for this is an estimated $317 per t$CO_2$–far above the current market price, which means that the policy is too costly.[a] An 11 percent increase in fuel taxes, which would cost much less, could both achieve the same emissions reduction and increase revenues (which could be used for mass transit and the like). The implied carbon price is more consistent with the market price. Another study similarly suggests that strengthening the CAFE standards would be too costly (Austin and Dinan 2005).

Comprehensive road user pricing, such as cordon pricing, also seems too expensive if only direct investment costs are considered. However, cordon pricing brought in $237 million in

box continues next page

Box 3.6 Policy Options Compared *(continued)*

Table B3.6.1 Fuel Taxes and Fuel Economy Standards: Cost and Emissions Benefits

Source	Policy	Welfare losses or direct costs	Savings[a]	Author's calculated carbon price
Kleit (2004)	3 mpg increase in CAFE standards in the United States	$4 billion a year	5.2 billion gallons of fuel (= 12.6 million tCO_2 a year assuming emission intensity of 2,421 gCO_2/gallon[b])	$317 per tCO_2
	11 cents per gallon increase in fuel tax in the United States	$290 million a year	Same	$23 per tCO_2
Austin and Dinan (2005)	10 percent (3.8 mpg) increase in CAFE standards in the United States	$3.6 billion a year	10 percent reduction in fuel consumption for new cars (= 101.5 million tCO_2 on average annually assuming a emission intensity of 2,421 gCO_2/gallon,[b] drives averaging 12,000 miles a year, annual new car sales of 13.3 million[c] and a fleet turnover of 14 years)	$282 per tCO_2
OECD/IEA (2009)	Cordon pricing in London	€90 million in direct investment in the system	120,000 tCO_2eq per year	$1,979 per tCO_2 (assume €/$ = 0.8)
	Cordon pricing in Stockholm	€5 million of direct investment in the system	43,000 tCO_2eq per year	$1,976 per tCO_2 (assume €/$ = 0.8)
JICA (2008)	20 km of rapid transit in Bangkok	121 billion bahts in capital investment and 2 billion in annual total expenses[d]	1,736,000 tCO_2 for 30 years, plus SO_2 and NO_2 reductions	$2,661 per tCO_2 (assume baht/$ = 40)
OECD/IEA (2009)	84 km of BRT in Bogota, Colombia	$554 million in capital cost and $7.8 million in annual operating costs	247,000 tCO_2eq per year	$144 per tCO_2
	20 km of BRT in Mexico City	$50 million in capital cost and $1.9 million in annual operating costs	18,000 tCO_2eq per year	$241 per tCO_2
	30 km of BRT in Pereira, Colombia	$72 million in capital cost and $2.8 million in annual operating costs	18,000 tCO_2eq per year	$237 per tCO_2
	82 km of BRT in Chongqing, China	$90 million in capital cost and $7.6 million in annual operating costs	18,000 tCO_2eq per year	$47 per tCO_2

Note: BRT = bus rapid transit, CAFE = Corporate Average Fuel Economy, CO_2 = carbon dioxide, NO_2 = nitrogen dioxide, SO_2 = sulfur dioxide.
a. Author's assumptions are in parentheses.
b. U.S. Environmental Protection Agency assumption.
c. U.S. new vehicle sales in 2006.
d. Based on Bangkok Metro Public Company Limited 2010.

box continues next page

Box 3.6 Policy Options Compared *(continued)*

Figure B3.6.1 Mexico: Expected Net Mitigation Benefits, Various Transport Intervention

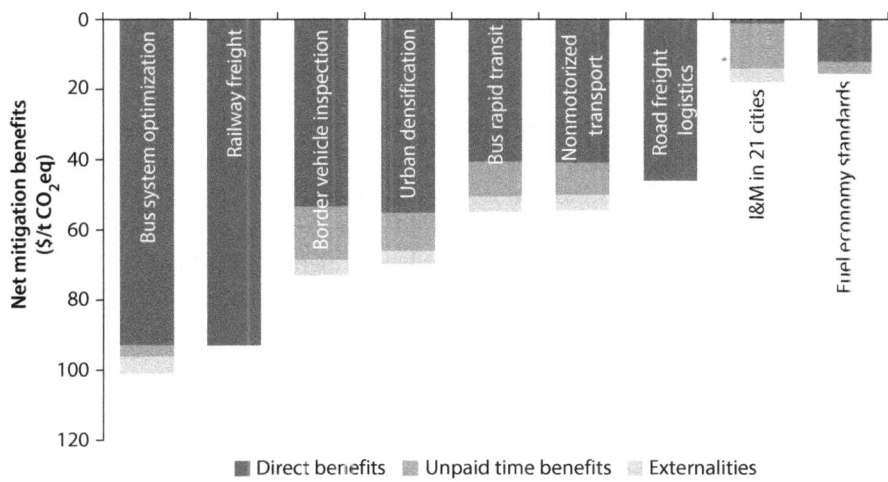

Source: Johnson and others 2010.
Note: CO_2 = carbon dioxide, I&M = inspection and maintenance.

revenue for London and $116 million for Stockholm (NSTIFC 2009), easily covering the costs of implementation.

From a cost/benefit perspective, rapid transit is more costly than a bus system. However, the feasibility and scope of these two options fundamentally differ, depending on customer density, geographic and environmental conditions, underlying assumptions, and how and whether other benefits are valued (such as whether the option raises additional revenues).

Since countries and cities have different cost structures, a country-specific evaluation may make more sense than a country-to-country comparison. For instance, in Mexico a comprehensive green-growth analysis found that fuel economy standards would not be most cost-effective (figure B3.6.1); optimizing bus and rail freight is preferable.

a. Another interpretation is that the current market price is too low, which is quite possible.

Designing Transport Projects from a Broader Point of View

The Preceding Discussion Has Important Policy Implications

Although technology may be a foundation for significant emissions reduction over the long term, advances are not likely to be dramatic. A broader policy approach should promote and accumulate new technologies. For example, technological transfer and trade liberalization could accelerate adoption of advanced low-carbon engine technologies. New technologies will be needed to make inspections and car repair more effective and regulations more enforceable.

Although appropriate alternative mass transit systems should be provided in a timely manner, they do not guarantee emission mitigation. Infrastructure should be used efficiently; operations and management can be improved without significant capital investment. Connecting different transport modes can make a city compact, so that people do not have to travel long distances. A policy framework that integrates transport, urban planning, and land management is needed.

Supply-side measures must be coordinated with demand-side policies. Pricing can guide people toward a low-carbon economy, with fuel pricing the most important policy tool. Road user pricing and parking policies are less effective but can be useful. Adopting vehicle-related taxes and charges based on emissions or vehicle miles traveled should motivate heavier users to refrain from car use. Subsidies for mass transit and rail freight can mitigate road dependency and emissions. Regulations can complement price incentives and increase the certainty that emissions will be reduced. But implementation may be too costly.

Finally, the carbon market price may not be high enough to effect mitigation, especially through costly infrastructure investment for multimodality. However, there are other options for mitigation. Road user pricing can discourage people from driving and motivate them to use public transportation. Road pricing also helps reduce costly congestion. Parking policies can change car use and encourage effective urban land planning. A significant portion of urban areas devoted to on-street parking aggravates congestion. Regulating speed limits can reduce vehicle fuel consumption and contribute to safety. Any evaluation of projects to mitigate emissions must account for all these benefits.

Notes

1. The total includes emissions from land-use change and forestry.
2. Transportation Research Board of the National Academies (2010). Until recently, diesel engines emitted more non-CO_2 pollutants, such as particulates, nitrogen oxide, and methane, (Defra 2009). These negative environmental effects have become more manageable thanks to advanced technologies, such as diesel particulate filters. However, proper environmental regulations are critical to control these other air pollutants.
3. *New York Times*, May 23, 2007.
4. *Seattle Times*, March 8, 2010.
5. Ministry of Land, Infrastructure, Transport and Tourism, Japan, 2010; http://www.mlit.go.jp/jidosha/jidosha_tk1_000003.html.
6. Based on National Association for Pupil Transportation http://www.napt.org/associations/3103/files/SBIC2007FactSheet.cfm.
7. California ZEBRA Electric School Bus Project; California Air Resources Board (2004).
8. This was a retrofitting project to repair malfunctioning electric buses. The incremental cost of replacing old batteries and other drive systems with new ones was $70,000 more than for a conventional diesel.
9. There are 535 electric recharging stations in the United States, compared to 161,000 conventional gas stations (U.S. Department of Energy, http://www.afdc.energy.gov/afdc/fuels/stations_counts.html).

10. The problems also apply to hybrid vehicles but are an especial concern for fully electric cars.
11. Once trains are electrified, the emission issues in the sector translate into the energy-sector efficiency problem (see figure 3.6).
12. http://www.eurostar.com.
13. It is assumed that B767 consumes 4,700 liter of fuel per hour on average (World Bank 2009a).
14. Though overloading would generate more emissions because overloading requires more power (see later in this chapter).
15. The distance from Johannesburg to Maputo is about 450 km; the distance to Durban is about 570 km.
16. Some studies have more detailed classifications; see, for example, OECD (2002b); Timilsina and Dulal (2009); and NSTIFC (2009). However, these four areas are most important for emissions reduction, and other measures can be considered as variations on these.
17. Advanced road or cordon pricing may also require the significant amount of costs to implement. For instance, the London system initially cost $275 million, and the annual operating costs are estimated at $158 million (NSTIFC 2009).
18. The elasticity was considered to be small, however, because of its small modal share at that time.
19. The price elasticities are –0.03 to –0.07 for those who are satisfied with the services and –0.26 to –0.37 for those who are not.
20. http://www.dieselnet.com/standards/eu/ghg_acea.php.
21. An inspection program may initially have a negative effect on emissions reduction, because it helps car owners to use their vehicles longer. Inspected cars are expected to generate fewer emissions than non-inspected cars but may generate more than brand-new vehicles (Yamamoto and others 2004).
22. This is a relatively successful case; most U.S. HOV lanes are underused, as will be discussed later.
23. Another view, however, is that reductions in size may make a vehicle more maneuverable, thereby reducing the potential for collision. The U.S. data contradict this hypothesis: smaller vehicles are actually involved in more collisions (National Academies 2002).

References

Amos, P., and L. Thompson. 2007. "Railways in Development: Global Round-Up 1996–2005." Transport Notes No. TRN-36, World Bank, Washington, DC.

Anable, J., B. Lane, and T. Kelay. 2006. "An Evidence Base Review of Public Attitudes to Climate Change and Transport Behaviour." U.K. Department for Transport, London.

Anas, A., and G. Timilsina. 2009a. "Lock-In Effects of Road Expansion on CO_2 Emissions: Results from a Core-Periphery Model of Beijing." Policy Research Working Paper 5017, World Bank, Washington, DC.

———. 2009b. "Impacts of Policy Instruments to Reduce Congestion and Emissions from Urban Transportation: The Case of Sao Paulo, Brazil." Policy Research Working Paper 5099, World Bank, Washington, DC.

Anable, J., B. Lane, and T. Kelay. 2006. *An Evidence Base Review of Public Attitudes to Climate Change and Transport Behaviour*. London: UK Department for Transport.

Arvis, J-F. 2005. "Transit and the Special Case of Landlocked Countries." In *Customs Modernization Handbook*, edited by L. De Wulf and S. Jose. Washington, DC: World Bank.

ATW Online. 2010. "American, Air France Conduct Green Transatlantic Flights." *Air Transport World Daily News*, April 5 2010.

Austin, D., and T. Dinan. 2005. "Clearing the Air: The Costs and Consequences of Higher CAFE Standards and Increased Gasoline Taxes." *Journal of Environmental Economics and Management* 50: 562–82.

Axsen, J., D. Mountain, and M. Jaccard. 2009. "Combining Stated and Revealed Choice Research to Simulate the Neighbor Effect: The Case of Hybrid-Electric Vehicles." *Resource and Energy Economics* 31: 221–38.

Bangkok Metro Public Company Limited (BMCL). 2010. *Annual Report 2009*.

Bonilla, D., and T. Foxon 2009. "Demand for New Car Fuel Economy in the UK, 1970–2005." *Journal of Transport Economics and Policy* 43: 55–83.

Brazil Institute. 2007. "The Global Dynamics of Biofuels: Potential Supply and Demand for Ethanol and Biodiesel in the Coming Decade." *Brazil Institute Special Report*, Issue No.3, Woodrow Wilson International Center for Scholars, Washington, DC. http://www.wilsoncenter.org/sites/default/files/Brazil_SR_e3.pdf.

California Air Resources Board. 2004. *Electric School Bus with ZEBRA Battery and Integrated Fast Charge: Final Technical Report*. California Air Resources Board ICAT Grant #01-1. Sacramento Municipal Utility District Electric Transportation Department.

Campbell, J. E., D. B. Lobell, and C. B. Field. 2009. "Supporting Online Material for Greater Transportation Energy and Ghg Offsets from Bioelectricity than Ethanol." *Science Express*. http://www.sciencemag.org/cgi/content/abstract/1168885v1.

Cervero, R., A. Golub, and B. Nee. 2007. "City CarShare: Longer-Term Travel-Demand and Car Ownership Impacts." *Transportation Research Record: Journal of the Transportation Research Board* 1992: 70–80. http://dx.doi.org/10.3141/1992-09.

Chamon, M., P. Mauro, and Y. Okawa. 2008. "Mass Car Ownership in the Emerging Market Giants." *Economic Policy* 23: 243–96.

Clerides, S., and T. Zachariadis. 2008. "The Effect of Standards and Fuel Prices on Automobile Fuel Economy: An International Analysis." *Energy Economics* 30: 2657–72.

Coad, Alex, Peter de Haan, and Julia Sophie Woersdorfer. 2009. "Consumer Support for Environmental Policies: An Application to Purchases of Green Cars, *Ecological Economics* 68 (7): 2078–86.

Corridor VIII Secretariat. 2007. *Corridor VIII: Pre-Feasibility Study on the Development of the Railway Axis*. Bari, Italy: Corridor VIII Secretariat.

Couto, A., and D. Graham. 2008. "The Impact of High-Speed Technology on Railway Demand." *Transportation* 35: 111–128.

Croezen, H. J., G. C. Gergsma, M. B. J. Otten, and M. P. J. van Valkengoed. 2010. *Biofuels: Indirect Land Use Change and Climate Impact*. Brussels: Transport and Environment.

Davis, S. C., and S. W. Diegel. 2004. "Transportation Energy Data Book: Edition 24." Report ORNL-6973. Oak Ridge, TN: Oak Ridge National Laboratory.

Defra. 2009. *2009 Guidelines to Defra/DECC's GHG Conversion Factors for Company Reporting: Methodology Paper for Emission Factors*. London: U.K. Department for Environment, Food and Rural Affairs.

Delucchi, M. 2007. "Do Motor-Vehicle Users in the US Pay Their Way?" *Transport Research: Part A* 41: 982–1003

Dissanayake, D., and T. Morikawa. 2010. "Investigating Household Vehicle Ownership, Mode Choice and Trip Sharing Decisions Using a Combined Revealed Preference/Stated Preference Nested Logit Model: Case Study in Bangkok Metropolitan Region." *Journal of Transport Geography* 18: 402–10.

Dreyfus, M., and K. Viscusi. 1995. "Rates of Time Preference and Consumer Valuations of Automobile Safety and Fuel Efficiency." *Journal of Law and Economics* 38: 79–105.

Eisinger, D. 2005. "Evaluating Inspection and Maintenance Programs: A Policy-Making Framework." *Journal of Air and Waste Management* 55: 147–62.

EC (European Commission). 2009. *EU Energy and Transport in Figures*. Directorate-General for Energy and Transport, European Commission, Brussels.

Echeverry, J., A. Ibáñez, A. Moya, and L. Hillón. 2005. "The Economics of Transmilenio, A Mass Transit System for Bogotá." *Economia* 5.2.

ECMT (European Conference of Ministries of Transport). 2003. *Implementing Sustainable Urban Transport Policies—National Reviews*. Paris: OECD.

Espino, R., J. de D. Ortúzar, and C. Román. 2007. Understanding Suburban Travel Demand: Flexible Modelling with Revealed and Stated Choice Data. Transportation Research Part A.

Faiz, A., B. B. Ale, and R. K. Nagarkoti. 2006. "The Role of Inspection and Maintenance in Controlling Vehicular Emissions in Kathmandu Valley, Nepal." *Atmospheric Environment* 40: 5967–75.

Fowles, R., and P. D. Loeb. 1995. "Effects of Policy-Related Variables on Traffic Fatalities: An Extreme Bounds Analysis Using Time-Series Data." *Southern Economic Journal* 62: 359–66.

Froidh, O. 2008. "Perspectives for a Future High-Speed Train in the Swedish Domestic Travel Market." *Journal of Transport Geography* 16: 268–277.

Frondel, M., J. Peters, and C. Vance. 2008. "Identifying the Rebound: Evidence from a German Household Panel." *The Energy Journal* 29: 145–63.

Frondel, M., and C. Vance. 2010. "Driving for Fun? Comparing the Effect of Fuel Prices on Weekday and Weekend Fuel Consumption." *Energy Economics* 32: 102–9.

Gao, O., and V. Kitirattragarn. 2008. "Taxi Owners' Buying Preferences of Hybrid-Electric Vehicles and Their Implications for Emissions in New York City." *Transportation Research Part A* 42: 1064–73.

Glazer, A., D. Klein, and C. Lave. 1995. "Clean on Paper, Dirty on the Road: Troubles with California's Smog Check." *Journal of Transport Economics and Policy* 29: 85–92.

Global Economic Research. 2010. *Global Auto Report*. Scotia Economics Canada. http://www.scotiabank.com.mx/resources/PDFs/G_economicas/Internacionales/2010/GAuto300310.pdf.

Godard, X. 2007. "Kyoto and the Double Trap for Public Transport." RTS, Issue No. 88, 2005.

Gonzalez-Savignat, M. 2004. "Competition in Air Transport: The Case of the High Speed Train." *Journal of Transport Economics and Policy* 38: 77–108.

GTZ (Gesellschaft für Technische Zusammenarbeit). 2009. *International Fuel Prices 2009*. Eschborn, Germany: Deutsche Gesellschaft für Technische Zusammenarbeit.

Harral, C., J. Sondhi, and G. Z. Chen. 2006. "Highway and Railway Development in India and China, 1992–2002." Transport Notes TRA-32, World Bank, Washington, DC.

Hensher, D., and T. Golob. 2008. "Bus Rapid Transit Systems: A Comparative Assessment." *Transportation* 35: 501–18.

Holmgren, J. 2007. "Meta-Analysis of Public Transport Demand." *Transportation Research Part A* 41: 1021–35.

Hou, J., J. Zhang, and Z. Zhao. 2002. *Clean Vehicle Action: R&D and Commercialization of Key Technologies*. Beijing: Office for Lead Group of Clean Vehicle Action.

Houston, David J., Lilliard E. Richardson, Jr., and Grant W. Neeley. 1995. "Legislating Traffic Safety." *Social Science Quarterly* 76: 328–45.

Hughes, J. E., C. R. Knittel, and D. Sperling. 2008. "Evidence of a Shift in the Short-Run Price Elasticity of Gasoline Demand." *The Energy Journal* 29 (1). http://web.mit.edu/knittel/www/papers/gas_demand_final.pdf.

Hughes, M. 2006. "High Speed Trains: A Second Golden Age for Railways?" *JE EAST Technical Review* 8: 42–51.

I-ce. 2000. *The Significance of Non-Motorised Transport for Developing Countries: Strategies for Policy Development*. Utrecht, the Netherlands: Interface for Cycling Expertise.

IEA (International Energy Agency). 2000. *Flexing the Link between Transport and Greenhouse Gas Emissions: A Path for the World Bank*. Paris: IEA.

INFRAERO. 2006. *Environmental Report 2005/2006*. Empresa Brasieira de Infraestrutura Aeroportuaria. INFRAERO Brazil. http://www.infraero.gov.br/images/stories/Infraero/Contas/ResAmbientais/relatorio ambiental 2006.pdf.

IPCC (Intergovernmental Panel on Climate Change). 2007. *Climate Change 2007: Synthesis Report*. Contribution of Working Groups I, II and II to the Fourth Assessment Report of the Intergovernmental Panel on Climate Change. Geneva, Switzerland: IPCC.

JBIC (Japan Bank for International Cooperation). 2003. *Ex Post Evaluation Report on ODA Loan Projects 2003*. Tokyo.

———. 2005. *Post Evaluation Report on ODA Loan Projects 2005*. Tokyo.

———. 2006. *Post Evaluation Report on ODA Loan Projects 2006*. Tokyo.

———. 2008. *Post Evaluation Report on ODA Loan Projects 2008*. Tokyo.

JICA (Japan International Cooperation Agency). 2008. *Annual Evaluation Report 2008*. Tokyo.

Johnson, T., C. Alatorre, Z. Romo, and F. Liu. 2010. *Low-Carbon Development for Mexico*. Washington, DC: World Bank.

JR East. 2009. *Sustainability Report 2009: Aiming for Sustainable Society*. Tokyo: JR East Group.

Kim, H. S., and E. Kim. 2004. "Effects of Public Transit on Automobile Ownership and Use in Households of the USA." *Review of Urban and Regional Development Studies* 16: 245–62.

Kleit, A. 2004. "Impacts of Long-Range Increases in the Corporate Average Fuel Economy (CAFE) Standard." *Economic Inquiry* 42: 279–94.

Kojima, M., and T. Johnson. 2005. *Potential for Biofuels for Transport in Developing Countries*. Energy Sector Management Assistance Programme (ESMAP). Washington, DC: World Bank.

———. 2006. *Potential for Biofuels for Transport in Developing Countries*. ESMAP Knowledge Exchange Series No. 4. Washington, DC: World Bank.

Kojima, M., R. Bacon, and S. Bhattacharya. 2010. *Expenditure of Low-Income Households on Energy: Evidence from Africa and Asia*. Extractive Industry Series. Washington, DC: IFC; World Bank.

Lave, C., and P. Elias. 1997. "Resource Allocation in Public Policy: the Effects of the 65-mph Speed Limit." *Economic Inquiry* 35: 614–20.

Lecocq, F., and Shalizi, Z. 2009. "Climate Change and the Economics of Targeted Mitigation in Sectors with Long-Lived Captial Stock." Policy Research Working Paper 5063, World Bank, Washington, DC.

Litman, T. 2005. "Transportation Land Valuation: Evaluating Policies and Practices That Affect the Amount of Land Devoted to Transportation Facilities." Victoria Transport Policy Institute, Victoria, BC, Canada.

Londono-Kent, P. 2009. "Road Freight." In *Freight Transport for Development Toolkit*. The Transport Research Support program. Washington, DC: World Bank.

Macedo, I. d. C., M. R L. V. Lea, and J. E. A. R. da Silva. 2004. *Assessment of Greenhouse Gas Emissions in the Production and Use of Fuel Ethanol in Brazil*. Government of the State of Sao Paolo, Brazil. http://www.wilsoncenter.org/sites/default/files/brazil.unicamp.macedo.greenhousegas.pdf.

Mandori-Perrott, C. 2010. *Private Sector Participation in Light Rail Light Metro Transit Initiative*. Washington, DC: World Bank and Public-Private Infrastructure Advisory Facility.

Martin, J. C., and G. Nombela. 2007. "Microeconomic Impacts of Investments in High Speed Trains in Spain." *Annals of Regional Science* 41: 715–33.

Mau, P., J. Eyzafuirre, M. Jaccard, C. Collins-Dodd, and K. Tiedemann. 2008. "The 'Neighbor Effect': Simulating Dynamics in Consumer Preferences for New Vehicle Technologies." *Ecological Economics* 68: 504–16.

McKinnon, A., and Y. Ge. 2006. "The Potential for Reducing Empty Running by Trucks: A Retrospective Analysis." *International Journal of Physical Distribution and Logistics Management* 36: 391–410.

Merrell, D., M. Poitras, and D. Sutter. 1999. "The Effectiveness of Vehicle Safety Inspections: An Analysis Using Panel Data." *Southern Economic Journal* 65: 571–83.

METI (Ministry of Economy, Trade and Industry), Japan, 2006. http://www.meti.go.jp/english/index.html.

Miravete, E., and M. Moral. 2009. "Qualitative Effects of Cash-for-Clunkers Programs." Centre for Economic Policy Research Discussion Paper Series 7517, London.

National Academies. 2002. *Effectiveness and Impact of Corporate Average Fuel Economy (CAFE) Standards*. Washington, DC: The National Academy of Sciences.

NBRTI (National Bus Rapid Transit Institute). 2006. Applicability of Bogota's TransMilenio BRT System to the United States—Final Report. Prepared for the U.S. Department of Transportation, Federal Transit Administration, Washington, DC.

NSTIFC (National Surface Transportation Infrastructure Financing Commission). 2009. *Paying Our Way: A New Framework for Transportation Finance*. Washington, DC: NSTIFC.

NPN (National Petroleum News). 2008. *MarketFacts 2008*. http://www.npnweb.com/me2/dirmod.asp?sid=A79131211D8846B1A33169AF72F78511&nm=Market+Data&type=MultiPublishing&mod=PublishingTitles&mid=8F3A7027421841978F18BE895F87F791&tier=4&id=2E2D50EEA5EF4382B431FB101A075383.

OECD (Organisation for Economic Co-operation and Development). 2000. *Environmental Effects of Liberalising Fossil Fuels Trade: Results from the OECD Green Model*. Trade Directorate Environment Directorate, Paris: OECD. http://search.oecd.org/officialdocuments/displaydocumentpdf/?doclanguage=en&cote=com/td/env(2000)38/final.

OECD (Organisation for Economic Co-operation and Development). 2002a. *Strategies to Reduce Greenhouse Gas Emissions from Road Transport: Analytical Methods*. Paris: OECD.

———. 2002b. *Road Travel Demand: Meeting the Challenge*. Paris: OECD.

———. 2002c. *Benchmarking Intermodal Freight Transport*. Paris: OECD.

———. 2004. *OECD Observer* 246/247, (December–January). http://www.oecdobserver.org/news/archivestory.php/aid/1505/Used_goods_trade.html.

OECD (Organisation for Economic Co-operation and Development)/IEA (International Energy Agency). 2004. *Oil Crises and Climate Challenges: 30 Years of Energy Use in IEA Countries*. Paris: OECD/IEA.

———. 2009. *Transport, Energy and CO_2: Moving toward Sustainability*. Paris: OECD/IEA.

Ornetzeder, M., E. Hertwich, K. Hubacek, K. Korytarova, and W. Haas. 2008. "The Environmental Effect of Car-Free Housing: A Case in Vienna." *Ecological Economics* 65: 516–30.

Pandey, R. 2006. "Looking beyond Inspection and Maintenance in Reducing Pollution from In-Use Vehicles." *Environmental Economics and Policy Studies* 7: 435–57.

Park, S., and G. Zhao. 2010. "An Estimation of U.S. Gasoline Demand: A Smooth Time-Varying Cointegration Approach." *Energy Economics* 32: 110–20.

Parry, I., M. Walls, and W. Harrington. 2007. "Automobile Externalities and Policies." *Journal of Economic Literature* 45: 373–99.

Pelletiere, D., and K. Reinert. 2006. "World Trade in Used Automobiles: A Gravity Analysis of Japanese and US exports." *Asian Economic Journal* 20: 161–72.

Poole, A. 2008. *The Procurement of Energy Efficiency Performance Contracts in Brazil's Public Sector*. Mimeograph.

Potoglou, D., P. Kanaroglou. 2007. "Household Demand and Willingness to Pay for Clean Vehicles." *Transportation Research: Part D* 12: 264–74.

———. 2008. "Modelling Car Ownership in Urban Areas: A Case Study of Hamilton, Canada." *Journal of Transport Geography* 16: 42–54.

Prasad, N., F. Ranghieri, F. Shah, Z. Trohanis, E. Kessler, and R. Sinha. 2009. *Climate Resilient Cities: A Primer on Reducing Vulnerabilities to Disasters*. Washington, DC: World Bank.

Ribeiro, S. K., and A. A. de Abreu. 2008. "Brazilian Transport Initiatives with GHG Reductions as a Co-Benefit." *Climate Policy* 8: 220–40.

Rotaris, L., R. Danielis, E. Marcucci, and J. Massiani. 2010. "The Urban Road Pricing Scheme to Curb Pollution in Milan, Italy: Description, Impacts and Preliminary Cost-Benefit Analysis Assessment." *Transport Research: Part A* 44: 359–75.

Sangkapichai, M., and J-D Saphores. 2009. "Why Are Californians Interested in Hybrid Cars?" *Journal of Environmental Planning and Management* 52: 79–96.

Schrank, D., and T. Lomax. 2005. *The 2005 Urban Mobility Report*. Texas Transportation Institute, Texas A&M University, TX.

Scuffham, P.A. 2003. Economic Factors and Traffic Crashes in New Zealand." *Applied Economics* 35.

Searchinger, T. 2009. "Evaluating Biofuels: The Consequences of Using Land to Make Fuel." Brussels Forum Paper Series, the German Marshall Fund of the United States, Washington, DC.

Singh, J., D. Limaye, B. Henderson, and X. Shi. 2010. *Public Procurement of Energy Efficiency Services*. Washington, DC: World Bank.

Small, K., and K. Van Dender. 2007. "Fuel Efficiency and Motor Vehicle Travel: The Declining Rebound Effect." *Energy Journal* 28: 25–51.

Sohn, K., and J. Yun. 2009. "Separation of Car-Dependent Commuters from Normal-Choice Riders in Mode-Choice" Analysis. *Transportation* 36: 423–36.

Solomon, B., and N. Johnson. 2009. "Valuing Climate Protection through Willingness to Pay for Biomass Ethanol." *Ecological Economics* 68: 2137–44.

SSATP (Sub-Saharan Africa Transport Policy Program). 2005. "Non-Motorized Transport in African Cities: Lessons from Experience in Kenya and Tanzania." SSATP Working Paper No. 80, World Bank, Washington, DC.

Suzuki, H., A. Dastur, S. Moffatt, and N. Yabuki. 2009. *Eco^2 Cities: Ecological Cities as Economic Cities*. Washington, DC: World Bank.

Swait, J., and G. Eskeland. 1995. "Travel Mode Substitution in São Paulo: Estimates and Implications for Air Pollution Control." Policy Research Working Paper 1437, World Bank, Washington, DC.

Takeuchi, A., M. Cropper, and A. Bento. 2007. "The Impact of Policies to Control Motor Vehicle Emissions in Mumbai, India." *Journal of Regional Science* 47: 27–46.

Tan, L. H. 2001. "Rationing Rules and Outcomes: The Experience of Singapore's Vehicle Quota System." IMF Working Paper No. 01-136, International Monetary Fund, Washington, DC. http://www.imf.org/external/pubs/ft/wp/2001/wp01136.pdf.

Teisl, M., J. Rubin, and C. Noblet. 2008. "Non-Dirty Dancing? Interactions between Eco-Labels and Consumers." *Journal of Economic Psychology* 29: 140–59.

Thanesuen, S., S. Kagaya, and K-e Uchida. 2006. "Sustainable Speed Limit with Optimal User Life Cycle Cost." *Studies in Regional Science* 36: 487–501.

Timilsina, G., and H. Dulal. 2009. "A Review of Regulatory Instruments to Control Environmental Externalities from the Transport Sector." Policy Research Working Paper 4867, World Bank, Washington, DC.

Transportation Research Board. 2010. *Transportation Research Circular E-C143: Modal Primer on Greenhouse Gas and Energy Issues for Transportation*. Washington, DC: Transportation Research Board.

UIC (International Union of Railways). 2006. *Rail Diesel Emissions: Facts and Challenges*. Paris: UIC.

———. 2007. *Railway and Biofuel*. Paris: UIC.

U.S. Department of Energy. 2010. "Transportation Energy Data Book." Edition 29, Oak Ridge National Laboratory, Oak Ridge, Tennessee. http://info.ornl.gov/sites/publications/files/pub24318.pdf.

U.S. DOT (U.S. Department of Transportation)/DOE (Department of Energy)/EPA (Environmental Protection Agency). 2002. *Report to Congress: Effects of the Alternative Motor Fuels Act CAFE Incentives Policy*. Washington, DC: U.S. DOT/DOE/EPA.

Wang, M., C. Saricks, and D. Santini. 1999. "Effects of Fuel Ethanol Use on Fuel-Cycle Energy and Greenhouse Gas Emissions." Center for Transportation Research, Argonne National Laboratory, Argonne, IL. http://www.transportation.anl.gov/pdfs/TA/58.pdf.

WBCSD (World Business Council for Sustainable Development). 2004. *IEA/SMP Global Transport Model, Mobility 2030: Meeting Challenges to Sustainability*. Geneva, Switzerland: WBCSD.

Woldeamanuel, M., R. Cyganski, A. Schulz, and A. Justen. 2009. "Variation of Households' Car Ownership Across Time: Application of a Panel Data Model." *Transportation* 36: 371–87.

World Bank. 1978. "Relieving Traffic Congestion: The Singapore Area License Scheme." World Bank Staff Working Paper 281, World Bank, Washington, DC.

———. 2006. "Albania: Restructuring Public Expenditure to Sustain Growth: A Public Expenditure and Institutional Review." Report No. 36453-AL, World Bank, Washington, DC.

———. 2007. *ICR for Trade and Transport Facilitation in South East Europe Project*. Washington, DC: World Bank.

———. 2008a. *World Development Report 2008: Agriculture for Development*. Washington, DC: World Bank.

———. 2008b. *Safe, Clean, and Affordable Transport for Development: The World Bank Group's Transport Business Strategy for 2008–2012*. Washington, DC: World Bank.

———. 2009a. "Air freight: A Market Study with Implications for Landlocked Countries." Transport Papers TP-26, World Bank, Washington, DC.

———. 2009b. *World Development Report 2009: Reshaping Economic Geography*. Washington, DC: World Bank.

———. 2010a. *World Development Report 2010: Development and Climate Change*. Washington, DC: World Bank.

———. 2010b. *A City-Wide Approach to Carbon Finance*. Washington, DC: World Bank.

———. 2010c. "Project Appraisal Document for Railway Modernization Project in Ukraine." Report No. 525310UA, World Bank, Washington, DC.

World Bank/ESMAP. 2002. *Urban Air Pollution: Tackling Diesel Emissions from In-Use Vehicles*. South Asia Urban Air Quality Management Briefing Note 10, World Bank and ESMAP, Washington, DC.

World Economic Forum. 2009. "The Global Competitiveness Report 2009–2010." World Economic Forum Geneva, Switzerland. http://www3.weforum.org/docs/WEF_GlobalCompetitivenessReport_2009-10.pdf.

Yamamoto, T., J-L Madre, and R. Kitamura. 2004. "An Analysis of the Effects of French Vehicle Inspection Program and Grant for Scrappage on Household Vehicle Trasaction." *Transport Research: Part B* 38: 905–26.

Zachariadis, T. 2006. "On the Baseline Evolution of Automobile Fuel Economy in Europe." *Energy Policy* 34: 1773–85.

Zhao, J. 2006. "Whither the Car? China's Automobile Industry and Cleaner Vehicle Technologies." *Development and Change* 37: 121–44.

CHAPTER 4

Climate-Resilient Investment in Transport

Mitigating and adapting transport will require considerable financing Individuals will pay a large part of the mitigation costs by buying energy-efficient vehicles, but governments must still cover incremental investment for adapting roads. And developing countries face large transport infrastructure deficits regardless of climate change.

Available funding, such as carbon financing and international assistance, cannot cover the adaptation and mitigation costs. Mitigation, including advanced technologies and electric and fuel cell cars, is particularly costly and will remain so for some time.

Factoring in all the benefits of mitigation measures dramatically alters the economics of transport investment. Accounting for negative externalities, such as congestion and pollution, could both reduce emissions and encourage policymakers to allocate more resources to transport.

Some measures, such as fuel taxation and road user charges, could bring in new resources relatively quickly. Minimizing harmful subsidies would also help. Immediate action is necessary; putting new institutions in place takes time and change becomes more costly once an economy is locked into high-carbon transport.

Financing Mitigation and Adaptation

Incremental costs for adaptation and mitigation are significant. Although future climate change, technology, and policy regimes may be uncertain, the costs are undoubtedly far beyond the resources of the developing world, even using the most conservative assumptions.

Investment in Mitigation
Few of the models that forecast future energy use and green house gas (GHG) emissions analyze the transport sector in detail. What role transport will play in emission reduction is therefore uncertain, as is the rate at which advanced transport technologies can be diffused. The International Energy Agency (IEA)

and the Pacific Northwest National Laboratory (PNNL) have markedly different views. While IEA estimates that transport can *reduce* emissions by 30 percent, PNNL predicts a 47 percent *increase* (table 4.1). The IEA model assumes that fuel use and CO_2 emissions/km by new vehicles could be cut 30 percent worldwide by 2020 and 50 percent by 2050; it also assumes that 50 million plug-in hybrid and electric vehicles will be sold by 2050 and that hydrogen fuel cell cars will be commercialized by 2020 and will promptly be widely distributed (OECD/IEA 2009b). Given current progress, those assumptions are optimistic.

The PNNL model assumes more limited technology diffusion, with only the United States adopting advanced vehicle technologies (plug-in hybrids and electric vehicles). Elsewhere, conventional internal combustion engines would remain dominant; their fuel efficiency is assumed to be 35–37 mpg. This model uses a discrete choice analysis (Clarke and Edmonds 1993) that reflects people's unwillingness to adopt vehicles that though more efficient are more expensive.

Depending on the model, mitigation costs vary substantially. Few models report sectoral emission reductions, including transport. The IEA estimates incremental investment for transport mitigation at $237 billion annually (table 4.2). This assumes international policies that limit GHG gases to 450 parts per million of carbon dioxide (CO_2) equivalent. It also accounts for about 45 percent of total additional mitigation investment needed in all sectors (buildings, power plants, industry, and biofuels supply).[1]

Table 4.1 Reduction of Energy-Related Emissions by 2050, by Sector

Sector	Estimated carbon to be removed (percent)	
	IEA	MiniCam[a]
Power	−71	−87
Building	−41	−50
Transport	**−30**	**47**
Industry	−21	−71
Total	−50	−50

Source: World Bank 2010a.
Note: IEA = International Energy Agency.
a. MiniCam is the Pacific Northwest National Laboratory model.

Table 4.2 Average Annual Incremental Mitigation Investment by 2030

	OECD/IEA (2009)		World Bank (2010)			
			McKinsey & Company		PNNL	
	$ billion	%	$ billion	%	$ billion	%
Total	525	100.0	563	100.0	384	100.0
Of which, infrastructure	324	61.7	—	—	—	—
Of which, transport	237	45.0	—	—	—	—
Of which, passenger cars	168	31.9	—	—	—	—

Sources: OECD/IEA 2009b; World Bank 2010a.
Note: — = not available, IEA = International Energy Agency, PNNL = Pacific Northwest National Laboratory.

The IEA model assumes that most mitigation investment (figure 4.1) will go into buying hybrid and electric cars. It focuses on changes in car technologies rather than behavior and modal shifts and may underestimate transport's capacity to reduce emissions (box 4.1). As the cost of low-carbon transport technology decreases and income increases, developing countries are expected to invest $52–$159 billion a year to reduce emissions (figure 4.2).[2]

Investment in Adaptation

Adaptation costs refer to the incremental investment needed to adapt to climate change. For infrastructure, the cost is calculated by multiplying baseline

Figure 4.1 Cumulative Incremental Transport Investment by Mode

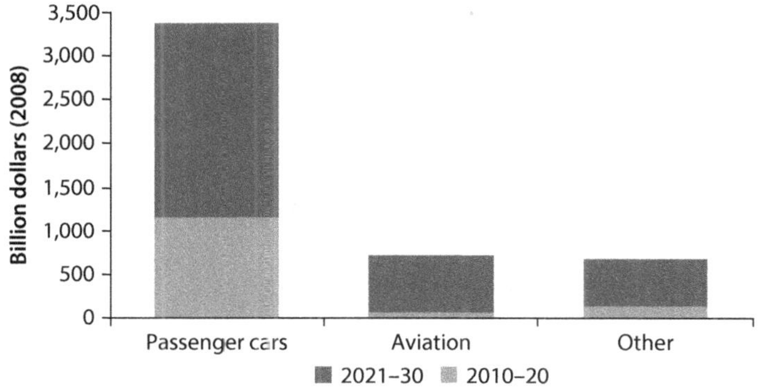

Source: OECD/IEA 2009b, figure 7.9, p. 275.

Box 4.1 IEA Assumptions in Estimating Mitigation Investment Needs

The International Energy Agency model, which emphasizes changes in car technologies, assumes that the cost of buying more efficient vehicles represents most of the additional mitigation cost. Engine-fuel efficiency standards for carbon dioxide (CO_2) emissions or fuel consumption per unit of service of passenger light-duty vehicles (fleet averages) for 2030 are assumed to be 80 $grCO_2$/km for Organisation for Economic Co-operation and Development and other European Union countries, 90 $grCO_2$/km for other major economies (Brazil, China, South Africa, the Russian Federation, and the Middle East), and 110 $grCO_2$/km for other countries. The scenario assumes that more efficient vehicles will increase their market share regardless of price: hybrid vehicles to 32 percent by 2020 and 29 percent by 2030, plug-in hybrids to 12 percent by 2020 and 21 percent by 2030, and electric vehicles to 12 percent by 2020 and 17 percent by 2030.

This scenario assumes fuel prices will hold steady, so that increases in fuel taxes would compensate for decreasing demand and downward pressure on fuel prices. It does not account for consumer reaction, regardless of fuel prices, except in terms of choices of vehicle type. Savings in transport CO_2 emissions would be 18 percent compared with the baseline and could slightly increase over time.

Figure 4.2 Cumulative Incremental Transport Investment by Regions and Sectors

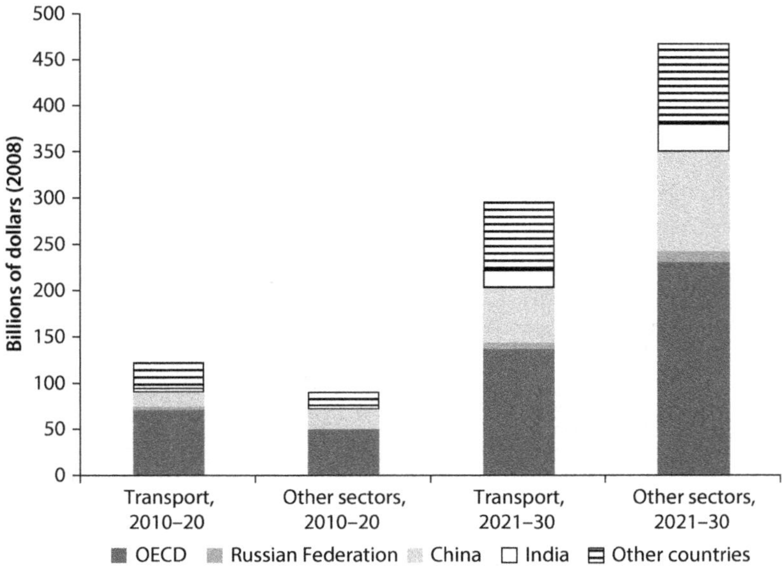

Source: OECD/IEA 2009b.
Note: OECD = Organisation for Economic Co-operation and Development.

Table 4.3 Average Annual Incremental Adaptation Cost through 2050

	World Bank (2010c) Delta-p only				UNFCCC (2007)	
	NCAR scenario		CSIRO scenario			
	$ billion	%	$ billion	%	$ billion	%
Total	89.6	100.0	77.7	100.0	28–67	100.0
Of which, infrastructure	29.5	32.9	13.5	17.4	2–41	—
Of which, transport	7.2	8.0	—	—	—	—
Of which, roads	6.3	7.0	—	—	—	—

Sources: UNFCCC 2007; World Bank 2010c.
Note: — = not available, CSIRO = Commonwealth Scientific and Industrial Research Organization, NCAR = National Center for Atmospheric Research, UNFCCC = United Nations Framework Convention on Climate Change.

projections of investment needs by the share of new investment vulnerable to climate change.[3] Because estimates of baseline infrastructure needs vary widely, particularly in developing countries, estimated adaptation costs also vary. With global warming of 2° C, total investment in transport adaptation for the world economy is an estimated $28–$100 billion a year (table 4.3). The World Bank's Economics of Adaptation to Climate Change (EACC) study offers two estimates based the different scenarios of the National Center for Atmospheric Research (NCAR) and the Commonwealth Scientific and Industrial Research Organization (CSIRO). Both estimates are higher than that of the UNFCCC (2007), which uses a narrower definition of adaptation needs (box 4.2).

Box 4.2 Methods of Estimating Adaptation Investment Needs

United Nations Framework Convention on Climate Change (UNFCCC) (2007) does not account for incremental operation and maintenance costs for existing infrastructure. It first estimates gross fixed infrastructure capital formation in 2030 at $22.27 trillion, three times the 2000 investment, based on annual growth of 5–6 percent. It then estimates how much of the new investment is vulnerable to climate change using insurance data on weather-related losses. Insurance company Munich Re counts 0.7 percent of all infrastructure as vulnerable, the Association of British Insurers (ABI) says 2.7 percent. Thus, estimates of vulnerable new investment in 2030 range from $153 billion to $650 billion. The UNFCCC study assumes that climate-proof infrastructure would cost 5–20 percent more, with incremental adaptation costs of $8–$31 billion using Munich Re data or $33–$130 billion using ABI data.

The Economics of Adaptation to Climate Change (EACC) study takes a different approach. It projects stocks of major types of infrastructure from 2010 to 2050, including roads, rail, and ports. Adaptation cost is computed as the additional cost of constructing, operating, and maintaining baseline infrastructure under the climate conditions projected by the National Center for Atmospheric Research (NCAR) and the Commonwealth Scientific and Industrial Research Organization (CSIRO).

The EACC study focuses on price and cost changes for fixed quantities of infrastructure (referred to as a delta-P component) but also calculates costs based on the impact of climate change on infrastructure service demand (delta Q component), including operating and maintenance costs. The NCAR model projects additional cost and maintenance expenditures for all sectors at $36.8 billion annually; the CSIRO model projects $28.6 billion.

Sources: Parry and Timilsina 2009; World Bank 2010c.

Infrastructure represents the largest share of adaptation costs. In the EACC model, infrastructure is 20–30 percent of the total, $14–$30 billion a year; this is consistent with the UNFCCC (2007). Infrastructure is also vulnerable to precipitation and humidity. The NCAR model assumes the wettest weather.

Adaptation needs for transport, mostly roads, are an estimated $7 billion a year for the next 40 years, 8 percent of total adaptation costs. Including maintenance costs raises the number to $10 billion—still much lower than estimated mitigation costs of $237 billion a year.

Adaptation and Development Deficits

Many adaptation cost estimates, even in the EACC study, ignore the close link between adaptation and development. In theory it is correct to distinguish the incremental cost of new climate-proofing infrastructure investment (the development deficit)[4] from the gap between current infrastructure and projected infrastructure needs to achieve a baseline (the adaptation deficit; World Bank 2010c). In addition, in theory adaptation costs are incremental and not directly related to development deficits. Therefore, most studies report only adaptation deficits.

However, many developing countries still have large infrastructure deficits, especially inadequate roads (World Bank 2008). Developing countries have only 5–30 percent of the paved roads per capita of high-income countries (figure 4.3). More than half their roads are unpaved, poorly maintained, and vulnerable to weather (ADB 2007).

Similarly, many railway assets, including locomotives, need to be upgraded to developed-country standards (World Bank 2005; JBIC 2006; World Bank 2010d). In Africa nearly half the railways are in urgent need of rehabilitation (Briceno-Garmendia, Smits, and Foster 2008). Airports have not yet reached international standards; some countries lack airport infrastructure, facilities, and oversight to enforce compliance with international safety and security standards (World Bank 2010e). According to the U.S. Civil Aviation Safety Assessment, about one-third of developing countries do not meet international standards and practices recommended for aircraft operations and maintenance (table 4.4).[5]

If development deficits are not taken into account, estimates for transport will be unrealistically low—a major criticism of the current estimation approach

Figure 4.3 Road Network and Population by Region, 2005

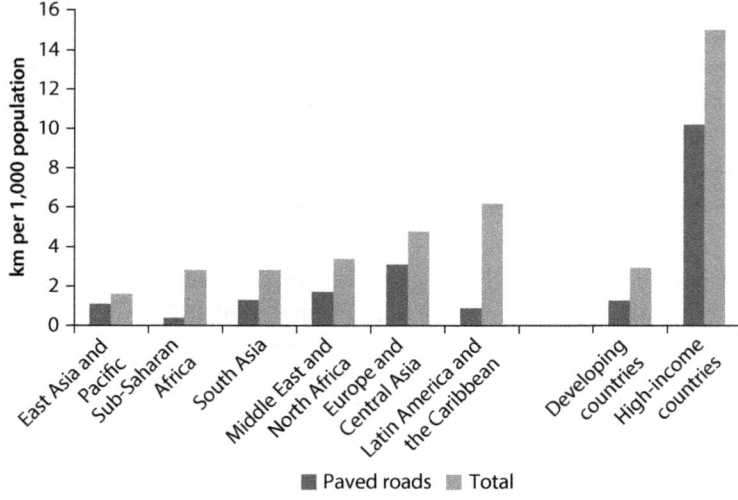

Source: World Bank 2008.

Table 4.4 U.S. Civil Aviation Safety Assessment, 2008

	Countries assessed	Countries meeting ICAO standards	%
High-income countries	45	43	95.6
Developing countries	62	42	67.7
Upper middle-income countries	27	24	88.9
Lower middle-income countries	27	16	59.3
Low-income countries	8	2	25.0

Source: U.S. Federal Aviation Administration.
Note: ICAO = International Civil Aviation Organization.

Climate-Resilient Investment in Transport

Table 4.5 Annual Adaptation and Infrastructure Deficits

	Parry and Timilsina (2009)		World Bank 2010c[a]			
	Infrastructure[b]		Infrastructure[c]		Transport only[d]	
	Annual average infrastructure deficit	Infrastructure adaptation cost	Baseline spending	Incremental adaptation investment	Baseline spending	Incremental adaptation investment
Asia	217.5	10.9–43.5	956.0	18.0	132.6	3.5
Latin America and the Caribbean	37.2	1.9–7.4	283.8	3.5	49.7	1.1
Africa	61.6	3.1–12.3	130.1	3.4	40.2	0.9
Others	—	—	531.3	4.6	89.3	1.7
Total	316.3	15.9–63.2	1,900.2	29.5	309.8	7.2

Sources: Parry and Timilsina 2009; World Bank 2010c.
Note: — = not available.
a. Based on the National Center for Atmospheric Research (NCAR) climate scenario.
b. Including housing and infrastructure.
c. Including health, education, power and wire, road, urban, water and sewage, and other transport infrastructure.
d. Including road and other transport.

(Satterthwaite and Dodman 2009). This could be particularly problematic for poorer countries with enormous development deficits.

Estimates of infrastructure deficits are sensitive to models and assumed goals and vary significantly, from $316 billion a year to achieve the Millennium Development Goals to annual baseline spending of $1,900 billion, which includes nonconventional infrastructure, such as health, education, and urban (table 4.5). For transport alone, including roads, estimated investment needs are $310 billion (World Bank 2010c). Estimated incremental adaptation costs are $7.2 billion a year, 2.3 percent of total investment.

Regardless of model, the incremental cost of adaptation is only a small fraction of total transport investment needs. A case study using highway development software found that in a "do the minimum" scenario the incremental road adaptation cost would be only 2 percent of total investment and maintenance costs (box 4.3). The case study also shows that regardless of climate change, more frequent road maintenance reduces not only maintenance costs but also eventual adaptation costs. Thus, timely building and maintenance of roads is a robust investment decision that should be a priority.

Insufficient Financing Available

At present the most important mechanism for financing mitigation and adaptation may be carbon markets. There are also a few other resources available internationally, but these mostly go to areas other than transport.

Carbon Markets

The Kyoto Protocol created three market mechanisms: emissions trading, the clean development mechanism (CDM), and the joint implementation mechanism. These offer developed countries an opportunity to buy carbon credits and

Box 4.3 A Numerical Example of Road Management: Applying HDM-4

The Highway Development and Management Model (HDM-4) version 2 is software that evaluates how climate affects highway development and maintenance. First, climate determines annual road deterioration. Humidity and low temperatures, for instance, quickly wear down road surfaces and shoulders. Second, seasonality and drainage affect road pavement strength, represented by the structural number of the pavement (SNP). SNP is calculated from the thickness of the base or surfacing layer and the depth of each layer from the top of the sub-base. It is reduced by seasonality, which is measured by the length of the wet season: water infiltrates cracks and joints, fracturing the pavement and increasing road roughness. Drainage, determined by the shape and type of drain, functions to reduce the length of the wet season. SNP is therefore a function of not only average temperature and precipitation but also seasonality and drainage.

In the case of a 10-km two-lane primary bituminous road in a tropical area, project life is assumed to be 20 years. The discount rate is 12 percent. There are two strategies. One is to do the minimum with routine pothole patching and edge treatment without major surface treatment until the International Roughness Index (IRI) reaches 10 m/km. The other is to do maintenance more often—before the surface is severely damaged—and assumes structural overlay at a lower IRI of 4.5 m/km, with routine pothole patching and edge treatment.

There are also two climate scenarios. One is the actual tropical condition; the other assumes more precipitation and humidity, which would increase the roughness environmental coefficient (road deterioration rate) from 2 to 2.5 percent.

In either scenario frequent maintenance is more cost-effective. Under actual weather conditions, total maintenance savings would be about 4 percent if maintenance were more

Figure B4.3.1 Road Maintenance Costs, Actual Maintenance, and Climate Change: An Example

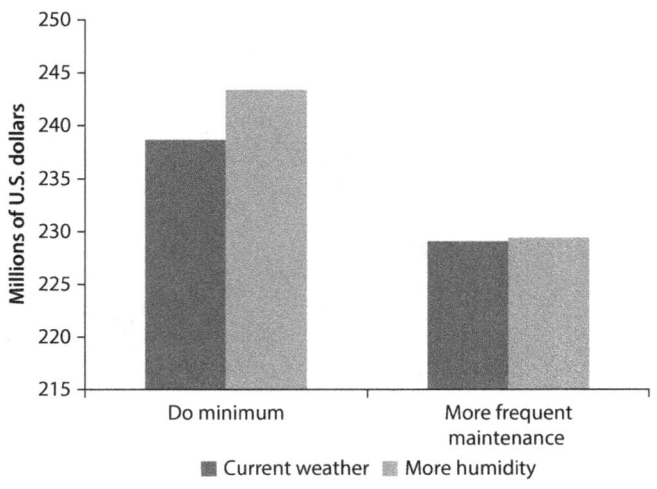

box continues next page

Box 4.3 A Numerical Example of Road Management: Applying HDM-4 *(continued)*

frequent. Over a longer period, the savings could be even greater. With the alternative weather scenario, savings would be 6 percent (figure B4.3.1).

Climate change would increase road maintenance costs only minimally, especially if the road were maintained properly. In the "do the minimum" scenario, the cost would increase by 2 percent. If the road were more frequently maintained, the cost would increase by only 1 percent. Thus, adaptation costs for roads would likely remain small relative to total investment needs, and additional costs could be minimized by appropriate maintenance.

Figure 4.4 Potential Annual Emission Reduction (Gt CO_2eq)

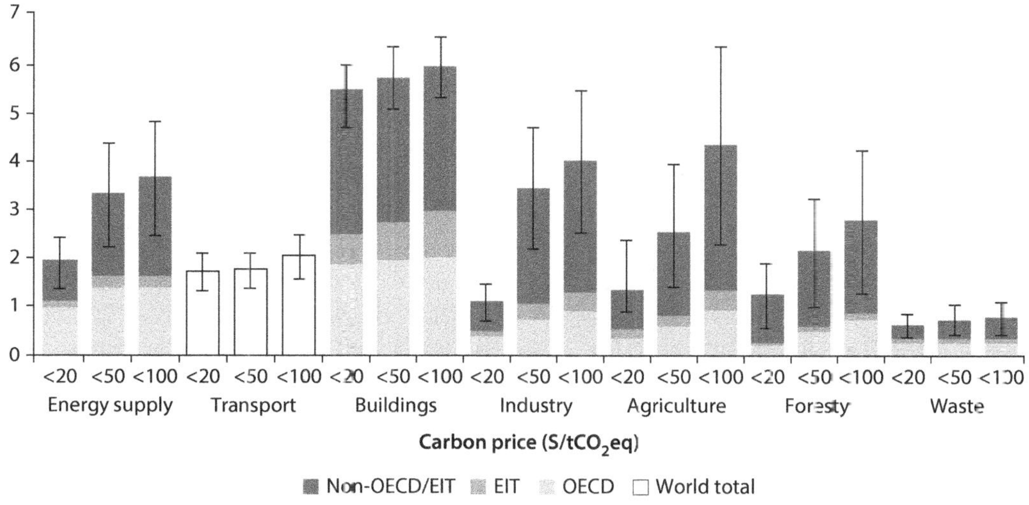

Source: World Bank 2010a.
Note: The ranges for global economic potentials as assessed in each sector are shown by black vertical lines. It's not just about energy: At high carbon prices the combined mitigation potential of agriculture and forestry is greater than that of other individual sectors of the economy. EIT = economies in transition, OECD = Organisation for Economic Co-operation and Development.

avoid more costly mitigation measures to meet their emission reduction commitments. They offer developing countries incentives for mitigation, can facilitate funding, and give access to emerging clean technologies. From 2000 to 2005 the CDM, one of the most promising mechanisms,[6] had more than 4,200 projects in the pipeline, with 2,246 of these approved.

However, CDM has only three registered transport projects: the Bogotá TransMilenio (BRT); installation of low-GHG rolling stock in rapid transit systems in Delhi; and the Cable Cars Metro in Medellin. These are expected to reduce emissions respectively by 246,563, 41,160, and 1,729 tons of CO_2eq. Even with fairly high carbon prices, it is unlikely that the private sector will be induced to adopt sufficient low-carbon transport technologies, which are expensive and difficult to commercialize (World Bank 2010a; figure 4.4). The limited impact of carbon markets may also be attributable to the current rigid framework for calculating emissions savings.[7] While mitigation intervention could help the carbon market mechanism, institutional reforms are needed if mitigation is to be significant.

Other International Funding Sources

Transport claims only a small share of other international funding. The Global Environment Facility (GEF), established in 1991 at the Rio Convention on Sustainable Development, commits about $250 million a year—largely in the form of grants to developing countries that are parties to the UNFCCC—in support of energy efficiency, renewable energy, new clean energy technology, and sustainable transport projects (table 4.6). In the past 20 years, the GEF has approved only 28 transport projects, 3.4 percent of the total; funding has been slightly higher at about 6.4 percent. On average, the GEF grant mechanism has mobilized about $120 million a year for transport, including cofinancing, but the sector needs $240 billion for mitigation[8] and $7–$10 billion for adaptation and it also needs to make up a transport development deficit of $310 billion.

Climate Investment Funds (CIF) is a family of funds devoted to climate change initiatives. Established in 2008, it is hosted by the World Bank and implemented by the Multilateral Development Bank. The Clean Technology Fund (CTF) is one of the most important funds, providing some grants, concessional loans, and partial risk guarantees of as much as $200 million per project to help countries scale up clean technology initiatives (table 4.7).[9] On average, 16 percent of CTF funding has been allocated to transport, although this varies significantly by country; the Colombia investment plan alone accounts for more than 77 percent. Transport is among the priority sectors in half the CTF investment plans.

Table 4.6 Global Environment Facility Funding, 1991–2010

	Projects approved		GEF grant		Cofinancing		Total	
	Number	Share (%)	$ Million	Share (%)	$ Million	Share (%)	$ Million	Share (%)
Transport	28	3.4	182.4	6.4	2,186.1	12.1	2,368.5	11.3
Other sectors	792	96.6	2,654.7	93.6	15,846.6	87.9	18,501.2	88.7
Total	820	100.0	2,837.1	100.0	18,032.6	100.0	20,869.7	100.0

Source: GEF project database.
Note: GEF = Global Environment Facility.

Table 4.7 CTF-Endorsed Country Investment Plans

	Total	Transport	
	$ Million	$ Million	Share (%)
Total investment	36,835	8,458	23.0
CTF funding	3,500	570	16.3
Private investment	7,329	1,983	27.1
Government and MDB	26,006	5,905	22.7

Source: CTF Country Investment Plans.
Note: CTF = Clean Technology Fund, MDB = multilateral development bank.

Box 4.4 Blending Carbon Finance Resources in Transport: An Example

Bringing together the agendas of local urban transport, national poverty reduction, and global climate change, the Mexico Municipal Transport Project (UTTP) aims to move urban transport to a lower carbon path. In many cities private cars account for 80 percent of all motor vehicles but just 30 percent of daily passenger trips. The goal is to reduce private trips despite high levels of motorization. The first UTTP phase focuses on improving transport policies and strengthening public transit institutions. The second addresses integrating transit systems, including mass transit corridors and other public transport. The third looks at stimulating the market for low-carbon buses and scrapping inefficient older buses.

Early Global Environment Facility support of the Climate Measures in the Transport Sector of Mexico City project, the Insurgentes bus corridor, and the testing of bus types helped demonstrate the importance of bus rapid transit systems and the clean development mechanism methodology. The UTTP experience in Mexico City can be transferred to other urban areas. The program builds on an International Bank for Reconstruction and Development Sector Investment Loan of $200 million and a Clean Technology Fund concessional loan of $200 million. The Banco Nacional de Obras channels resources, serves as financial intermediary, and lends the funds to participating municipalities. These loans will be combined with up to $900 million from the National Trust for Infrastructure. The private sector is expected to contribute up to $2.3 billion and municipalities up to $150 million. Estimated carbon revenue is another $50 million. Cities that submit Integral Transport Plans are eligible for funding.

Source: GEF webpage, http://www.thegef.org/gef/gef_projects_funding.

Although the sum of this fragmented funding is small compared with total investment needs, the combination of resources may create synergies sufficient to finance mitigation and adaptation, as in the case of Mexico City (box 4.4; World Bank 2010b). Early in the market's transformation, the GEF piloted innovative approaches and helped countries to create effective policies and regulations. CTF resources support low-carbon infrastructure investment on favorable terms, helping the market to scale up or move innovation toward maturity. Carbon revenues improve investment profitability and strengthen the financial viability of projects that do not depend on carbon finance.

Different financial sources have different comparative advantages (figure 4.5). Since the GEF's mandate is to innovate and remove barriers, its limited funds focus on early stages in technology adoption. These are often risk-prone, and resources are rarely sufficient to transform markets completely. CTF funds, by contrast, are technologically conservative and figure relatively little in early phases. They contribute to demonstration, deployment, and transfer of low-carbon technologies. Carbon finance can significantly affect the second stage, improving investment return on relatively new, initially marginal technologies. To initiate a shift to low-carbon development and avoid high-carbon technology lock-in, concessional funding and revenue enhancement are needed.

Figure 4.5 Climate Funds and Transition to Low-Carbon Technologies

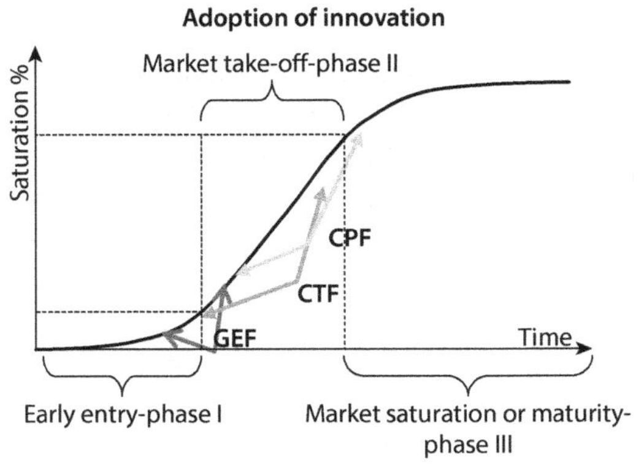

Source: World Bank 2009.
Note: CPF = Carbon Partnership Facility, CTF = Clean Technology Fund, GEF = Global Environment Facility.

At the mature stage, when carbon finance provides the most significant push into maturing markets, the CTF may still have an important role but GEF resources will be phased out.

Domestic Spending on Transport

In theory, domestic sources could address development deficits. Routine transport infrastructure maintenance, for instance, is financed domestically rather than through international funding.[10] Meeting development deficits with domestic resources could substantially reduce additional investment.

In reality, however, securing internal resources has long been difficult for developing countries. Spending on infrastructure is easily marginalized under fiscal pressures, as in Latin American countries during the 1990s (Calderón and Servén 2004b). Although developing countries spend hundreds of millions of dollars annually on transport development and maintenance, accounting for several percent of gross domestic product (GDP), the amounts are still insufficient. In Africa, for example, most countries have underinvested in transport, with a total of 22 countries together spending only about $11 billion annually on transport investment and maintenance (figure 4.6). About $4 billion was spent on transport projects (Briceno-Garmendia, Smits, and Foster 2008), although an estimated $8 billion is needed (this is exclusive of South Africa; Carruthers and others 2009).[11,12] Thus, at only half of what is needed, fiscal resources cannot close development deficits, let alone respond to adaptation or mitigation needs.

Economics of Climate-Resilient Transport Financing and Mitigation

A narrow view of the costs and benefits of transport helps to keep funding low. If local externalities, such as congestion, local pollution, and safety, are factored into policy evaluations, however, the economics of transport investment change dramatically, supporting more resources for the sector.

Climate-Resilient Investment in Transport

Figure 4.6 Actual Transport Spending and Estimated Requirements, Sub-Saharan Africa

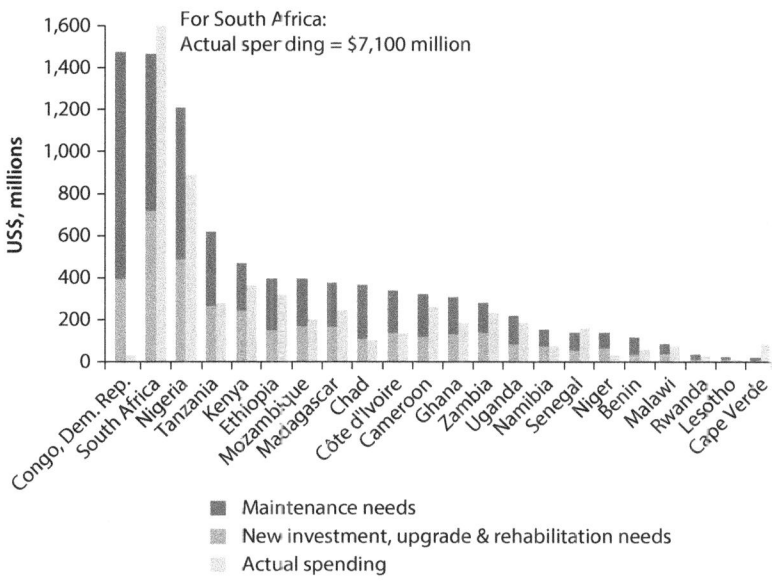

■ Maintenance needs
▨ New investment, upgrade & rehabilitation needs
▨ Actual spending

Sources: Briceno-Garmendia Smits, and Foster 2008; Carruthers and others 2009.

Table 4.8 Estimated Costs External to Transport, United States

Externality	Cents/gallon	Cents/mile
Central values of marginal external costs		
Greenhouse warming	6	0.3
Oil dependency	12	0.6
Local pollution	42	2.0
Congestion, cents/mile	105	5.0
Accidents	63	3.0
Total	228	10.9

Source: Parry, Walls, and Harrington 2007.

The Magnitude of Transport Externalities

Externalities in transport are estimated at 11 cents a mile (Parry Walls, and Harrington 2007), about the same as the cost of fuel for a standard passenger car in the United States (table 4.8).[13] In aggregate the cost of externalities would exceed 10–11 percent of GDP in Organisation for Economic Co-operation and Development (OECD) countries (table 4.9).[14] Removing these externalities would thus be beneficial.

Traffic congestion is a major externality. The estimated cost of congestion is 5 cents a mile and adds up to 8.5 percent of GDP. Road congestion is particularly costly in urban areas. In the United States, urban congestion delays increased from 16 hours a year to 47 between 1980 and 2003, pushing up the annual

Table 4.9 Estimated Costs External to Transport, OECD Averages
% of GDP

Externalities	Road	Other modes	Total
Travel time	6.8	0.07	8.5
Local pollution	0.4	—	0.4
Global pollution	—	—	1.0–10.0
Accidents	2.0	—	1.5–2.0
Noise	0.1	0.01	0.3

Sources: Banister 1998; reproduced in OECD 2002b.
Note: — = not available, GDP = gross domestic product, OECD = Organisation for Economic Co-operation and Development.

national time loss cost from $12.5 to $63 billion (Schrank and Lomax 2005). Congestion will increasingly be a problem for developing countries that are urbanizing rapidly. Road congestion that reduces mobility for freight and individual travel undermines city productivity—traditionally the most important growth center in any economy (World Bank 2009).

Benefits of Coping with Transport Social Costs

Policies to internalize or mitigate transport externalities could also help mitigate emissions. For instance, traffic congestion clearly increases emissions: cars emit more CO_2 when traffic is moving slowly (Davis and Diegel 2004; Anas, Timilsina, and Zheng 2009), and congestion and idling increase local pollutants and noise. Optimizing traffic signals not only alleviates congestion and saves travel time but also increases fuel efficiency. In California, synchronizing traffic signals at 3,172 intersections reduced congestion and lowered fuel consumption by 8.6 percent (OECD 2002a). Realigning intersections can also reduce congestion. In Tokyo improving an intersection of rail tracks and trunk roads doubled traffic speed, reducing CO_2 by an estimated 12,000 tons per year.

These supply-side measures may be enough to alleviate congestion and some emissions, but demand-side interventions are also needed. For instance, improving traffic flow alone could motivate people to drive more. In Niort, France, traffic signal synchronization improved average speeds, but traffic volume also increased 7 percent and emissions 6 percent. Fuel taxation, road user pricing, parking policies, and vehicle-related charges can all discourage individual car use, thus alleviating traffic congestion and lowering emissions. Particularly promising are high congestion charges during peak periods.

There are also safety benefits. Mass transportation is usually much safer than car travel. In Japan the road fatality rate is eight times that of rail (table 4.10). Road fatality rates are also noticeably different between developed and developing countries. The road injury/fatality rate in high-income countries is 10.3/100,000 a year; in low-income countries it is 21.5/100,000 (table 4.11). Promoting mass transit in large cities could reduce both fatalities and emissions.

Similarly, lower speed limits can reduce fatalities and mitigate emissions. Accidents typically increase with open road speed limits. In New Zealand the elasticity of total fatal accidents is estimated at 1.2 (Scuffham 2003).

Table 4.10 Transport Fatality and Injury, Japan, FY2008/09

	Fatalities	Injured persons	Fatality rate per million passenger-km	Injury rate per million passenger-km	Passenger-km (millions)
Road	5,155	945,504	5.7	1,043.7	905,907
Railway	300	397	0.7	1.0	404,585
Air	7	10	0.1	0.1	80,931
Waterborne[a]	2,414	n.a.	687.7	n.a.	3,510
Total	7,876	945,911	5.6	678.1	1,394,933

Sources: Ministry of Land, Infrastructure and Transport 2008.
Note: FY = fiscal year, n.a. = not applicable.
a. Including all marine perils.

Table 4.11 Road Traffic Injury and Fatality Rates
per 100,000 people

Region	High-income	Middle-income	Low-income	Total
Africa	—	32.2	32.3	32.2
The Americas	13.4	17.3	—	15.8
South East Asia	—	16.7	16.5	15.6
Eastern Mediterranean	28.5	35.8	27.5	32.2
Europe	7.9	19.3	12.2	13.4
Western Pacific	7.2	16.9	15.6	15.6
Global	10.3	19.5	21.5	13.8

Source: WHO 2009.
Note: — = not available.

In the United States, the fatality rate—defined as the number of fatalities per billion vehicle miles travelled—would decrease by 5 percent if the speed limit were 55 mph (88 km/h) instead of 65 (110 km/h; Houston and others 1995). Emissions would also decrease.

Vehicle inspection and maintenance increase safety and reduce emissions. Spending for vehicle maintenance would reduce fatal accidents (Houston and others 1995), and inspections encourage the scrapping of old cars that do not meet safety standards. Fleet transition to newer vehicles would decrease fatalities (Fowles and Loeb 1995). In Rio de Janeiro the state light-vehicle inspection and maintenance program is expected to reduce carbon monoxide by 16–44 percent and hydrocarbons by 9–37 percent (Ribeiro and Abreu 2008).

Potential health benefits from local pollution policies, such as diesel particulate filter regulation, are significant. In sunlight, air pollutants react to form ozone (smog), which affects pulmonary function in children and asthmatics and reduces visibility. Fine particles are small enough to reach lung tissue, and particulate exposure can cause death (Schwartz 1994). Lower-middle-income and low-income countries are exposed to 50 percent more particulate pollution than high-income countries (figure 4.7).

Other antipollution policies also have health benefits and reduce emissions. For instance, converting diesel buses to CNG is a common pollution control

Figure 4.7 Average Particulate Matter Emissions, 10 Micrometers or Less, 2006

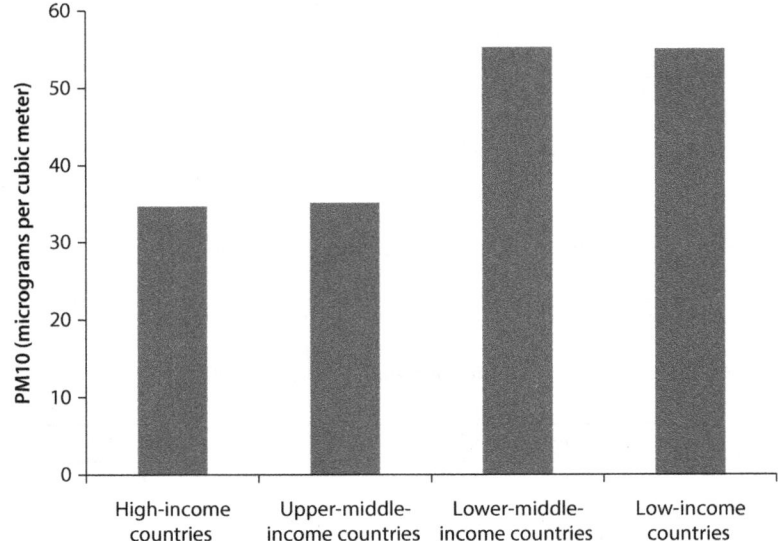

Source: World Bank 2011.
Note: PM = particulate matter.

measure that has proved effective in Mumbai. Based on observation of passengers, a 5–10 percent increase in bus fares could cover the cost of converting all 3,400 Mumbai buses, which travel 240 million km a year. It would reduce PM10 by 662 tons a year (Takeuchi and others 2007), as well as reduce CO_2 emissions. In Madrid, one of the most polluted cities in the European Union (EU), a new metro line, Arganda, that came into service in 1999 has reduced a number of pollutants (CO, NOx, SO_2, and particulates) by more than 20 percent and also reduced emission intensity. Although the number of vehicles on alternative roads has increased, that increment is smaller, and the slowdown is 2–16 percent less than it would have been without the Arganda (Zamorano and others 2006).

Generating New Resources

Addressing negative externalities like congestion and local pollution is good for economies and helps justify funding of transport, but it does not create the additional fiscal space needed for mitigation and adaptation.

Reducing Harmful Subsidies

Removing fuel subsidies can create significant financial resources (Nash and others 2002) and be accomplished at fairly low cost. The IEA estimates 2008 fossil fuel subsidies at $557 billion, where the implicit subsidy is the difference between a reference price and the actual end-user price. Oil products received $312 billion in subsidies and natural gas $204 billion, with the rest going to coal (IEA, OECD, and World Bank 2010).

Figure 4.8 Implicit Subsidies to Gasoline and Diesel, 2007–08

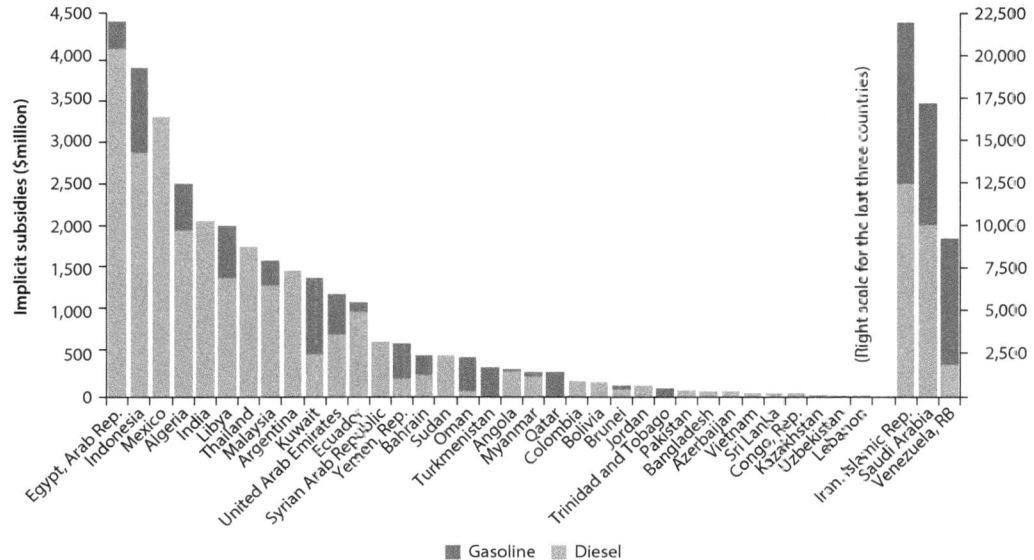

Source: Based on GTZ 2009 and World Bank 2010.

Thirty-seven developing countries subsidize gasoline and diesel fuel at more than a million dollars a year (figure 4.8), an amount calculated using a price-gap approach where U.S. fuel prices are assumed to be subsidy-free.[15] In many countries, diesel prices are more heavily subsidized not because its carbon content is lower but because diesel affects the movement of goods. Iran could increase revenues by more than $20 billion and Saudi Arabia by more than $17 billion if they abolished all gasoline and diesel subsidies. Many other countries could gain more than a billion dollars a year.

Mobilizing Revenues from Mitigation Measures

A fuel tax is the best way to create fiscal space fairly quickly and motivate people to reduce energy intensity (table 4.12). Fuel tax rates vary considerably by country (see figure 3.22). While many European countries, as well as such countries as Malawi, Mongolia, and Zambia, tax fuels heavily, many developing countries do so at relatively low rates (GTZ 2009). The transaction costs of fuel taxation are relatively low (Kleit 2004) and applying the carbon price to pump prices can generate significant revenue. A gallon of gasoline contains 0.0024 tons of carbon. Thus a market carbon price of $20, $30, and $300 per ton would translate into 5, 12, and 72 cents per gallon, respectively. While these numbers appear small, carbon pricing could increase annual revenues by about $10 billion, $24 billion, and $145 billion a year, based on U.S. fuel consumption.

Other economic measures, such as road user pricing and parking policies, can generate revenue, but particularly in developing countries initial transaction costs can be high. In London, cordon pricing generates $237 million

Table 4.12 Emission Reduction: Effect, Benefits, and Fiscal Potential of Various Interventions

Measure	Primary benefits	Impact on fiscal balances
Economic		
Fuel taxation	Congestion mitigation	++
Road user charges	Congestion mitigation	+
Parking policies	Efficient urban land use	+
Vehicle-related charges		+
Cash for clunker programs	Competitiveness of auto industry	–
Low mass transit fares	Congestion mitigation; safety	–
Regulatory		
Fuel economy standards	Competitiveness of auto industry	–/+
Inspection and maintenance	Safety	–/+
Traffic rules	Safety	–/+

annually at an operating cost of $158 million (NSTFC 2009). The initial investment of $275 million will thus be paid back relatively quickly (see box 3.6).

The revenue potential of vehicle-related charges, such as registration fees and customs duties, is subject to political acceptability and may not be particularly effective in mitigating emissions. Parking policies are less likely to create fiscal space; violations are widespread, and the cost of enforcement is high in developing countries.

Subsidies to new vehicle buyers and mass transit passengers can help alleviate transport emissions, but the costs may be too high for the expected benefits. They may still, however, be an appropriate counterpoint to huge implicit road subsidies.

As long as car users pay transaction costs, regulatory measures are generally fiscally neutral. Of course, inspection fees can be too high, and traffic tickets can also be set very high. Even when they are, though, revenues are relatively small. Regulatory measures are in general very costly (Austin and Dinan 2005; Merrell, Poitras, and Sutter 1999). Therefore, while these measures can help mitigation, they cannot be relied on to generate revenue.

Conclusion

Measures to reduce GHG emissions will reduce the costs of congestion, local air pollution, and safety risks. Policies to reduce these social impacts of transport also reduce GHG emissions. They have the potential to make transition to a low-carbon transport sector largely self-financing. Policies to convey all environmental, safety, and congestion costs to users will reduce the social costs of transport. To give an example, without such policies transport users have no opportunity to learn about the health costs of local air pollution and no incentives to change their behavior to reduce them. The policy deficit in making such costs felt is enormous. The highest social costs are due to

- congestion,
- local air pollution,
- road accidents, and, last but not least,
- GHG emissions.

Efforts to reduce these costs do more to reduce GHG emissions than a narrow climate change agenda (Parry 2007). Moreover, removal of these deficits would create revenues to finance the transition to a low-carbon environment. In addition to the global public good of reducing damages from climate change, this would also provide local political motivation because it creates local benefits in terms of reduced time losses and health costs.

An obvious reform—one that reduces the social costs of transport and creates fiscal opportunities—is to remove subsidies that give the wrong signals. Most important in this respect are subsidies for gasoline and diesel. U.S. pump prices for gasoline and diesel are taken to be a good approximation for tax- and subsidy-free consumer prices (GTZ 2009). In addition to countries like Iran and Saudi Arabia, poorer countries could also have important savings: Myanmar, for instance, could save more than $300 million in transport fuel subsidies. Iran, Colombia, and other countries are now making major strides toward reducing transport subsidies.

The most direct way to convey the costs of transport's contribution to climate change is by setting a price for carbon. A gallon of gasoline contains 0.0024 tons of carbon (Parry, Walls, and Harrington 2007). As already discussed, setting a carbon price of, say, $20 per ton would lead to only a moderate change of 12 cents in consumer prices. If there were no changes in travel behavior, a carbon charge that small could bring in revenues of $10 billion a year in the United States.

The fiscal consequences of charges for local air pollution differ substantially. In some cases they can be very high. For the Los Angeles area, Small and Kazimi (1995) estimated charges to contain the health costs of local pollution of 1–8 cents per mile for 2000. Given the number of vehicle miles driven in the area, they would bring in revenues of $40 million to $3.26 billion. Willingness to pay to avoid the health costs will depend on the local context. Functions for how willingness varies with income and household characteristics remove the need to collect primary data in each locality. Applying such functions shows that valuations differ much less than income differences suggest (For example, Loehmann and others 1997). The health costs for Beijing, for instance, were estimated at $3.5 billion in 2007, equivalent to 3.5 percent of local GDP (Creutzig and He 2009). Similar estimates can be done for congestion and accident costs. Signaling the true costs of transport to users should open considerable fiscal opportunities. These could be used to address the chronic underfinancing of transport and the incremental costs of climate-related transport policies.

The measures discussed above generate substantial income and welfare benefits. They are designed to maximize the development gains from limiting GHG emissions, local air pollution, costs of congestion, and accidents.

They bring net benefits to both consumers (benefits from transport minus the costs of the charges) and revenue. Rough estimates of the revenue potential suggest that it could be even higher than the additional funding required for the low-carbon transition. If so, efforts to increase the efficiency of the transport sector could make it possible to reduce taxes that are harmful to growth and welfare. A broad agenda to make the sector more efficient provides far stronger incentives to reduce GHG emissions than a narrow climate policy program that implicitly assumes that all other inefficiencies have been removed. An efficient transport sector protects the environment and advances development.

Annex 4A City Examples: How Carbon Pricing Can Produce Benefits

Studies have looked at measures to simultaneously address the environmental costs of transport, road safety, and congestion for Beijing, Mexico City, and Washington. The following gives an approximation of the fiscal space such measures would earn.

Beijing

The most recent transport study for Beijing analyzes optimal policies for containing not only GHG emissions but also air pollution, congestion, and noise. The study assumes a price of $70 per ton of carbon, and an annual social cost of $205 million. It relates concentration levels of PM 10 to cases of chronic bronchitis and asthma and premature death from lung cancer. These health effects are converted to monetary values using a willingness-to-pay function from a study by Deng (2000). The values are corrected for health cost increases, growth in motorization, and reduced emissions per vehicle-km if the fleet were modernized. Health costs were $3.5 billion for 2007, equivalent to 3.5 percent of local GDP. Motorized transport's share in total emissions is a function of population density and vehicle emission standards.

Accident costs are based on the number of fatalities and severe injuries reported by the Beijing Transportation Research Center for 2005 and have been corrected for underreporting. The study assumes that 25 percent of accident costs are external and not covered by insurance. Values for a statistical life and severe insurance are from the EU handbook (Maibach and others 2008). Total external safety costs are valued at $147 million a year.

Time lost in traffic is valued at $3.35 billion a year for car drivers and $853 million for bus riders. By implementing all measures, the most important being those related to congestion and air pollution, the metropolitan area of Beijing could bring in $6.5–$13.56 billion a year in revenue.

Another study analyzed CO_2 emission charges versus congestion charges. A congestion toll in Beijing would earn $5.5 million daily, reducing travel time by about 20 percent and CO_2 emissions by 36 percent. A fuel tax would earn the same amount, reduce time loss even more, and reduce emissions by 45.3 percent. The toll reduces car fuel use by 34 percent and the fuel tax by 43 percent. The toll, however, would have less effect on transport user income. The lowest two income quintiles would benefit most and the highest three quintiles least from a congestion toll and the differential would be even larger with a fuel tax.

The study also compares fuel taxes versus technical standards. Regulations affect user income less because they affect car use less. However, that is without taking into account changes in the prices of fuel-efficient cars or that revenues could contribute to other benefits. It also does not include the combined effect of fuel taxes and per-km charges on government revenue and user well-being. Fuel taxes could lead to trips outside the high-price region to refuel vehicles and to even higher transport demand. National carbon pricing would not have this localized problem.

Mexico City

Fuel taxes and congestion tolls were similarly compared for Mexico City. Here the optimal gasoline tax to reduce negative externalities would be $2.72 a gallon, much higher than the current excise tax of 17 cents a gallon. Such a tax would increase the pump price by 215 percent, from $2.21 per gallon to $4.76. It would also reduce GHG emissions by 37 percent with high welfare gains, assuming high fuel costs could not be avoided. An optimal average toll on car mileage is 20.3 cents per vehicle mile. At current fuel standards, this is the equivalent of $3.50 a gallon. Current mass transit prices (50 percent of operating costs are subsidized) are roughly in line with optimal prices.

High optimal fuel and congestion charges would increase transport revenue and help shift demand from cars to rail or other mass transit. Microbuses would become less attractive, with an optimal vehicle-mile tax of 34.2 cents a mile and a fuel tax equivalent of $2.67 a gallon. However, high taxes and tolls may not be politically feasible. A more modest fuel tax of $1 a gallon could achieve 60 percent of these benefits. There is still a strong bias toward individual car use: 600 cars are registered in Mexico City every day. Thus, increasing mass transit capacity without demand-side measures risks a mismatch between supply and demand (see chapter 2).

Washington

Correcting for the social costs of congestion, air pollution, and road safety is also relevant in developed countries. As an analysis of urban transport in Washington shows, congestion, accident, and local air pollution costs are of far greater economic importance than a charge for GHG emissions (table 4A.1).

Table 4A.1 External Costs of Passenger Transport, Washington, 2007

	Cent/gallon	Cents/mile
Fuel-related costs		
Global warming	6	0.3
Oil dependency	12	0.6
Total	18	0.9
Distance-related costs		
Local pollution	42	2
Congestion	105	5
Accidents	63	3
Total	210	10

Source: Parry, Walls, and Harrington 2007.

Notes

1. The 20-year cumulative cost to the transport sector is about $4,700 billion, followed by buildings at $2,533 billion, and power generation at $1,745 billion.
2. The requirements are exclusive of OECD member countries.
3. Normally, no retrofitting required for existing infrastructure assets is considered in estimating adaptation costs, but the World Bank EACC model includes incremental operation and costs of maintaining existing assets.
4. This is also referred to as infrastructure deficit (Parry and Timilsina 2009).
5. The U.S. Federal Aviation Administration's foreign assessment program looks at the ability of the country, not individual air carriers, to adhere to international standards and recommended practices for aircraft operations and maintenance established by the International Civil Aviation Organization (ICAO), the United Nations technical agency for aviation. Data are as of December 2008. http://www.faa.gov/about/initiatives/iasa/.
6. The EU Emissions Trading System is by far the most important carbon market. Others, including the Kyoto Protocol Joint Implementation and international emissions trading Switzerland, New South Wales, the U.S. Regional Greenhouse Gas Initiative, the Chicago Climate Exchange, and voluntary markets, are tiny by comparison and irrelevant for transport (Kossoy and Ambrosi 2010).
7. See, for example, the methodology UNFCCC, ACM 0016: Baseline Methodology for Mass Rapid Transport Projects—Version 1, Tool for the demonstration and assessment of additionality and Tool to calculate baseline, project and/or leakage emissions from electricity consumption. http://cdm.unfccc.int/methodologies/PAmethodologies/approved.html.
8. $50–$150 billion for developing countries only.
9. In Indonesia and Kazakhstan transport components may be added later.
10. It is well known that there is a general bias toward new investment in the international donor community for various reasons. See, for instance, Briceno-Garmendia, Smits, and Foster (2008).
11. The financial requirements are calculated based on the assumptions that the levels of connectivity comparable to those in developed countries would be achieved with all transport assets maintained in good condition. See Carruthers and others (2009) for more details.
12. Other estimates for the whole of sub-Saharan Africa are even larger. For instance, the World Bank (2010c) estimates baseline transport spending at $40 billion a year for sub-Saharan Africa.
13. It is assumed that vehicle fuel economy is 30 mpg and gasoline costs $3 per gallon.
14. The external costs in tables 4.8 and 4.9 are evaluated based on shadow prices in the United States or OECD member countries, prices that are presumably higher than in developing countries. However, the relative costs to GDP, as in table 4.9, should apply in developing countries as well.
15. As discussed in chapter 3, it must depend on the price elasticity of fuel. For simplicity, fuel consumption would not change even if the pump price is increased by the abolition of subsidies.

References

Austin, D., and T. Dinan. 2005. "Clearing the Air: The Costs and Consequences of Higher CAFE Standards and Increased Gasoline Taxes." *Journal of Environmental Economics and Management* 50: 562–82.

Acemoglu, A., P. Aghion, L. Burszlyn, and D. Hemous. 2010. *The Environment and Directed Technical Change*. Harvard Economics Discussion Papers, Cambridge, MA.

Alberini, A., M. Cropper T-T. K. Fu, J-T. S. Liu, and W. Harrington. 1997. "Valuing Health Effects of Air Pollution in Developing Countries: The Case of Taiwan". *Journal of Environmental Economics and Management* 34: 107–26.

ADB (Asian Development Bank). 2007. *Timor-Leste: Road Sector Investment Planning in the Pacific: An Example of Good Practice*. Philippines: ADB.

Anas, A., G. R. Timilsina, and S. Zheng. 2009. "An Analysis of Various Policy Instruments to Reduce Congestion, Fuel Consumption and CO_2 Emissions in Beijing." Policy Research Working Paper 5068, World Bank, Washington, DC.

Arnott, R., A. De Palma, and R. Lindsey. 1993. "A Structural Model of Peak-Period Congestion: A Traffic Bottleneck with Elastic Demand." *American Economic Review* 83: 161–72.

Banister, David. 1998. *Transport Policy and the Environment*. Routledge, UK.

Beijing Transportation Research Center. 2005. *Measuring Transportation in Beijing*. Beijing.

Bovenberg, A. L. 1999. 'Green Taxes and the Double Dividend: An Updated Reader's Guide." *International Tax and Public Finance* 6: 421–43.

Briceno-Garmendia, C., K. Smits, V. Foster. 2008. "Financing Public Infrastructure in Sub-Saharan Africa: Patterns and Emerging Issues." Africa Infrastructure Country Diagnostic, Background Paper 15, World Bank, Washington, DC.

Brueckner, J. 2005. "Internalization of Airport Congestion: A Network Analysis." *International Journal of Industrial Organization* 23: 599–614.

Calderón, C., L. Servén. 2004b. "Trend in Infrastructure in Latin America, 1980–2001." Policy Research Working Paper 3401, World Bank, Washington, DC.

Carruthers, R., R. R. Krishnamani, S. Murray, N. Pushak. 2009. "Improving Connectivity: Investing in Transport Infrastructure in Sub-Saharan Africa: Cross-country Annex and Sample Country Annex." Africa Infrastructure Country Diagnostic, Background Paper 7, Phase II, World Bank, Washington, DC.

Clarke, J. F., and J. A. Edmonds. 1993. "Modeling Energy Technologies in a Competitive Market." *Energy Economics* 15 (2): 123–9.

Creutzig, F., and D. He. 2009. "Climate Change Mitigation and Co-Benefits of Feasible Transport Demand Policies in Beijing." *Transportation Research, Part D* 14: 120–31.

Davis, S. C., and S. W. Diegel 2004. *Transportation Energy Data Book: Edition 24*, ORNL-6973. Knoxville TN: Oak Ridge National Laboratory, Center for Transportation Analysis.

Deng, X. 2000. "Economic Costs of Vehicle Emissions in China: A Case Study." *Transportation Research Part D* 11: 216–22.

Doll, C. 2002. *Unification of Accounts and Marginal Costs for Transport Efficiency (UNITE)*. Deliverable 7: User Cost and Benefit Studies. Leeds, U.K.

Edlin, A. 2003. "Per-Mile Premiums for Auto Insurance." In *Economics for an Imperfect World. Essays in Honor of Joseph Stiglitz*, edited by R. Arnott, B. Greenwald, R. Kanbur, and B. Nalebuff, 53–82. Cambridge, MA: MIT Press.

Edlin, A. S., and P. Karaca-Mandic. 2006. "The Accident Externality from Driving." *Journal of Political Economy* 114 (5): 931–55.

Fowles, R., and P. D. Loeb. 1995 "Effects of Policy-Related Variables on Traffic Fatalities: An Extreme Bounds Analysis Using Time Series Data." *Southern Economic Journal* 62: 359–66.

Foster, V., and C. Briceno-Garmendia. 2010. "Africa's Infrastructure. A Time for Transformation." Washington, DC: World Bank.

GTZ (Gesellschaft für Technische Zusammenarbeit). 2009. *International Fuel Prices 6th ed.* Eschborn, Germany: GTZ.

Hall, J., A. Winer, M. Kleinman, F. Lurmann, V. Grajer, and S. Colome. 1992. "Valuing the Health Benefits of Clean Air." *Science* 255: 812–17.

Houston, David J., Lilliard E. Richardson, Jr., and Grant W. Neeley. 1995. "Legislating Traffic Safety." *Social Science Quarterly* 76: 328–45.

Hughes, G., P. Chinowsky, and K. Strzepek. 2010. "The Costs of Adapting to Climate Change for Infrastructure." Paper of the World Bank Economics of Adaptation to Climate Change Study, Washington, DC.

IEA (International Energy Agency), OECD (Organisation for Economic Co-operation and Development), and World Bank. 2010. "Analysis of the Scope of Energy Subsidies and Suggestions for the G-20 Initiative." Paper prepared for submission to the G-20 Summit Meeting, Toronto, Canada, June 2010.

JBIC (Japan Bank for International Cooperation). 2006. *Post Evaluation Report on ODA Loan Projects 2006*. JBIC, Tokyo.

Kleit, A. 2004. "Impacts of Long-Range Increases in the Corporate Average Fuel Economy (CAFE) Standard." *Economic Inquiry* 42 (April): 279–94.

Kossoy, A., and P. Ambrosi. 2010. *State and Trends of the Carbon Market 2010*. Washington, DC: World Bank.

Kuik, O., L Brander, and R. Tol. 2009. "Marginal Costs of Greenhouse Gas Emissions: A Meta Analysis." *Energy Policy* 37: 1395–404.

Loehman, E., S. Berg, A. Arroyo, R. A. Hedinger, J. Schwartz, M. E. Shaww, R. W. Fahien, V. H. De, R. P. Fishe, and D. E. Rio. 1997. "Distributional Analysis of Regional Benefits and Cost of Air Quality Control." *Jornal of Environmental Economics and Management* 34: 107–26.

Maibach, M., C. Schreyer, D. Sutter, H. van Essen, B. Boon, R. Smokers, A. Schroten, C. Doll, B. Pawlowska, and M. Bak 2008. *Handbook on Estimation of External Costs in the Transport Sector. Produced within the Study Internalisation Measures and Policies for All External Costs of Transport (IMPACT)*. Delft, the Netherlands.

Mayeres, I., S. Ochelen, and S. Proost. 1996. "The Marginal External Costs of Urban Transport." *Transportation Research: Part D: Transport and Environment* 1: 111–30.

McCubbin, D. R., and M. A. Delucchi. 1999. "The Health Costs of Motor-Vehicle Related Air Pollution." *Journal of Transport Economics and Policy* 33: 253–86.

Merrell, D., M. Poitras, and D. Sutter. 1999. "The Effectiveness of Vehicle Safety Inspections: An Analysis Using Panel Data." *Southern Economic Journal* 65: 571–83.

Ministry of Land, Infrastructure and Transport 2008. White paper on traffic safety in Japan.

Nash, C., P. Bickel, R. Friedrich, H. Link, and L. Stewart. 2002. *The Environmental Impact of Transport Subsidies*. Paris: OECD Workshop on Environmentally Harmful Subsidies.

Nordhaus, W. 2008. *A Question of Balance: Weighing the Options on Global Warming Policies*. New Haven CT: Yale University Press.

NSTIFC (National Surface Transportation Infrastructure Financing Commission). 2009. "Paying Our Way—A New Framework of Transportation Finance." NSTIFC, Washington, DC. http://financecommission.dot.gov/Documents/NSTIF_Commission_Final_Report_Mar09FNL.pdf.

OECD (Organisation for Economic Co-operation and Development). 2002a. *Benchmarking Intermodal Freight Transport*. Paris: OECD.

———. 2002b. *Road Travel Demand: Meeting the Challenge*. Paris: OECD.

OECD (Organisation for Economic Co-operation and Development)/ECMT (European Conference of Ministers of Transport). 2007. *Transport Infrastructure Charges and Capacity Choice-Self Financing of Maintenance and Construction*. Paris: OECD.

OECD (Organisation for Economic Co-operation and Development)/IEA (International Energy Agency). 2009a. *Transport, Energy and CO_2: Moving toward Sustainability*. Paris: OECD/IEA.

———. 2009b. *World Energy Outlook 2009*. Paris: IEA.

Parry, I. 2004. "Comparing Alternative Policies to Reduce Traffic Accidents." *Journal of Urban Economics* 56 346–68.

Parry, I. W. 2007. "Are the Costs of Reducing Greenhouse Gases from Passenger Vehicles Negative?" *Journal of Urban Economics* 62: 273–93. http://ac.els-cdn.com/S0094119006001197/1-s2.0-S0094119006001197-main.pdf?_tid=a64366e2-84f0-11e2-be35-00000aacb361&acdnat=1362418169_4f5bf02bef1c5b7a8222 1ef3cbf9e1ed.

Parry, I. W., and K. A. Small. 2005. "Does Britain or the United States Have the Right Gasoline Tax?" *American Economic Review* 95: 1276–89.

Parry, I. W., and G. R. Timilsina. 2009. "Pricing Externalities from Passenger Transport in Mexico City." Policy Research Working Paper 5071, World Bank, Washington, DC.

Parry, I., M. Walls, and W. Harrington. 2007. "Automobile Externalities and Policies." *Journal of Economic Literature* 45: 373–99.

Ribeiro, S. K., and A. A. de Abreu. 2008. "Brazilian Transport Initiatives with GHG Reductions as a Co-benefit." *Climate Policy* 8 (2): 220–40.

Sachs, J., Earthscan, United Nations Development Program, and the United Nations Millennium Project. 2005. *Investing in Development: A Practical Guide to Achieve the Millennium Development Goals*. London and Sterling, VA.

Santos, G. 2004. *Road Pricing: Theory and Evidence*. Vol. 9. Amsterdam: Research in Transportation Economic.

Satterthwaite, D., and D. Dodman. 2009. "The Costs of Adapting Infrastructure to Climate Change." In *Assessing the Costs of Adaptation to Climate Change: A Review of the UNFCCC and Other Recent Estimates*, edited by M. Parry, N. Arnell, P. Berry, D. Dodman, S. Fankhauser, C. Hope, S. Kovats, R. Nicholls, D. Satterthwaite,

R. Tiffin, T. Wheeler. 73–89. London: International Institute for Environment and Development.

Schrank, D. and T. Lomax. 2005. *The 2005 Urban Mobility Report.* TX: Texas A&M University, Texas Transportation Institute.

Schwartz, J. 1994. "Air Pollution and Daily Mortality: A Review and Meta Analysis." *Environmental Research* 64: 36–52.

Scuffham, P.A. 2003. "Economic factors and traffic crashes in New Zealand." *Applied Economics* 35.

Small, K. A. 1992. "Using the Revenues from Congestion Pricing." *Transportation* 19: 359–81.

Small, K. A., and C. Kazimi. 1995. "On the Costs of Air Pollution from Motor Vehicles." *Journal of Transport Economics and Policy* 29: 7–32.

Takeuchi, A., M. Cropper, and A. Bento. 2007. "The Impact of Policies to Control Motor Vehicle Emissions in Mumbai, India." *Journal of Regional Science* 47: 27–46.

Tol, R. S. 2005. "The Marginal Damage Costs of Carbon Dioxide Emissions: An Assessment of the Uncertainties." *Energy Policy* 33: 2064–74.

UNFCCC (United Nations Framework Convention on Climate Change). 2007. "Investment and Financial Flows to Address Climate Change." UNFCCC, Bonn.

World Bank. 2005. "Results of Railways Privatization in Latin America." Transport Papers TP-6, World Bank, Washington, DC.

———. 2008. *Transport Business Strategy for 2008–2012: Safe, Clean, and Affordable… Transport for Development.* Washington, DC: World Bank.

———. 2009. *World Development Report. Reshaping Economic Geography.* Washington, DC: World Bank.

———. 2010a. *World Development Report 2010: Development and Climate Change.* Washington, DC: World Bank.

———. 2010b. *Beyond the Sum of Its Parts: Blending Financial Instruments to Support Low-Carbon Development.* Washington, DC: World Bank.

———. 2010c. "The Costs of Developing Countries of Adapting to Climate Change: New Methods and Estimates." The Global Report of the Economics of Adaptation to Climate Change Study, World Bank, Washington, DC.

———. 2010d. "Project Appraisal Document for Railway Modernization Project in Ukraine." Report No. 525310UA, World Bank, Washington, DC.

———. 2010e. *Air Transport Annual Report 2009.* Washington, DC: World Bank.

———. 2010f. *World Development Indicators 2010.* Washington, DC: World Bank.

———. 2011. *World Development Indicators 2011.* Washington, DC: World Bank.

WHO (World Health Organization). 2009. *Global Status Report on Road Safety. Time for Action.* Geneva, Switzerland: WHO.

Zamorano, Clara, Amparo Moragues, and Adela Salvador. 2006. "Analysis of the Impact of the Arganda Metro Line on Alternative Road Route Emission Levels." *Journal of Environmental Planning and Management* 49 (4): 475–94. http://www.tandfonline.com/doi/pdf/10.1080/09640560600747521.

Environmental Benefits Statement

The World Bank is committed to reducing its environmental footprint. In support of this commitment, the Office of the Publisher leverages electronic publishing options and print-on-demand technology, which is located in regional hubs worldwide. Together, these initiatives enable print runs to be lowered and shipping distances decreased, resulting in reduced paper consumption, chemical use, greenhouse gas emissions, and waste.

The Office of the Publisher follows the recommended standards for paper use set by the Green Press Initiative. Whenever possible, books are printed on 50% to 100% postconsumer recycled paper, and at least 50% of the fiber in our book paper is either unbleached or bleached using Totally Chlorine Free (TCF), Processed Chlorine Free (PCF), or Enhanced Elemental Chlorine Free (EECF) processes.

More information about the Bank's environmental philosophy can be found at http://crinfo.worldbank.org/crinfo/environmental_responsibility/index.html.

www.ingramcontent.com/pod-product-compliance
Lightning Source LLC
Chambersburg PA
CBHW081939170426
43202CB00018B/2948